Screen
Experience:
an Approach
to Film

Screen
Experience:
an Approach
to Film

Edited by SHARON FEYEN
for the National Curriculum Commission of
the Journalism Education Association and
DONALD WIGAL *for Geo. A. Pflaum,*
Publisher, 1969

Copyright 1966 United Feature Syndicate

Library of Congress Catalog Card Number: 71-84448
Copyright © 1969 by JOURNALISM EDUCATION ASSOCIATION, INC.
GEO. A. PFLAUM, PUBLISHER, *38 West Fifth St., Dayton,*
  Ohio 45402

Manufactured in the United States of America by Vail-Ballou Press, Inc., New York,
  New York

Overview

SHARON FEYEN - DONALD WIGAL

We do not know which television program prompted Linus to advise Lucy so wisely, but we agree that "adults are different" and "you have to be able to read them." While we wait for Linus to write his book of advice to adults, we offer SCREEN EXPERIENCE: AN APPROACH TO FILM as an aid for adults to "read" themselves and others through experiencing motion pictures.

Pictures are constantly being made and adults are being asked "Which one do you think is the better?" When someone can predict what the "average adult" will say or do in almost any given situation, including his response to a film, this response is not going to educate. SCREEN EXPERIENCE does not wish to formulate pat answers, rather it intends to encourage discovery. It does not attempt to cover all areas exhaustively or to give definitive or comprehensive commentary on the rapidly expanding art form of film. It hopes to stimulate, encourage and expand the awareness which is brought to and from the film experience.

It is not possible, of course, that we can like two pictures with equal intensity; they both cannot be equally "very nice." When we are asked for our reaction to a picture we are being asked to reveal something of ourselves, at least a statement on what we like or do not like. An intelligent answer demands an appreciation and knowledge of pictures.

Adults in general and educators in particular are more aware of this today than ever before. The TV generation and the highly visual environment of today excite questions and discussions which were never

[v]

formulated before. Because of this growing awareness on the part of teachers, students, and the general public of the art of film, the National Curriculum Commission of the Journalism Education Association initiated the following guide.

CONTENTS

An outline history of film styles is followed by a chapter on the present scene and probable future of movies. The succeeding chapters each cover specific aspects of film. A chapter with suggestions for a film series and another on several possible groupings of films are included to help plan a worthwhile film program. Next, the language of film and its properties introduce the *what* and *how* of movies. Finally, an annotated index to films (Appendix I), a list of film distributors (Appendix II), and a general bibliography, are followed by an index of all the films mentioned in the book.

[SPIN-OFFS]

Each chapter offers "spin-offs." These are discussion starters, projects, and a selected bibliography. There are no "correct answers" to any of the discussion questions. There is no one direction which the projects should take. Their only purpose is to stimulate personal discovery.

In EXPLORING THE FILM, William Kuhns and Robert Stanley announce that "the following two pages give the standards for judging a good film." Turning the page, however, the reader finds that the next two pages are absolutely blank. These answer-less pages underline the statement of Randi Brehm, education director of the American Film Academy: "There is no pat answer to the question of what a film is all about. Each individual brings to it his own experiences, his own criteria . . . his own values." He adds, moreover, that these personal standards may change through the experience of watching a film, but will do so successfully "only when the change comes from within—from an extended or renewed perception" ("Film as Film" TAKE ONE, Vol. 1, No. 10, p. 19).

There is no substitute for actually screening a film if we desire to experience it and share as much of this experience as we can with others. Obviously, SCREEN EXPERIENCE is not intended to take the place of experiencing film. In fact, the best film study guide is film itself. Film-on-film would be more ideal than a text-on-film. The "spin-offs" will help as we wait and prepare for better film-on-film techniques.

The suggested projects come close to film-on-film when they suggest the actual making of a motion picture. Those who choose to do so will probably want to work with 8mm. film and a taped soundtrack. They will also try to write their own script, complete with filming instructions (close-ups, long shots, and the various properties mentioned in Chapter Thirteen). Besides the many fine books on amateur film making which are available at photo shops, we also recommend MOVIES: THE UNIVERSAL LANGUAGE by Bede Sullivan (South Bend: Fides Press, 1967). Her suggestions for student film making are practical and flow from her successful experience. Some help for film making is also given in EXPLORING THE FILM by William Kuhns and Robert Stanley (Dayton, Ohio: Geo. A. Pflaum, Publisher, Inc., 1968).

Most advice to beginning film makers tends to be very complicated. François Truffaut's suggestion is very simple. "There is no limit to what can be done. There are no rules." Truffaut, the director of THE 400 BLOWS, JULES AND JIM, SHOOT THE PIANO PLAYER and THE BRIDE WORE BLACK, adds that a good preparation for the film maker would be to go to the movies and sit through the same picture, provided it's a good one, as many times as possible. "It's better to see a movie you like twenty times than to see twenty movies of average quality once" (Richard Nusser, "An Interview with François Truffaut" AFTER DARK, Vol. 10, No. 4, August 1968, p. 25-27).

This sort of *intensive* viewing is encouraged by the chapters of SCREEN EXPERIENCE which often deal specifically with a particular film. *Extensive* viewing is encouraged by the suggested film groupings and the annotated film list.

Both intensive and extensive viewing can be meaningless, however, if students merely look at movies. The program is incomplete if the students do not in some way experience making their own filmed creation. The "spin-offs" try to encourage this creativeness but it will be the individual enthusiasm of the group leader which can cause it to really happen. Just as with the impossibility of giving the ultimate standards for judging a good film, there is no pat answer to the question of "How do you get a group to create?"

ACKNOWLEDGEMENTS

Recognition is made here of the generous help of contributors, educators, students, film distributors, and critics in many parts of the country. In particular, acknowledgement is given to Professor James W. Arnold of the College of Journalism, Marquette University, Milwaukee, whose advisory and editorial work, along with that of Dr. Richard B. Byrne, Radio, Television and Film Department, University of Texas, Austin, was indispensable.

[vii]

Additional valuable and informative data were contributed by the following members of the Film Study Committee of the Journalism Education Association: Frances Bock, University of Wisconsin—Milwaukee; Sister Carol Casper, S.D.S., Divine Savior High School, Milwaukee; Michael M. Dorcy, S.J., Regis College, Willowdale, Ontario; Sister Ann Christine Heintz, B.V.M., St. Mary's High School, Chicago; Betty Ihlenfeldt and Marlene Ott, both of South Milwaukee Senior High School; William D. Kwapy, St. Louis University; Patrick Samway, S.J., Woodstock College, Woodstock, Maryland; and Ray Sanders, S.M., McBride High School, Saint Louis.

Deep gratitude is expressed to the Research Library of the Performing Arts at Lincoln Center in New York City; to Florence Rydell and the Ohio Society of New York for their hospitality; to Mary Yushack of the Museum of Modern Art, as well as to Henry G. Kier and Gene Andrewski for making their collections of stills available; to Michael Silver and Nat Gartsman of CBS-TV News; to Miles Kreuger, William Kuhns, Robert Stanley, Thomas Giardino and Gertrude Foley for their expert advice; to Joan Auber and Sister Mary Ann Chrzan, S.D.S., for their tireless typing; to Jack Heher and Marlene Shebu for their patience.

ABOUT THE AUTHORS

JAMES W. ARNOLD is an associate professor of journalism at Marquette University, Milwaukee, Wisconsin. His past experience includes: teaching journalism and creative writing at Creighton University, Omaha; news reporting and editing; reviewing film, TV, music and drama; and writing fiction. Arnold teaches critical writing—dealing primarily with literary, stage and film criticism—as well as courses on film as communication, and documentary film. He is now a candidate for the Ph.D. in mass communication at the University of Wisconsin, Madison.

FRANCES BOCK, a member of the National Curriculum Commission of the Journalism Education Association, is an instructor in media and an M.A. candidate at the University of Wisconsin—Milwaukee, pursuing her degree in communication. Miss Bock has taught high school English and communications courses, moderated student film seminars, and advised student publications. She has also served for several years on the executive committee of the Wisconsin Journalism Teacher-Adviser Council.

RICHARD B. BYRNE is a professor of radio, TV, film and drama at the University of Texas, Austin. Dr. Byrne has also served as associate professor in the School of Speech, University of Wisconsin. He is a native of Independence, Missouri and received his advanced degrees in speech and dramatic art at the University of Iowa. He has published articles in the field of multi-media, and instructional art and film.

MICHAEL M. DORCY, M.S., has taught English at St. Louis University and courses in literature, film, and communications at Marquette University High School, Milwaukee. He has contributed articles to *College English, Media and Methods, Revue de l'Universite d'Ottawa,* and *Commonweal.* He resides in Toronto, Ontario.

WILLIAM KWAPY, a native of Milwaukee is presently pursuing his master's degree in English at St. Louis University. An avid film and media fan, he taught English at Marquette University High School in Milwaukee, where he moderated a group of young men who called themselves "Media Diggers." His students have experimented in film and other forms of media. During the summer of 1968, Kwapy taught film making to a group of inner-city youths in Milwaukee.

PATRICK SAMWAY, S.J., is finishing his studies at Woodstock College, Maryland. He has studied English and philosophy at Fordham University and has taught at McQuaid Jesuit High School in Rochester, New York.

RAY SANDERS, S.M., initiated film study in a Milwaukee-area school system and taught film and communications courses at Don Bosco High School there. Sanders is presently coordinator of Educational Television at McBride High School in St. Louis, and works with teachers in that city and around the country in various in-service education programs, workshops, and institutes. He has published several articles on film study and related fields, and is now completing his master's degree in communications arts at Notre Dame University.

SHARON FEYEN, co-editor of *Screen Experience,* is a candidate for the master's degree at the University of Iowa. She has taught high school journalism and communications in Milwaukee and has been adviser to student publications. A member of the National Curriculum Commission of the Journalism Education Association, she has published articles on media and education, and has been active in student journalism and film groups for the past six years. Other past communications experiences include public relations and magazine editing work and a summer internship on the staff of the *Milwaukee Sentinel.* Miss Feyen has also been an active member of the executive committee of the Wisconsin Journalism Teacher-Adviser Council.

DONALD WIGAL, co-editor of *Screen Experience,* is a free-lance writer and director of adult education projects for Herder and Herder. He is also the director of film festivals for Stage Left, an off-Broadway theater group. He has contributed to several publications including *Media and Methods* and *New Book Review,* and is a regular columnist for *Interface,* the newsletter of the Institute of Environmental Response. Mr. Wigal received his master's from Notre Dame and has taught film, music, art and theology in several schools including Antioch College, where he was a coordinator of experimental seminars in multi-media. Besides writing the "Spin-Offs" accompanying each chapter, Mr. Wigal wrote the bibliography and expanded the film annotations.

[ix]

[x]

Contents

[xi]

Part One

An Introduction to Film

STAR, *1968, Julie Andrews*

One

An Outline History of Film Styles

RICHARD B. BYRNE

INTRODUCTION

The motion picture has developed as an art form in cycles, which is to be expected. Since the motion picture has been a medium of mass entertainment, films which are new and startling soon achieve popularity and are followed by a flock of imitators. If the influence of an extraordinary film is sufficient, it establishes a tradition against which other innovators react. Finally, a movement is usually reduced to cliché and even self-parody, or is supplanted by a new movement.

The following are capsule descriptions of a few major film styles or movements. In the interest of brevity, generalizations are offered in place of detail. Being so brief they constitute only a glossary of characteristics, and the listing of major periods or styles could probably be doubled with ease. Because of its importance, the documentary is treated at length in Chapter Eight rather than here. For a fuller understanding of the evolution of film styles consult the bibliography of film history listed at the close of this chapter.

THE RECORD

In the earliest years the motion picture was used merely as a recording device. Cameramen and the public were fascinated with the simplest of subject matter. The fact that events could be preserved and reproduced on a suspended sheet or bare wall was reason enough to watch the "movies." The same impulse provides the appeal of the millions of home movies now shot every year.

The first film records were called "one-shots," since they were essentially the work of still photographers and were filmed from a stationary camera position. In Europe these were called "one-shot actualities" and showed events of daily life. "Actualities" are illustrated by such films of Louis Lumière and his brother Auguste as THE ARRIVAL OF THE PARIS EXPRESS (1895), BREAKFAST FOR THE BABY, and FEEDING THE DUCKS AT TAMPA BAY.

Americans seemed less satisfied with reproductions of daily life, and their films were mainly "one-shot theatricalities." From the beginning Thomas Edison's Kinetoscope showed the admiring public views of current stage attractions. Among the stars of these brief displays were Annie Oakley, the famed strongman Professor Sandow, and John C. Rice and May Irwin, whose innocent kiss in 1896 precipitated an early censorship debate.

ARRANGED SCENES

Film took a major step toward the fulfillment of its technical and artistic potential when it was used by George Méliès. This versatile, talented, and wealthy young Frenchman was a magician, cartoonist, designer, actor, and machinist. Combining his talents, he was able to discover and develop new technical abilities of the motion picture medium in a series of delightful "trick and fantasy" films.

By both accident and design Méliès introduced the concept of disjunctiveness to film structure. He broke scenes up into more than one shot. By stopping and starting the camera in various ways, he produced cuts, superimposures, double exposures, slow and fast motion. He called the magical appearances, disappearances, and transformations which he produced in film "arranged scenes." Although his films were a great stride beyond the "one-shots" which preceded them, they were still filmed versions of static stage magic acts. They were more akin to theatre than to film, as we know it today.

FILM SYNTAX

The development of "film language" cannot be attributed to a single director. Many early directors experimented with the camera and with the arrangement of single shots in an attempt to tell stories in new and more compelling ways.

Two American pioneers who deserve a large share of this credit are Edwin S. Porter and David Wark Griffith. Porter's film THE LIFE OF AN AMERICAN FIREMAN (1902) was divided into seven distinct scenes. THE GREAT TRAIN ROBBERY (1903) went even further, using alternate

THE THOMAS CROWN AFFAIR, *1968, Steve McQueen and Faye Dunaway*

close-ups and long shots, a moving camera, intercutting of scenes in separate locations, and the technique of "matching action" to bridge the cut between adjacent shots. Porter established the early American editing style and the 8-to-12-minute film.

D. W. Griffith, working with cameraman G. W. "Billy" Bitzer, developed most of the story-telling techniques which are still used today. His BIRTH OF A NATION (1915) was perhaps the most important single picture in the evolution of the film as a narrative medium. Produced at a time when most films contained only 25 to 50 shots, BIRTH was originally divided into 1500 separate shots, of which 1375 remained after some highly inflammatory racial material was eliminated. Among the techniques demonstrated so effectively in this film were the "long shot—medium shot—close-up" establishing sequence, the isolation of significant detail by close-ups, high speed traveling shots, symbolic intercutting of actions in two locales, and unprecedented spectacle. Griffith's next film, INTOLERANCE (1916) was an even more colossal spectacle, but being far in advance of its times, it met with little critical or financial success.

Film D'Art was a misguided attempt to bring respectability to the motion picture and culture to the masses. The American counterpart of the European Film D'Art was called Famous Players in Famous Plays. This project eventually merged with Jesse Lasky's productions and later became Paramount Pictures.

Famous Players were brief films of notable stage dramatic stars of the day in their most famous roles. One of the earliest was THE ASSASSINATION OF THE DUC DE GUISE (1908). Other silent records of famous players included the divine Sarah Bernhardt in QUEEN ELIZABETH, Joseph Jefferson in UNCLE TOM'S CABIN, James K. Hackett in THE PRISONER OF ZENDA, James O'Neill in THE COUNT OF MONTE CRISTO, and Minnie Fiske in TESS OF THE D'UBERVILLES.

The obvious aesthetic flaws of the Film D'Art arose from the camera technique employed and the absence of sound. The producers mistakenly believed that in placing the camera "third row center" in the orchestra, the resulting unbroken record of a brilliant performance would be the equivalent of having attended the original performance. This was an unfortunate step backward toward the "one-shots" of fifteen years earlier. Furthermore, without sound, the verbal richness of the performance was lost, and all that remained was a slow and static pantomime, small pleasure for a public being thrilled with the constant movement and visual delight provided by Porter and Griffith.

AMERICAN SILENT COMEDY

American silent comedy, referred to also in Chapter Seven, exerted world-wide appeal. It was characterized by speed, reckless abandon, spontaneity, and improvisation. The sources of most humor were wacky

A rare 1921 shot of David Wark Griffith

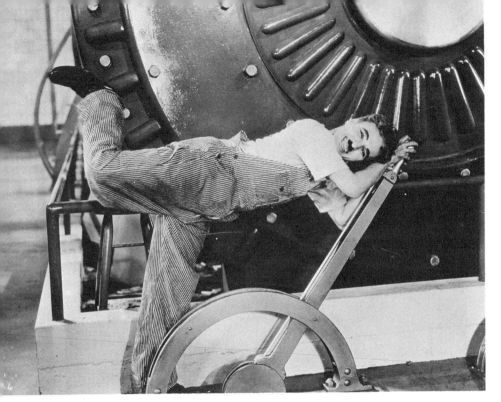

Charlie Chaplin
in MODERN TIMES, *1936*

incongruities and broadly violent slapstick action. These traits were almost a formula for the laugh factory headed by Mack Sennett. His zany comic shorts, starring the Keystone Kops and the Sennett Bathing Beauties, were the training ground for many comedians who later attained stardom with their own individual comic styles.

The most famous of these comic stars was Charlie Chaplin whose films were announced on theater marquees throughout America by the words "He's here!" His films combined pratfalls with poignancy, showing the downtrodden "tramp" struggling to protect his self-respect. Chaplin's comic style approached ballet, since his sure sense of timing and his consummate physical skill raised simple acts like roller skating or walking through a pawn shop to the level of artistry.

Other American comedians with distinctive styles were Harold Lloyd, Joseph Francis "Buster" Keaton, and Harry Langdon. Lloyd wore tortoise-shell glasses and moved with great nimbleness, but he developed no clearly defined screen personality. His youthfulness and naiveté were emphasized in such films as GRANDMA'S BOY (1922), GIRL SHY (1924), and THE FRESHMAN (1925).

"Buster" Keaton was the son of circus acrobats, who spent his childhood working in American vaudeville knockabout routines. Throughout his career he capitalized on his tumbling skills and his unchanging facial expression. He was billed as "the man who never smiles." When placed in a desperate or incredible situation, the disparity between his circumstances and his passive acceptance of them provoked unfailing laughter. His best films include SHERLOCK JR. (1924), THE NAVIGATOR (1924), and THE GENERAL (1926).

Harry Langdon was less successful with the general public, although his comic invention was remarkable. His screen personality was like an undeveloped child. His pale innocence, his complete inability to cope with any situation, the almost sadistic violence done to him, made him unsympathetic to the masses. His most notable films were THE STRONG MAN (1926), LONG PANTS (1927), and SHY BOY (1929).

GERMAN EXPRESSIONISM

Expressionism is a Movement in film which reflected the political and social chaos of a defeated Germany after World War I. Expressionism marked a departure from previous film styles, which had been generally realistic, since even the work of George Méliès had attempted to create "realistic" illusions of magical feats.

Expressionism is an attempt to shatter the reality of surface appearances to reveal the reality of inner experience. As in expressionist paintings and stage plays, the desire to externalize inner emotional responses results in symbolism, morbidly neurotic themes, and emphasis upon the importance of dreams as revelation of the subconscious.

The visual style of expressionism was most striking. The settings were frequently almost cubistic—jagged and fragmented jumbles of nightmarish landscape, a pasteboard wasteland through which zombie-like figures stalked. Among the memorable films done in this style were R. Wiene's THE CABINET OF DR. CALIGARI (1919), A. Robinson's WARNING SHADOWS (1923), and Paul Leni's WAXWORKS (1924).

SOVIET MONTAGE

Lenin said, "Of all the arts, the cinema is the most important for us." From the time of the nationalization of the Soviet cinema in 1919, the key task of film directors was to use the medium in support of the primary goal of the state: to convince the masses that they should labor unceasingly to build a new social and economic community.

In their search for new ways to influence mass opinion, the Soviet directors experimented with film form. Working with newsreel footage, or films shot to look like newsreels of actual events, they placed shots in startling arrangements to make symbolic comment. Their style was called "montage," and was based upon the effect of conflicts in structure. A shot placed alongside another shot with which it conflicted in subject matter, visual appearance, or apparent meaning, resulted in a new concept or offered a new insight into the subjects being shown. Several examples of films using montage are given in Chapter Thirteen, Property one.

Dziga-Vertov produced a series of twelve newsreels called KINO-PRAVDA ("Cinema Truth") in 1922. These episodes used explanatory titles, emotional appeals, and films of current events to influence social conduct.

Most influential of the Soviet directors was the brilliant intellectual, Sergei Mikhailovich Eisenstein (1898-1948). His films STRIKE (1924), THE BATTLESHIP POTEMKIN (1925), and ALEXANDER NEVSKY (1938), stand as milestones in Soviet cinematic achievement. Program 36 in Chapter Twelve lists some of these early Russian films.

THE COMING OF SOUND

Popular opinion seems to hold that the "first sound film" was THE JAZZ SINGER (1927), starring Al Jolson. In fact, as early as 1889 Thomas Edison and W. K. L. Dickson had apparently synchronized sound and pictures. In the years which followed, many systems for synchronizing pictures with sound and music were developed and demonstrated for the public. Sound film was definitely not a development of the late 1920's.

However, with THE JAZZ SINGER and other "talkies" to follow, audiences were seized with a mania for sound films. Since they were obviously good box office, producers converted almost their entire output to sound.

The introduction of sound had far-reaching effects upon the star system. Some feature players in the silent films had voices which destroyed the romantic illusions created for film-goers by their handsome faces and beautiful figures. These unfortunates were replaced by Broadway stars, who were in great demand because of their training in diction and dialogue delivery. A new star system was born.

The 1952 musical SINGIN' IN THE RAIN (discussed in Chapter Seven) deals with the transition period from silents to talkies. The era is personified in this film's leading man—a silent star with a speech problem.

The coming of sound also changed the forms and techniques of film. Since sound technology was not highly developed at this time, the camera and microphone could not move freely, as they could in silent films. The camera was immobilized in a soundproof room like a large telephone booth, and all action had to be staged before it. The resulting tyranny of technicians and sound equipment set the aesthetic achievements of the motion picture back several decades, but sound also offered the potential for later artistic accomplishments never considered previously.

NEO-REALISM (c. 1943-1952)

The application of the principles of documentary filming to a specific social environment, post-World War II Italy, resulted in a style called "Neo-realism." These films were a reaction against the escapist epics of gladiatorial rebellions in imperial Rome and the "white telephone" films which showed bourgeois Italian life as a lark in sumptuous surroundings, white interior decors complete with the coveted "white telephone."

The neo-realists wanted to show the devastating effects of war on the middle and lower classes. The films presented the life of the poor in the streets of Rome and Milan. As in the documentary film, neo-realism used non-professional actors, real settings in the cities, natural lighting, and themes of implicit social criticism. Outstanding examples of neo-realism are Luchino Visconti's OSSESSIONE (1942), Roberto Rossellini's ROME: AN OPEN CITY (1945), Vittorio de Sica's BICYCLE THIEF (1948) and UMBERTO D (1952). Chapter Twelve, program 37, lists some early Italian directors and some of their films.

FOREIGN INDEPENDENTS

During the mid-1950's the forceful personalities and highly individualistic film styles of several directors began to exert international influence. These directors fit no particular school. Their themes and techniques are as different as their own personalities.

Ingmar Bergman creates a Nordic form of expressionism. His themes are deeply intellectual, full of psychoanalytical ideas, dealing with religious and philosophic issues such as life, death, reality, the nature of God, and the role of the artist. Symbolism, a slow tempo, formal graphic compositions, and many long passages of silence mark THE SEVENTH SEAL (1956), WILD STRAWBERRIES (1957), THE MAGICIAN (1958), THE VIRGIN SPRING (1959), THE SILENCE (1963), and PERSONA (1965). Chapter Twelve, program 40, lists several Bergman films.

Michelangelo Antonioni tries to show the loneliness, the boredom, the emptiness of modern urban life. Existence seems to be meaningless, indeterminate. Man is estranged, alienated, without hope for love or a productive life. L'AVVENTURA (1960), LA NOTTE (1961), and L'ECLIPSE (1962) provide a slow journey across a plain of despair. Antonioni presents an even more complex view of life in love in BLOW-UP (1966).

Federico Fellini says his task in making films is "to take the temperature of a sick world." LA DOLCE VITA (1959) and 8½ (1963) blend sensationalism and almost surrealistic symbolism to condemn a corrupt and insensitive society. Fellini's art is discussed at length in Chapter Nine. Several Fellini films are listed in Chapter Twelve, program 37.

THE NEW WAVE ("Nouvelle Vague")

The "new wave" is not a movement at all, but a journalistic catchphrase which was applied at random to almost anyone directing films during a sudden surge of film creativity. First used in reference to films shown at the Cannes Festival in 1959, the term included films by veteran directors as well as neophytes offering their first films. In a more restricted sense, the term is best applied to films made from 1958 to 1961 by a group of French directors, especially a group of young critics-turned-directors who had written for the film magazine, LES CAHIERS DU CINÉMA.

François Truffaut was one such critic, whose first film, THE 400 BLOWS, won the prize for Best Direction at that 1959 Festival. His films, such as SHOOT THE PIANO PLAYER (1960) and JULES AND JIM (1961), move swiftly and seem to have been shot candidly with natural lighting and a hand-held camera. Truffaut is captivated with the process of making films, and his gaiety and enthusiasm are reflected in the frolicsome improvisation of his actors.

Alain Resnais also labeled a "new wave" director, could scarcely have developed a style more different from that of Truffaut. He has been called the "Schoenberg of the cinema," indicating his interest in formal structural innovation. His films progress like a chess game, with elaborate ritualistic regularity. HIROSHIMA, MON AMOUR (1959) and LAST YEAR AT MARIENBAD (1961) have little plot and they ignore chronology in their narrative. Their enigmatic dialogue and slow, rhythmic pace attempt to produce an almost hypnotic effect. Chapter Twelve, program 39, lists several "new wave" directors and their films.

The "New American Cinema" or the "Underground" is a fairly well-organized avant-garde movement in the United States. The present situation and a projection towards the future of film is treated in the next chapter.

A SELECTED BIBLIOGRAPHY OF FILM HISTORY

See the literature marked "1" in the Bibliography at the close of the book for complete data on these and other related readings.

Barnouw *A History of Broadcasting in the United States.*
Ceram *Archaeology of the Cinema.*
Griffith (Mrs.) *When the Movies Were Young.*
Griffith *The Movies.*
Jacobs *The Rise of the American Film.*
Knight *The Liveliest Art.*
Lindgren *A Picture History of the Cinema.*
McGowan *Behind the Screen.*
O'Leary *The Silent Cinema.*
Ramsaye *A Million and One Nights.*
Rotha *The Film Till Now.*
Schickel *Movies.*
Tyler *Classics of the Foreign Film.*
Wood *The Fabulous Films of the Twenties.*

[SPIN-OFFS]

Discussion

1. Are there some parallels between the history of painting, music, architecture and the evolution of motion pictures? Is there a Gothic,

Romanesque and Baroque period in motion pictures? Were there revolutions in other arts similar to the coming of sound to film? Were there experiments in the other arts like 3-D in motion pictures?

2. Does the music of impressionistic composers "fit" best with an impressionistic painting, rather than with a painting of another style? What happens when we hear music of a distinctive style while seeing a painting of a radically different period? Picture cool jazz being played in the Rembrandt room of the Metropolitan Museum of Art in New York City, or Palestrina being sung in the Picasso collection. Some films have used the musical classics well. How was music used in THE GOSPEL ACCORDING TO SAINT MATTHEW (during the carrying of the cross), ELVIRA MADIGAN (during the closing scene), THOROUGHLY MODERN MILLIE (when she sees her new boss for the first time), LORD OF THE FLIES (when the choir boys first appear). Each of these examples use music from the classics in a different way to fit various effects. Do you recall other examples?

Projects

1. In SOUND OF MUSIC a singer lists a few of her "favorite things." These included a variety of sights, sounds, smells, tastes and touches. Leo Lewis and William Sherman do a similar self-disclosure when they list "Things we dig the most." They include Akim Tamiroff's death-scene in ALPHAVILLE and the singing of Blake's "Jerusalem" in THE LONELINESS OF THE LONG DISTANCE RUNNER. (LANDSCAPE OF CONTEMPORARY CINEMA, Buffalo, New York: Spectrum Press, 1967, p. 91-95. Reprinted in TAKE ONE, Vol. 1, No. 10, p. 27.)

List a few of your "favorite things" from films. Imagine a film composed of nothing but highlights of your favorite scenes from several movies. Could this collection make a worthwhile film for others to see?

2. Take a tape recorder to the next film you see and record the initial reactions of volunteers from the audience after the film. You should have specific questions to ask each person: What scene impressed you the most in the film? Did you also read the book—see the play? Would you recommend this film to your friends? Edit this tape and share it with a group. If well done, it could provide an interesting soundtrack for a collection of slides taken from stills of the film. Such a report could also make interesting newspaper copy.

Two

Film Today and Tomorrow

DONALD WIGAL

The sixties are an era of cinematic revolution. The contemporary camera is liberated from its mechanical anchor and can zoom in and out from life at any angle. The contemporary film maker is also liberated; he need not live in Hollywood or subscribe to any social or moral code; he need not have great financial backing or appeal to the masses. The camera and the film maker are evolving hand-in-hand, each feeding back to the other a dialogue leading to the next cycle of cinematic change.

Some scholars in the fifties were concerned with what they said was the age of pictorialization. They thought of the pictorial deluge as the last stage of an evolution which they traced back to the beginnings of human culture. Others disagreed and thought that the pictorial deluge was not all bad and certainly solvable. Neither group seemed to adequately anticipate the even greater revolution about to take place in *moving* pictures.

Engineering and general technical know-how has decreased radically the time which evolves from the point of "discovery" to the point of "developed." The years it took photography to develop are many times the months between the discovery of the transistor and its practical use around the world. We can expect today's discoveries in multi-media to be perfected faster and phased out sooner.

The 16mm camera has improved to a point where the 35mm camera is far less needed, yet the 70 mm camera is being adopted more than ever before. The 8mm camera is as domesticated as the television set and nearly as numerous. With such availability some observers predict

[15]

that movies will soon be as commonplace and as "throwaway" as pen and paper.

But, the rate and speed at which film and television will develop into an art will not depend on its technical improvements. The advent of color to television has not made it an art, any more than sound automatically made film more artistically perfect. The use and even perfection of technique does not, of itself, guarantee quality.

The history of art is not a succession of "advances"—from Bach to Bruckner, from Giotto to Picasso, from Sir Christopher Wren to Frank Lloyd Wright. The Romanesque was not "perfected" by the Gothic, nor was Baroque the epitome of the Renaissance. There is not an improvement, but a diversity of means and interpretations. As our conception of God, man, time and space change our pictorial representations also change.

Natural Vision and its 3-D glasses were born and discarded in nearly the same year. Cinerama and its practical cousin CinemaScope caused a revolution nearly as radical as the introduction of sound to film, bringing wide-screen systems that are here to stay.

The wide screen offered a unique opportunity to revive David Griffith's theory of fifty years previous: the full screen need not always be used; it can be split up into smaller units, reserving the total area only for those shots which can best employ the full screen.

Despite the varieties of techniques existing today, the most practical and flexible employment of variable screen size is still, as it was for Griffith, those projections made from a single strip of film. The multi-image is in full revival.

Multi-image combines several images on one film print and projects them on one screen, whereas multi-screen is the simultaneous projection of several film images using a number of film projectors with an equal number of fixed screen areas. While the multi-screen is technically not yet practical for universal adoption, the multi-image is an alternative which is more authentic to what film is. This was dramatized at Expo '67.

Thousands of viewers at Expo '67 saw the kind of experimentation which had been alive and well and living in the underground for years. Graeme Ferguson's POLAR LIFE used twelve screens and a revolving theater; the Walt Disney studios presented a 360° screen; the United Kingdom pavilion was flooded with images from 69 projectors; and in the Czechoslovakia pavilion the audience decided, by pushing buttons, how the plot would proceed at various points in Raduz Chinchera's KINOAUTOMAT.

A PLACE TO STAND, *directed by Christopher Chapman, from Expo 67, Ontario pavilion*

Yet, amid all this, it was Christopher Chapman's comparatively simple A PLACE TO STAND that most highly influenced the future of film making. It presented up to 11 different images from a single 70mm film.

Even when limited to the small area of a television screen, the multi-image offers a more intense involvement of the viewer than would a single image picture. What too often interests the television commercial maker: multi-image also offers an increase in the amount of "information" that can be communicated. The technique is abused when various images really are giving the identical message.

Increasing the quality of "information" which can be seen at one time will most likely soon be integrated with recent efforts in "accelerated speech." These experiments use tapes which are sped up without changing the pitch of the normal speaking voice. It is staggering to imagine the result of coupling such a system with a multi-station visual simulation unit for classroom use.

The multi-station visual simulation units researched in 1968 at the University of Dayton are already somewhat sophisticated. Each of these units uses 16mm film loops with silent picture projectors and rotary trays with 35mm slide projectors, all operated by specially designed control units. Each unit simultaneously reads four channels of control information from a repeating loop of magnetic tape. Signals from the unit are fed into the switching unit which can turn on or off either a motion picture projector or slide projector, advance a slide, or reverse the direction of the slide magazine. The consequences of designing feedback into the system and further experimentation with inter-disciplinary programs should excite the educator to expect multi-image aids sooner than he expected.

Yet, the students who see and especially those who make film will soon desire more multi-media in their learning environment. And this desire increases as more and more students are actually making films.

The availability of relatively inexpensive equipment permits young men to put their visions on film, while old men find new ways to film their dreams. The results range from passionate attempts which are often poorly made, to equally passionate efforts which border on genius. Either way they are threatening the "established" film world and are keeping alive the cycles of art history.

According to the extraordinary film maker Stan VanDerBeek, some of the ideas that are of particular interest to the contemporary film maker are:

1.) simultaneous images and compression,

2.) abstractions, superimpositions,

3.) discontinuous information,

4.) social surrealism,

5.) episodic structure,

6.) loop film (continuous projection),

7.) film as a reflection of private dreams, hallucinations . . .

Some predict that, sooner or later, the experimenters will have to discipline themselves and face the fact that movies' main function is intelligible communications. Others wonder if communication itself is undergoing a revolution and redefining what it means to be intelligible. The latter would seem to be the message being massaged on the mass-age by the Marshall McLuhan masses.

Whether or not the "experimenters" will eventually become disciplined, there is a pattern—not entirely forboding—of organization and collaboration in the underground.

On the high school level a full program of research, study, publishing and film production was made available in 1968 to high school teachers by the American Film Institute.

Also in 1968 Filmways, Inc., gave a commercial outlet to films made by college students. Filmways began to duplicate and release the "best" college-produced films to the college theater circuit—beginning on the West coast and, reversing the usual flood of underground film's flow, gradually spreading to the East coast. After this service to college campuses, Filmways offers the films to commercial movie houses.

Of all the significant organizations, Filmmakers' Cooperative is still outstanding. It was the first to help finance and distribute avant-garde films, largely because of the pioneering efforts of Jonas Mekas. In fact, the underground "movement" could be said to have been established by Mekas, the publisher and editor of FILM CULTURE magazine and film critic for THE VILLAGE VOICE.

Mekas and his followers argue that Hollywood feature films are aesthetically obsolete, thematically superficial, and generally offensive. The position seems justified when we see Hollywood releasing GONE WITH THE WIND for the sixth time in 1968, this one in wide screen and stereo sound at a cost of twenty-five million dollars. The thirty-year-old "classic" was the biggest financial success of any film before the profits of SOUND OF MUSIC topped sixty-six million. Apparently measuring by box office returns, these two films have been called the most "successful" films of all time.

The regrettable influence of the familiar myth—"nothing succeeds like success"—will continue, despite the efforts of Jonas Mekas and the nonconformists. Innumerable deformed offspring will claim "success"

THE GRADUATE, *1968, Dustin Hoffman and Katharine Ross*

as their parents: romanticized violence flowing from BONNIE AND CLYDE; phony space extravaganzas attempting to imitate 2001: A SPACE ODYSSEY, sentimental nostalgias swinging from STAR! But, optimistically, revolutionary schools of film makers will continue to flunk the box office test and will continue to promote new graduates searching for the real world.

SUGGESTED READINGS

See the literature marked "2" in the Bibliography for further information on these and other related readings.

Battcock *The New American Cinema.*
Renan *An Introduction to the American Underground Film.*
White-Averson *Sight, Sound and Society.*

[SPIN-OFFS]

Discussion

1. What examples of multi-image technique have you noticed recently on television and in movies? Do you agree with the statement that the multi-image is abused when various images are giving the identical message? Is it ever possible for two different images to give the identical message? Recall the Peanuts cartoon at the beginning of the book.

2. What are the comparative merits of a "live" and a "taped" television show? What are the comparative merits of a television show in color and a show in black and white? Are there similar comparisons to make concerning movies?

3. There are over seven thousand films released for television use. Does this mean that eventually all the "oldies but goodies" will be seen on television? Is there any advantage to watching some of the poorly made films which are often offered on television?

4. What are some examples of pictorial representations changing throughout history as man changed his concepts of God, man, time and space?

5. Can you give examples from films of each of the ideas mentioned by Stan VanDerBeek quoted in this chapter?

6. What could be the dangers of the pattern of organizing the underground? Can the independent film makers ever actually become totally united or unionized?

Projects

1. Go through newspapers or local magazines and see which type of films are being shown by the major movie houses in town. Draw some conclusion about the apparent policy of each theater. Are there certain types of films which never are booked in your town?

2. Invite a local film maker to show and discuss his films with your group. (Local photo supply shops usually can name the independent film makers in the area.)

3. Cut out at random several interesting pictures from magazines. Which seem to fit together and could be presented on a multi-image screen?

4. Recall a feature film which could have used masks (blocking out all but a small section of the total screen) during particular scenes. Make a few masks of different shapes out of cardboard, place over the same still picture and demonstrate how the shape of the frame affects the impact of the shot.

5. If your school or organization has a newspaper, check to see if it has news on current film. If so, evaluate it. If not, see what can be done about starting such a service.

6. Using the suggested readings, recent magazines, and papers, find current information on a few of the following independent film makers:

Kenneth Anger	Ken Dewey	Jonas Mekas
Bruce Baillie	Ed Emshwiller	Marie Menken
Jordan Belson	Peter Emmanuel Goldman	Andy Meyer
Charles Boultenhouse	Storm De Hirsch	Robert Nelson
Stan Brakhage	Ken Jacobs	Ron Rice
Robert Branaman	Larry Jordan	Harry Smith
Robert Breer	Stanton Kaye	Jack Smith
Rudy Burckhardt	Mike and George Kuchar	Warren Sonbert
Bruce Conner	George Landow	Stan VanDerBeek
Trudy Conrad	Carl Linder	Andy Warhol
Carmen D'Avino	George Markopoulos	Robert Whitman

Part Two

Putting it Down
on Film

THE GRAPES OF WRATH, *1940, Henry Fonda*

Three

Literary Adaptations

WILLIAM KWAPY

The written word by its nature is private, personal, and intimate—"Take my word for it." A person's word is interchangeable with his self. This personal word demands that the reader be involved in the subject as well as in time, if he is to understand it. Writing will always be the most complete private human expression. The photograph and movies, on the other hand, are more public than writing in communication, but more shareable; they reach more people at a single viewing.

Our point of interest here is the problem of transferring the basic message of the word or story to the images of film and observing what advantages and disadvantages are brought about by this shifting of media.

The film is instantaneously communicative, while reading is slow, lineal, complex and often a monotonous experience, insofar as authors "tell" about it instead of "show" it. But the visual picture and the soundtrack flood our senses, our eyes, ears, and minds with the simultaneous revelation of scene, mood, atmosphere, beauty—elements that are most difficult to communicate by means of words.

The film is by its special nature an audio-visual medium. As such, it is not readily or easily conductive of intellectual content. It requires special handling in order to convey *inner* feelings; by *inner* feelings I mean the nonsensible or intangible elements of human nature such as emotions, memories, thoughts, fears, and psychological motivation and experience. The thoughts of Dr. Zhivago on art and culture and poetry were lost in the film. Exterior documentation or even artistic suggestion will often still leave something to be desired to "complete the picture of what is going on 'inside' a character." Obviously, outer events cannot tell all there is to know, though the camera can tell all the outer events.

The soundtrack is the film maker's means of intensifying, deepening, and multi-dimensionalizing the visual picture. It will carry the basic dialogue, music, songs, and authentic sounds. We are reminded that, although the blind are more handicapped in active movement than the deaf, their communicative abilities (mainly speech) are normal. But the deaf are excluded from the world of conversation. Sound does not lie. Sound supports the image on the screen and dispels the ambiguity of pictures. Homer, the master communicator, story teller, and cultural influence of ancient Greece, was blind.

Ideally, the moving pictures and soundtrack tell all. Such an ideal becomes difficult when the written story to be filmed contains a large number of inner events.

Another ideal is that music (soundtrack) and action should work together somewhat like a ballet: action wedded to sound. The soundtrack can link the inner with the outer events, superimposing one on the other, intensifying the significance and power of the film—much as in THE DIARY OF ANNE FRANK (1958), the outer events which we could *see,* were deepened by the voice of Anne reading her diary which we *heard.*

The film, then captures the sensual or outer actions, such as movement, scenic background or setting, objects, such objects as symbols, sounds, strong passion, gestures, and facial expressions, to a high degree of authenticity. But it is less sensitive to the inner events; it can only suggest them.* Even with a soundtrack films tend naturally to be low in information about these inner events. Oddly enough, we find the greatest film makers are the most skillful in presenting the inner events, sometimes to the detriment of the outer.

Some scenes from the famous short film AN OCCURRENCE AT OWL CREEK BRIDGE will, perhaps, enlighten us on these matters. The original prose short story was written by Ambrose Bierce. Its film counterpart was done by Robert Enrico, a Frenchman.

Compare the prose story to the film story at three specific events in the story: the opening and scene setting, the execution, and the event of the victim's realization that he's alive. Another, and more technique-oriented method of approach will be presented in Chapter Five, in the unit on the short film as a cinema genre.

---

*Consider what I have called "introceptive camera", property 10 in Chapter Ten.—D. Wigal, ed.

In a scene from Thursday's Children (*made by World Wide Pictures Ltd.,
1952*) *deaf children are taught to sense 'sound' vibrations they cannot hear*

THE OPENING AND SCENE SETTING

> A man stood upon a railroad bridge in northern Alabama, looking down into the swift water twenty feet below. The man's hands were behind his back, the wrists bound with cord. A rope loosely encircled his neck. It was attached to a stout crosstimber above his head, and the slack fell to the level of his knees. Some loose boards laid upon the sleepers supporting the metal of the railway supplied a footing for him and his executioners—two private soldiers of the Federal army, directed by a sergeant who in civil life may have been a deputy sheriff.

Bierce's story begins with this description of preparations for an execution. Later the narrator mentions the railroad tracks, the stockade, the soldiers standing like statues, and the sentinels. The atmosphere is evoked by Bierce's fine poetic observations:

> Death is a dignitary who when he comes announced is to be received with formal manifestations of respect, even by those most familiar with him. In the code of military etiquette silence and fixity are forms of deference.

The scene and mood are set.

Enrico's film version of the same OCCURRENCE opens with a long shot nearly a quarter-mile away. The soldiers on the bridge are not noticed until the drum roll promptly communicates their presence and intimates a military rite of some kind. The camera swings an arc around the bridge at treetop level catching the still setting of this death-event within peaceful nature. The cries of some mournful southern birds cut the air and are resonant with the gravity of this incident in the framework of a high and bitter war.

From the first shot onward we are immediately present at the scene, seeing and hearing what is happening. The bird cries conjure up dark omens. The rugged bridge structure stands out with rigidity and foreboding, like the military company with their "formal manifestations of respect and deference" for the coming dignitary, in the wilderness of natural forms. Enrico translates into the film medium all that Bierce wrote.

Enrico drops all irrelevant information in the film and keeps only a minimum. Whereas Bierce gave us the man's name, Peyton Farquhar, and partly explained this treason, Enrico omits this information. The film maker supplies the locale and mood, but allows the audience to piece together the happenings leading up to this point. As a result, perhaps, the viewer gets more involved than the reader.

THE EXECUTION AND ESCAPE

The opening of the film conveys the scene more immediately and the atmosphere more effectively than did the written account. The content delivered favored the movie, since film and sound track are high in sensual data. The action, from the point of execution, rope breaking, struggling, to the apparent escape, baffles the camera, which tries to show what happens, but can't handle the feelings (inner feelings) of near-execution and escape. The camera chooses to document the event. Bierce, however, at this point demonstrates his finest writing as he enters into the event fully with a brilliant understanding of a tortured psyche. He stops the action in order to reveal the psychologically subtle changes and quirks of emotion as Peyton's rope breaks and he struggles to free himself. The film merely records a splash and a slow struggle: the soundtrack fails to inform us of any of these inner flashes of a highly complex state of mind:

> As Peyton Farquhar fell straight downward through the bridge he lost consciousness and was as one already dead. From this state he was awakened . . . by the pain of a sharp pressure. . . . Keen, poignant agonies seemed to shoot from his neck downward. . . . These pains . . . beat with an inconceivably rapid periodicity. They seemed like streams of pulsating fire heating him to an intolerable temperature. . . . he swung through unthinkable arcs of oscillation, like a vast pendulum. . . . Then it (gleam of light) began to grow and brighten, and he knew that he was rising toward the surface—knew it with reluctance, for he was now very comfortable. . . . trying to free his hands. He gave the struggle his attention, as an idler might observe the feat of a juggler, without interest in the outcome. . . (after ridding himself of the noose) 'Put it back! Put it back!' He thought he shouted these words to his hands . . . his brain was on fire; his heart, which had been fluttering faintly, gave a great leap, trying to force itself out at his mouth.

The written version from the fall to the bursting out of the water free, comprises sixteen per cent of the total written story, while the film version uses only seven per cent of its time on this tense psychological movement. The written section completely outcommunicates the film by venturing into the inner soul at the second of the execution. The film medium is not introspective on this point. In such a situation as this hanging, its limitation with the visual and with the action hinders it from entering "inside."

The film, then, records the outer event, and the written word describes the inner, but since the real event in this instance is the "inner" the camera fails to "let us in" on the real story. The film, however begins to take over with a splendid shot of the prisoner bursting out of the water and sucking in the air of life.

THE TURNED-ON ESCAPEE

There is a paragraph of Bierce's with one hundred and fifty words describing Farquhar experiencing a conscious expansion, of a "turning-on" after his escape and realization that he is alive. Bierce tells us that Farquhar now sees directly "individual trees," "the veining of each leaf," "the very insects upon them . . . the brilliant-bodied flies." Bierce says Peyton "noted the prismatic colors in . . . the dewdrops," and heard the "strokes of the waterspider's legs, like oars." As narrator, he *tells* us these things and we can imagine what it must be like for Peyton.

But Enrico's camera *shows* us and lets us hear these fantastic things. Close-ups of insects, leaves, and the song "Livin' Man" by a highly syncopated Negro voice implode upon the perceiver who identifies with Peyton. This relief of escape and hypersensitivity is experienced by the audience. In retrospect, the intensity of this sense-communication informs the preceding scene of the agony of the hanging in Peyton's mind. We were not told visually or orally what emotions Peyton experienced, but now we have an implicit knowledge of what it must have been like.

If we put the scenes back to back the total effect of the film is better because of its brilliant "turned-on" scene of the resurrection, even though we lose the well-written introspective psychology of a man dying and thinking he is being freed. This psychology as Bierce wrote of it must be supplied by the individual observer-listener in order to get the full impact of the film. Enrico was simply not able to tell it all, but he had to emphasize what his medium could do most effectively.

To sum up, the written medium favors the inner action, intellectual, spiritual, psychological or what have you. The camera cannot follow easily into such places, and if it does, it will have to modify the original, which is perfectly legitimate. The viewer-listener must watch for what is implied and supply his own insight. But where it is a question of presenting action or outer events the film can hardly be equaled.

A SELECTED BIBLIOGRAPHY ON LITERARY ADAPTATIONS IN FILM

See the literature marked "3" in the Bibliography at the close of the book for complete data on these and other related readings.

Bluestone *Novels into Films.*
Ross *Picture.*
Sheridan *The Motion Picture and the Teaching of English.*

[SPIN-OFFS]

Spin-offs concerning film adaptations in general are given at the end of Chapter Four. The following are specifically about AN OCCURRENCE AT OWL CREEK BRIDGE. These discussions and projects, so closely related to the more familiar world of prose, will act as a transition to discussions on the film as film.

One of the most helpful guides to the appreciation of Bierce's short story is given in the teacher's edition of the series entitled *Insights Into Literature*. (Boston: Houghton Mifflin, 1965, pp. 145-153. See also the teacher's handbook, pp. 42-43.) The short story is in various anthologies and collections of Bierce's works.

Discussion

1. Where is the action taking place in Peyton Farquhar's experience? Is this really action? How much of Farquhar's *real* time elapses from the beginning to the end of this 27 minute film?

2. The soundtrack is often poor on rented copies of AN OCCURRENCE. Could you make out the words to the song sung as Peyton reached shore? A refrain was "I'm a livin' man." Could you suggest other music appropriate for this scene?

3. Adults may profit from comparing Enrico's direction of AN OC-CURRENCE to his direction of ZITA (1967), written by his wife, Lucienne Hamon. In ZITA, a young girl, filled with the horror of death, runs in panic through the streets of Paris in search of life. What similarity do you find with the story-line of AN OCCURRENCE?

4. What meanings do military drums have? How were they used at John F. Kennedy's funeral? (See the film YEARS OF LIGHTNING, DAY OF DRUMS.) How were military drums used in AN OCCURRENCE?

5. In what ways do "entertainment films" and "art films" differ in their use of symbols and subtle meaning? Is AN OCCURRENCE more of an art film than an entertainment film? Or, is it both? Give examples of films which are extreme opposites in terms of entertainment and art. Define your use of the terms "art" and "entertainment". Is it legitimate to attempt a distinction between the two?

6. Do you agree with the chapter's ideas on the difficulty of the film to express inner feelings? Are there some contradictory statements made? Write out your opinion on this difficult matter.

7. In what way is the film inhibited from expressing just what people think, do, and feel? In what way is the film superior to other art media in this respect?

8. Recall the point in the film AN OCCURRENCE after Peyton bursts out of the water. How does the film differ from the following section in the short story?

> He looked at the forest on the bank of the stream, saw the very individual trees, the leaves and the veining of each leaf—saw the very insects upon them: the locusts, the brilliant-bodied flies, the gray spiders stretching their webs from twig to twig. He noted the prismatic colors in all the dewdrops upon a million blades of grass. The humming of the gnats, the beating of the dragonflies' wings, the strokes of the water-spider's legs, like oars which had lifted their boat—all these made audible music. A fish slid along beneath his eyes and he heard the rush of its body parting the water.

Projects

1. Decide how *you* would film the scene in which Peyton comes out of the water. Try to decide how to portray the inner joy of Peyton to be alive. Try to express what Ambrose Bierce has written, as well as how *you* would feel if suddenly "brought back to life".

2. Collect a series of slides of stills which depict some of the sensations and impressions Peyton saw. Add whatever sound background you need, as well as any effects required to create the total impression. Present the program to your group.

Four

The Stage Play Adapted

SHARON FEYEN ·

The film is an art form and the stage play is an art form. Each is a distinctive medium. Each must be allowed to speak through its own specific form and focus. Thus the stage play relies heavily on words and gestures for interpretation and explanation, whereas the film can use mountains, oceans, deserts, mob scenes, weather, phenomena.

Far too often movie goers have judged and criticized film adaptations by their fidelity to the minutiae of the original form. They have judged all the media by the same standards and have failed to recognize the unique aspects of each, aspects which create a special interpretation, give a particular impression.

The stage play and the movie make use of sight and sound. Both present their messages before a seated audience. But the playgoer remains stationary. He sits before the stage. He can see only what is large and prominent, and rely on the dialogue to fill in what he cannot see or understand.

Film is more completely visual. It is free of the somewhat confining limits of stage and boundaries. It can more easily jump the barriers of time and space, can more convincingly juxtapose settings and situations and images to create the desired effects. It can interpret through cinematic technique and in brief span of time what the play does primarily through words. It can show vast deserts, forests, oceans, city slums, where the play can only talk about or suggest them through props. It can give insight *into* situations through one glance of a well-placed camera.

[33]

The object of this chapter is not to show how one medium is better than the other, but how each medium must be critically evaluated in terms of how fully it exploits its own peculiar abilities. So, the good film must be *good film,* and the good stage play must be *good stage.*

William Gibson once wrote, "The camera is the most facile medium in the world to write for; with the free run of time and space it can untie one story knot at a time and skip on, and has such transparency that it does not need, but is burdened by, too many words."

In comparing the stage play STALAG 17, a smash hit on Broadway in 1951, and director Billy Wilder's film version of the same name which appeared in 1953, it is well to keep the media differences in mind. While both versions show a group of men in conflict with situations enclosed within the cramping and threatening confines of a Nazi prison camp, the methods of presentation are different. The stage version is confined, of necessity, to the building and an outer court. If the camera retained the limitations demanded by the original stage presentation, the viewer would soon become tired and impatient. Instead, the film makes use of a wider range of field, uses larger, more diversified settings and more space.

Thus the film opens a night before the play does. We watch the men in the stalag making final preparations for the escape of Johnson and Manfredi. We watch as Sefton lays bets on the odds for the successful attempt. We crawl with the two men, being brought into the actual scene of escape through a careful use of subjective camera. And we are kept aware of the tension in the barracks as the camera cuts back and forth between the escaping men and the rest of the company in the stalag.

The play opens with the morning roll call and the announcement, as much for the benefit of the men in the stalag as to let the audience know what has happened, of the death of Johnson and Manfredi. The Americans are called out and made to stand at attention. In the film, the morning scene is made dramatic as the camera pans in a slow, painful sweep down the line of men standing at attention. This silent, relentless movement of the camera is used to advantage when the German commandant discovers the radio which the prisoners throughout the camp have been smuggling from barracks to barracks. The film viewer realizes that the discovery has been made, but the men in the stalag do not. A slowly moving camera pans the radio cord and settles on the set itself, just as Schultz's eyes would have done. In the stage play the men themselves announce the confiscation of the radio set. It is a case of "tell," instead of "show," again necessitated by the stage medium.

Students of the two versions will find other examples in which the unique abilities of the camera contrast with the word-oriented stage play

STALAG 17, *1959*

form. The highlighting of the light cord, the chess set, the Christmas tree and record player, and the sweeping shots made through the subjective eye of the camera as it pans the prison courtyard in search of the hidden prisoner Dunbar—all are peculiar to the film medium. All lend an intensity and interpretation impossible on stage.

A SELECTED BIBLIOGRAPHY ON THE STAGE PLAY ADAPTED

See the literature marked "4" in the Bibliography at the close of the book for complete data on these and other related readings.

Arnheim *Film as Art.*
Gibson *Dinny and the Witches, The Miracle Worker: Two Plays.*
McAnany *Film Viewer's Handbook.*
Sheridan *The Motion Picture and the Teaching of English.*

COLLECTIONS OF TELEVISION PLAYS

Chayefsky, Paddy *Television Plays.* New York: Simon and Schuster, 1955.

Foote, Horton *Harrison, Texas.* New York: Harcourt, Brace and World, 1956.

Mosel, Tad *Other People's Houses.* New York: Simon and Schuster, 1956.

Rose, Reginald *Six Television Plays.* New York: Simon and Schuster, 1956.

Serling, Rod *Patterns; Four TV Plays.* New York: Simon and Schuster, 1957.

[SPIN-OFFS]

Discussion on STALAG 17

1. What are the major differences and similiarities between the play and film versions? Compare the first scene of Act One of the play and the opening scenes of the film. Why do you think these differences were introduced into the film?

2. Compare the percentage of dialogue in the two versions. What would you say is the reason for any difference you may discover?

3. What is the place of background sound and/or music in the two versions? Does either one use sound for ironic or dramatic effects? How is light used and controlled in the two versions?

4. What is the place of Horney in the story? How is this shown in each version?

5. Why do you think the individual versions used the method they did of telling the audience who the traitor was?

6. What are some of the most outstanding portions of the film which would not have taken place in the stage version? Compare the final scene in both versions. Why the difference? Why would you not want either substituted in place of the other?

7. What is the value of black and white instead of color in this particular film? (Recall the discussion Chapter Three AN OCCURRENCE AT OWL CREEK BRIDGE. Was there one section that may have been effectively done in color, while the rest of the film remained in black and white?)

8. How do the various camera angles and positions add to the impact of the film? Recall details to prove your point.

Discussion on Literary Adaptions in General

1. After writing the movie script ON THE WATERFRONT, Budd Schulberg developed it into a novel. His essay "Why write it if you can't sell it to pictures?" tells of his experiences in both ways of storytelling. In this essay Schulberg states that "a filmplay seems to be related more closely to the short story than to the novel." He explains:

> The film is an art of high points. I think of it as embracing five or six sequences, each one mounting to a climax that rushes the action onward. The novel is an art of high, middle, and low points and, though I believe its form must never be overlooked, it's the sort of form you lock the front door against, knowing full well it will climb into one of the small back-windows thoughtfully left open for it. The film does best when it concentrates on a single character. It tells the "Informer" superbly. It tends to loose itself in the ramifications of "War and Peace." It has no time for what I call the essential digression. The "digression" of complicated, contradictory character. The "digression" of social background. The film must go from significant episode to more significant episode in a constantly mounting pattern. It's an exciting form. But it pays a price for this excitement. It cannot wander as life wanders, or pause as life always pauses, to contemplate the incidental or the unexpected. The film has a relentless form. Once you set it up it becomes your master, demanding and rather terrifying. It has its own tight logic, and once you stray from that straight and narrow path the tension slackens—or, you might say, the air is left out of the balloon.
> Budd Schulberg, "Why Write It When You Can't Sell It To The Pictures?", SATURDAY REVIEW, Sept. 3, 1955. Copyright 1955 The Saturday Review Associates, Inc.

1. Can you think of exceptions to Schulberg's complaint that film is an art of high points? What essential "digressions" can the novel include

that are usually not put into a film? Are there some "digressions" which a film can employ that a novel cannot?

2. There has been an increasing number of books written after a screenplay, reversing the usual practice. Can you name a few of these?

3. Are there more novels put into film than plays? Is there less "distance" from a play (especially a television play) to film, than from a novel to film? Or, is each case different and are there no guidelines?

4. Are certain types of fantasy or high imagination impossible to stage and difficult to film? There are at least three film versions of Lewis Carroll's ALICE IN WONDERLAND. The animated version seems to be closest to the original spirit, yet other versions could also be good movies. Is animation more conducive to fantasy than "live film"? What technique was used in THE WIZARD OF OZ, MARY POPPINS, PINOCCHIO, and 2001: A SPACE ODYSSEY? Each achieved fantasy in different ways. Was each equally effective?

5. Suggest a specific scene of a novel or play which would be very cinematic. How would you direct this scene? Would you have to take certain liberties with the original in order to display the potential of your camera?

6. Very often films adapted from novels or plays are disappointing to a person who experiences the original version. Could you offer some observations on what makes this happen, or why the opposite is also often the case?

7. Compare a movie, play, or television presentation that you have seen and that is an adaptation of something you have read, or could read. Be specific in comparing the two, as was done with AN OCCURRENCE AT OWL CREEK BRIDGE in Chapter Three.

Projects

1. What is your stand on the issue of whether film or written literature best captures and/or expresses psychological states? To support your opinion, write a few paragraphs in which you try to capture a mood or state of mind. Then try the same with 8mm. film, and attempt to capture the mood or state of mind through camera work and editing.

2. Take a poll on the magazines most often read by people of all ages. Does the inclusion of photography seem to affect the public's choice? Does it affect your choice?

3. Make a word-only collage and then a picture-only collage, each expressing your impressions of a particular film. Can people guess which movie you have "illustrated"? Are there any differences between the word-only and the picture-only collages? Which collage do you prefer

and which did people find the better expression of the film being illustrated?

4. Make or take two filmed versions of an event, one from a stationary
viewpoint (as in a stage play) and one from a movable camera and
edit-able footage point of view. Keep this simple, limited to some basic
action, including facial as well as bodily gestures. Discuss the differences
in the end result.

5. Study sections of a film with the sound turned off. Without sound
would PYSCHO be just as mysterious, SOUND OF MUSIC just as entertaining, THE ODD COUPLE just as funny, or A MAN AND A WOMAN just as
beautiful? Which type of films seem to rely most on the soundtrack?
Which type seems to rely the least on the soundtrack?

Part Three

Forms of Film

The River, *1937*

Five

The Short Film

RAY SANDERS, S.M.

Television commercials may have much to do with civil rights revolution as court decisions. The one inescapable message is—here is a world that is attractive and that you should live in.—(Former F.C.C. Commissioner Lee Loevinger)

Only recently has the American citizen come to realize the titanic significance of screened images. Only recently, through the pop-writing of Marshall McLuhan, have the insights of communication theorists like Innis, Schramm, Greenhill, Ong, Bluem, and Lynch been translated into the language of mass media. A need has been created: the need to understand the visual language, the primary vehicle of the twentieth-century communicator.

One way of meeting this need is through a more considerate use of the short film in the humanities classes of the high school curriculum. Social studies, language arts, fine arts, and guidance classes often use a selection of short films. If these films are used, not as icing on the cake but as part of the main course of the curriculum, there is no reason why they should not serve as a basis for developing a greater appreciation of visual language.

The purpose of this chapter is to demonstrate how by using short films teachers and students of the humanities can enhance their understanding and appreciation of film as art.

Practically all films demonstrate a reality. They might introduce: a new product (commercial); report on the latest world events (news); probe a social problem (documentary); point out life's incongruities

[43]

(comedy); elicit sympathy for a fallen man (tragedy); reflect on the purpose of life (philosophy); visually interpret a literary classic (adaptation); or visually reflect on society (social commentary). Used in the humanities classes, films can be a visual experience of what it is like to be a human being.

However, perception and understanding of content do not just happen. Reflection and intelligent discussion should follow each screening (presuming, of course, that the film selected has a visual content worthy of inductive, communal understanding). It is precisely in the contemplation and guided dialogue that education will take place. Unless feelings, criticisms, judgments, and suggestions are aired and shared, there will be no chance for a development of real understanding and appreciation of the demonstrated reality.

A familiarity with the grammar and properties of camera-ville is an important step in developing a taste for the artistic film. Chapter Thirteen presents film grammar and cinematic properties with examples to illustrate each property. Without an understanding of these elements of film, technique is easily confused with content, and this confusion renders aesthetic appreciation most difficult. Technique is to be appreciated, but in terms of the reality created or reported in the film. The *how* is important only because of its ability to enhance the *what*. Artistic taste is not proportionate to knowledge of artistic means, but understanding the means enhances our realization of the artist's intentions.

For example, Willard Van Dyke and R. Steiner's THE CITY, made some thirty years ago, contains some shocking juxtapositions of slum living and suburban living, a marvelously humorous bit of editing, satirizing unconscious mouth-stuffing in a crowded luncheonette. It is important to recognize these clever cinematics; but it is more important to relate this four minutes of film to the other 26 to appreciate the worth of the whole film. After a class has seen a film, been given some time for reflection, and reviewed the film, discussion (or some type of group activity leading to communal understanding) is necessary. Initial remarks will focus on the particular means used by the director. But subsequent discussion should dwell on the relevance of the director's point of view, his presentation of reality. (See the stills from THE CITY on page 73.)

It must be remembered that the art of film lies in its representation of reality. It presents a virtual reality—a reality condensed by the limits of space and time. To appreciate film is to pass an informed, critical judgment on the meaningfulness of the image of reality and the beautiful manner in which that reality is presented. Short films offer especially good examples of concise and compact presentation.

THE CITY reflects sharp contrasts which are at times faintly visible and at times poignantly evident. As discussions progress, viewers may note that the director's vision seems slightly blurred. The community life presented is too perfect; the city life, too sterile. And the film becomes, noticeably, a propaganda piece for suburban land developers.

A criticism of the film, such as the one just presented, does not diminish the beauty of its presentation. Nor does Lee Loevinger imply (in the quotation cited at the outset of this chapter) that TV commercials are not well made. Indeed, no company is going to spend $50,000 producing a commercial and another $100,000 or so on air time unless the mass audience is attracted by the commercial and persuaded to try, buy, sell, or whatever. Loevinger's implied concern is with the inability of the viewing public to distinguish fantasy from reality; to distinguish Disneyland from Detroit. And this ability to distinguish is not a skill to be learned but rather a sense to be cultivated. It is a type of growth which requires experience, time, and critical openness to the opinions of others.

FILM TECHNIQUES

A good beginning could be made with such films as PACIFIC 231, THE TENDER GAME, "Diving Sequence" from OLYMPIC GAMES, 1936, DREAM OF THE WILD HORSES, NIGHT MAIL, SKY, LITHO, NANOOK OF THE NORTH, or BOILED EGG. After the screening, discussion could center on questions such as:

1. How does the film differ from drama? from TV? from poetry? from the other visual arts?

2. Does film need sound to qualify as art? Could a story be presented without dialogue?

3. What was the director trying to show in this film?

4. What is the difference between the film(s) screened here and the last one you saw in a movie theater?

Editing patterns discussed in Chapter Ten can be brought out especially well in the films already mentioned. Other good short films are SKYSCRAPER, THE RIVER, GRANTON TRAWLER, the "Odessa Steps" sequence from POTEMKIN, HAVE I TOLD YOU LATELY THAT I LOVE YOU?, NIGHT AND FOG, VERY NICE, VERY NICE, and THE PLAIN MAN'S GUIDE TO ADVERTISING.

The various types of shots, camera angles, and camera movements can be studied in shorts such as CORRAL, TIME IS, THE RED KITE, THE CHICKEN, and LANGUAGE OF FACES. Also, the principles of continuity could be discussed after the screening of any of these films.

Areas of symbolism are well illustrated in THE RED BALLOON, GOOD NIGHT, SOCRATES, STRINGBEAN, A TIME FOR BURNING, SUNDAY, and OH, DREAMLAND. Screening prior to class will suggest other possibilities.

Character development is shown through subjective camera, through reaction to environment, through dialogue, and through juxtaposition of images (visual metaphor). PHOEBE, NO REASON TO STAY, THE GOLDEN FISH, A TIME OUT OF WAR, TWO MEN AND A WARDROBE, NANOOK OF THE NORTH, BUSTER KEATON RIDES AGAIN, and THE HAND are a few of the shorter films which would be helpful in coming to understand cinema's way of character development. A few of the feature films which achieve "character development" are given in Chapter Thirteen, No. 11.

FILM TYPES

In writing, the "report" is distinguished from the: "essay," "poem," "parable," "short story," "drama," and the "novel." Likewise, there are films that record (documentary, *cinéma vérité* photoplay); film using selective representation (revelation of character through symbol); interpretive films (novel to film, play to film, film about film, social commentary, moral fable, original films); discovery films (pure film and the animated cartoon).

The recording film, like the newspaper article, visually and more or less objectively reports a situation. The documentary usually treats one subject. NANOOK OF THE NORTH (the Eskimo), THE DETACHED AMERICANS (apathy of U.S. citizenry), HARVEST OF SHAME (migrant worker problem), A TIME FOR BURNING (racial bias in a Lutheran parish), and THE CITY (importance of city planning). These are some of the documentaries which might be screened for discussion. (In this regard, see Chapter Eight on the documentary film. Chapter Twelve, programs 4 and 29, also recommends some documentary films.)

Cinéma vérité allows the camera to roam, to stalk, to probe its subject matter, making a visual point here and there but interfering as little as possible with the actuality of what it is studying. It relies on the viewer to synthesize its presentation and derive meaning. In its handling of dramatic time, cinéma vérité is somewhat similar to stream-of-consciousness writing. LONELY BOY and DON'T LOOK BACK (two probing studies of two different folk singers), SUNDAY (a sharp look at the New York upheaval over Sunday park restrictions), and BLIND GARY DAVIS (impressionistic view of a Negro street singer), as well as PRIMARY (the John F. Kennedy campaign in Wisconsin), would provide interesting and beneficial discussion of this genre.

Photoplays are filmed stage presentations, with only a minimum of film technique. Most of the short photoplays are poor fare.* It would be well to stay with the feature-length presentations, such as Olivier's OTHELLO. It would also be well to keep in mind the difference between the photoplay and the stage adaptation. The latter was considered in Chapter Four.

"Films about films" are available from many libraries and distributors. The 1966 *JEA Media Guide* contains an extensive list of related short films. Social commentary is strong in THE CITY, PHOEBE, THE RIVER, 21-87, and GOOD NIGHT, SOCRATES. Moral fables to be considered include THE HOLE, CLAY, I WAS A NINETY-POUND WEAKLING, CROSS-COUNTRY RUNNER, HELP! MY SNOWMAN IS BURNING DOWN, THE HAT, THE EYE OF THE BEHOLDER, and BOUNDARY LINES.

Discovery films challenge even the experienced cinemaniac. They invite a high degree of involvement and often divergent interpretation. Among the pure films that might be used are PANTA PHEI, N.Y., N.Y., MOSAIC, BEGONE DULL CARE, ORANGE AND BLUE, VERY NICE, VERY NICE, NEIGHBORS and A CHAIRY TALE. Animated films that would lend themselves to discussion here include FIDDLE-DE-DEE, CHRISTMAS CRACKER, THE TOP, THE ADVENTURES OF *, AUTOMANIA 2000, BOILED EGG, SCRAP OF PAPER AND A PIECE OF STRING, and HEN HOP. Chapter Twelve, programs 10 and 35, lists several other short films.

The two approaches sketched above (analysis of film by technique and by film type) should prove more than ample for beginning a film education (or film appreciation) course. Some films, because of their scope and style, have been suggested under several headings. The study group will, no doubt, find other suggested films that will fit several categories. Association and discovery are two indications of an interested and visually aware group.

Many resources and resource people are available to the group or school interested in inaugurating a cinema program: public libraries, museums, university A-V centers, college film teachers, film critics, photographers, camera shop and TV studio personnel, as well as local film societies and independent film buffs. These individuals are interested in helping film educators and will add a professional luster to the school's film program. Whenever possible, the class members themselves should preview the films and lead the ensuing discussion.

---

*For this reason many short photoplays often listed in guides to short films are not included in listings in Chapter Twelve or the Appendix I.—D. Wigal, ed.

A SAMPLE APPROACH

VERY NICE, VERY NICE, by Arthur Lipsett of the National Film Board of Canada, runs seven minutes, and both startles and intrigues the observant viewer. A screening of the film offers an excellent opportunity to engage in the kind of analysis we have been discussing.

The group studying the film will have two main purposes in mind: 1.) to visualize man's tendency to generalize existing problems to the extent that he is no longer conscious of them, nor responsible for their correction; and 2.) to appreciate the contemporary film maker's ability to state today's problems in an artistic way.

The film should be screened twice toward the end of the period on the first day of the unit. No orientation is necessary, but the class should be encouraged to discuss the film among themselves after the period. In preparation for the next day, the class should develop (individually) pictorial satires of well-known TV commercials or role-plays. Without any discussion of the presentation, re-screen VERY NICE, VERY NICE. After the screening, the discussion leader elicits the class's initial impressions of the film. Most of the initial comments will probably concern technique, since this is the first impressive element that strikes the viewer. The rapidity of the grotesque still pictures, the meaningless babble of the sound track, and the confusing order of the juxtapositioning are typical of first impressions of this film.

If this "initial reactions" probe does not unearth a good sampling of viewer comment, the discussion leader might ask for comment on ideas such as:

1. Did the third screening prompt different impressions than the first?
2. Did any particular images seem more memorable than others?
3. Does anyone recall any phrases from the soundtrack of the film?

After the discussion has begun, the initial impressions or particularly vivid images, snatches of dialogue, or hinted meanings can be applied to the content:

1. What is the director trying to show by any initially striking image mentioned in the earlier discussion?
2. Is what the director showing us worthwhile? That is, does it bring us to any greater realization of what it means to be human?
3. What has this film to do with the members of this particular group?

As a follow-up, the class could try to locate records, plays, feature films, novels, poetry, TV shows, or art of other media which satirically illustrate and illuminate one of the social problems considered in the editorial stances of the local papers.

Subsequent class discussion, while naturally focusing on man's needs, will also work toward an understanding of film as a collage of all the arts. With this insight comes an appreciation of the task of the film critic and a heightened need to grow in appreciation of the film as art.

The approaches to discussion set down in this chapter will not suit the needs of every humanities class. "Approaches" must be individually tailored and adapted to local needs and possibilities. The advice of local film experts, other media faculty and students, and various publications should be utilized.

SUGGESTED FOLLOW-UP

But what advantages will accrue to the class members as they continue viewing and discussing? Very few will move to Hollywood, although a few might attempt to make their own films. The day of the 8mm and Super 8 movie camera is here, and the home movie is as popular as the snapshot album. The noticeable development for the individual members of the class and/or film club will be a growing appreciation of the artist's ability to enable the viewer to live a more conscious, autonomous, and communal human life. Class study and consideration of film art will develop the discernment powers of students. They will promote greater depth in seeing, and greater creativity in composition. Cinema sophistication will also enhance the ability to use the camera in a really artistic and interpretive manner. Thus, the "home movie" might well become a medium for experimentation in a new and vital form of communication. And after the last film has been rewound (or earlier), the group will ask about making their own films.

A SELECTED BIBLIOGRAPHY ON THE SHORT FILM

See the literature marked "5" in the Bibliography at the close of the book for complete data on these and other related readings.

Kuhns *Short Films in Religious Education.*

Kuhns *Themes: Short Films for Discussion.*

Kuhns and Stanley *Exploring the Film.*

McCaffrey *A Guide to Short Films for Religious Education.*

Parrington *An Educator's Guide to the Use of Film.*

Sullivan *Movies: The Universal Language.*

Wigal "Feature Book Review," *Ave Maria,* December 2, 1967. (A review of books by Kuhns and McCaffrey.)

[SPIN-OFFS]

Discussion

There are several helpful discussion guides on short films. Films marked "s" in Appendix I are less than sixty-one minutes long. Many of these have a key to discussion questions offered by Patrick McCaffrey (M and M2) and/or William Kuhns (K).

Projects

1. Work up a scenario (a film script) for a short film. A good beginning would be to try a script for an original filmed television commercial, or a visual interpretation of a popular song.

2. Prepare a tape-recorded sound track for this film, or to accompany a collection of slides.

3. Analyze the visual ads presented on television: try to find out what makes each appealing, convincing, different. Compare these same ads to static, on-paper counterparts. How does film differ from the print media? (Another worthwhile comparison would be to consider the movie, phonograph record and book of Marshall McLuhan's THE MEDIUM IS THE MASSAGE. See the Bibliography.)

4. Follow a television advertising campaign for a single product, idea, or issue. Try to find ways in which the producers use visual materials such as light, symbolism, movement, that could not be employed by any other medium. (The large book THE BEST TELEVISION COMMERCIALS may help here, as well as the last section of TV 68, TV 69, etc.)

Six

The Western

JAMES W. ARNOLD

The western has been a staple subject for motion pictures from the very beginning, which is usually marked from Edwin S. Porter's GREAT TRAIN ROBBERY (1903), a half-western, half-gangster film. The reasons for the perennial popularity of the cowboy movie are many and complex, but some of them are clearly aesthetic. There are many reasons the western is ideally suited to the medium of motion pictures.

The locales are vast and photogenic, and have become increasingly so with technical developments in color and wide-screen cinematography.

The western traditionally uses a maximum of action and movement, and a minimum of dialogue. Audiences simply will not tolerate westerns that are overly theatrical or literary.

The breadth and unsettled nature of the setting, the American West of the late 19th century, lend themselves to stories involving movement. Not only is the typical hero a wanderer, who never stays too long in any one town or place, but often the whole cast is moving (the wagon train, stagecoach, cattle drive, search or escape plots). And the action is usually so spread out geographically, with related events occurring simultaneously, that it is ideal material for the skill of the film editor.

The lawless, primitive background allows conflicts to be worked out legitimately in terms of physical violence, which is, of course, external by nature and much more easily photographed than more civilized, internal human conflicts.

The growth of a stylized western mythology, involving only a few basic plots and a perennial set of recurring characters, makes for sim-

[51]

plicity. A few broad strokes will usually establish all the story and characterization a western needs, and these can be readily achieved in visual terms. The film maker can quickly get on with the drama and action.

Thus one needs only to know whether a new western is about 1.) the good sheriff, 2.) the reformed gunfighter, 3.) the hero searching for a lost enemy or loved one, 4.) the group against the wilderness, perhaps seeking gold or treasure, 5.) the cavalry vs. the Indians, or 6.) the cattlemen vs. the farmers or settlers. When the story-type has been determined, the rest falls into a pattern with chiefly only stylistic variations and differences in complexity and maturity.

The basic character-types include the Hero, who is always competent and virtuous, usually a lonely outsider who is merely pausing on a melancholy journey to Someplace Else; the Good Woman, a symbol of culture and civilized values who seldom understands or gets her man; the Villain, frequently a symbol for pure evil, especially of greed and cruelty, often as competent as the hero and usually surrounded by lesser allies; the Bad Woman, the unattached and unvalued female who understands the hero but seldom wins him, and the Innocent (a child, an old man, an Indian, a younger brother), who admires the protagonist's heroism and skill in violence but does not understand his complex moral doubts: he is either killed or lives on to build the hero's legend.

There are probably as many favorite westerns as there are movie fans, but two of the best and most famous were made within a year of each other in the early 1950's: Fred Zinnemann's HIGH NOON (1952) and George Stevens' SHANE (1953). Chapter Twelve, programs 5 and 30, recommends several western films.

HIGH NOON is the modern prototype of the "good sheriff" western: the story of the lawman who stands alone, out of sheer integrity, courage and devotion to justice, against the massed forces of evil. Visually, the veteran cowboy-hero Gary Cooper, his face etched and shoulders stooped by decades of experience and frontier wisdom, was perfect for the role. The film also offers first-rate portrayals of the classic villain and the good and bad women (played by Grace Kelly and Katy Jurado).

The quality of the film hangs on its beauty and simplicity of technique, and on the mature and insightful variations it plays on the traditional plot. In contrasting the integrity of the hero with the meanness and cowardice of the town's good citizens, who abandon him as well as the concepts of Right and Law at a time of crisis, the film makes important comments about the meaning of democracy and social responsibility. Of course, it also tells an exciting story, with atmosphere and suspense built inexorably, as the clock approaches the crucial hour of noon. The

HIGH NOON, *1952, Gary Cooper*

movie is an excellent example of the flexibility of "time" in the film, and of the use of theme music to support both mood and motivation. The final shoot-out on the abandoned streets is superbly staged and imaginatively edited.

SHANE has been described as a perfect film, a virtual apotheosis of the western form using the traditional "reformed gunfighter" plot. It is one of the few movies of any kind whose excellence depends entirely on the beauty of its technique; in story, character and dialogue it is really more trite than exceptional, and unlike HIGH NOON, it has no social message.

Stevens takes advantage of the sculpture-like good looks of Alan Ladd, a quiet-spoken god in fringed buckskins, to capture once and for all the image of the western hero: haunted, noble, fierce in his independence yet envying the lot of ordinary men, pausing briefly on his competence in violence. The Ladd of SHANE is pure hero, and Stevens emphasizes his stature by allowing us to see him through the eyes of a good-but-mortal family (Van Heflin, Jean Arthur, Brandon DeWilde).

The movie is full of virtuoso touches: the stark, ugly town, a mere collection of clapboard in the lovely Wyoming prairie; the frontier funeral on the windswept hill, its participants shot against the endless blue sky, the barroom brawl *par excellence* between Ladd and Ben Johnson; villain Jack Palance's brilliantly moody murder of Elisha Cook as thunderclouds bristle overhead; and the little boy's touching cries of "Come back, Shane!" as the wounded hero rides off into the darkening hills of his destiny. With SHANE our memories of *what* happened are forever joined with our images of *how* it happened, the sign of a great film.

Perhaps the outstanding quality of SHANE is its subtlety. We are not told, but rather are allowed to sense, the growing admiration of Ladd by the mother and the boy; the mutual respect but vague rivalry between Ladd and Heflin; the evil of the Palance character; Ladd's professional respect for Palance and his reluctance and sadness at the final need for violence.

The care with which the film is made is perhaps best revealed in the differences even in which the hero and villain ride their horses. Sound is manipulated beautifully so that we clearly hear dialogue in the town from the distant cemetery, and then when Ladd whispers his final challenge to Palance, the words reverberate through the theater.

In accord with western tradition, the hero of SHANE is willing to suffer early humiliations, and he takes his guns from the wall only when some crisis brings on his moral resolve. He goes to fight the villain alone, and he does it with honor: how he used the violence is very important to

SHANE, *1953, Alan Ladd*

him. The western hero is described fittingly as a kind of celibate knight who has relevance only where there is no established justice. As civilization comes and bad men die, he moves on to another frontier. Where there are no more frontiers, he becomes a figure of pathos, as in LONELY ARE THE BRAVE. The western is the last domain of the ancient hero; in other genres, the hero declines, either in skill or moral stature, and the resulting drama tends to be thin, unresolved, and unsatisfying.

The critical viewer must deal with each new western in relation to the classic tradition: what is the story, who are the characters, how, if at all, are they changed or given new depth, has the film maker provided any freshness in style and choreography (e.g. of gunfights, chases, battles)? Above all, as with any film one asks: has the film medium, with all its peculiar affinity for the western form, been fully used?

With a type as stylized as the western, it is perhaps dangerous to be too revolutionary: it goes against the grain of decades of tradition, for example, to allow the cruel exploitation of the innocent. Both the psychological and social-message western, as well as the spoof, tamper with the sense of tradition at great risk.

A SELECTED BIBLIOGRAPHY ON THE WESTERN FILM

See the literature marked "6" in the Bibliography at the close of the book for complete data on these and other related readings.

Cowie "The Growth of the Western," in his *International Film Guide, 1966.*

Eyles *The Western.*

Everson "The Western Outlaws," in his *The Bad Guys.*

Fenin and Everson *The Western.*

Gruber "The Western," in Yoakem's *TV and Screen Writing.*

Kitchen "Decline of the Western," *The Listener,* July 14, 1966.

Speed *The Western Film Annual* and *The Western Film and TV Annual.*

Vallance *Westerns: A Preview Special.*

Warshow "The Westerner," *The Immediate Experience.*

Whitehall "The Heroes Are Tired," *Film Quarterly,* XXII (Winter, 1966), pp. 12-14.

[SPIN-OFFS]

Discussion

1. Could the character of the boy in SHANE be eliminated without harming the picture? Could the same be said for the boy in HUD? How

do the closing scenes of these two great films differ? What was the role of the young boy in THE OLD MAN AND THE SEA?

2. Why is the villain of SHANE more memorable than the villain of HIGH NOON? Compare the techniques of building up to the final shoot-outs in these two westerns. Compare the two films also on grounds of believability and realism. Is the Heflin-Ladd fight better as cinema than the Cooper fight with Lloyd Bridges?

3. Cite examples of the use of the moving camera, subjective (intro-ceptive camera, aesthetic use of long shots, cutting to simultaneous events.

4. Which westerns have you seen recently on television or in the movie houses? Which did you enjoy the most? Compare its hero, villain and leading female characters with those in SHANE and HIGH NOON.

5. Which western elements were in BONNIE AND CLYDE? What comparisons could be made between the horse and the car, the barmaid and the moll, the sheriff and the police, etc? Have you seen other "non-western" films which employ many patterns more proper to western movies?

6. A film with many western elements and excellent for discussion of Christ-symbols was entitled THEY CAME TO CORDURA, directed by Robert Rossen in 1959. A "way-out" comparison could be made with DON QUIXOTE and/or the play THE MAN OF LAMANCHA. (For "star lovers," by the way, THEY CAME TO CORDURA featured Gary Cooper, Rita Hayworth and Van Heflin.)

Projects

1. Take a western spoof and indicate what classic western elements it changes. Are any changes made in camera, sound, editing? Besides the perennial spoofs offered on television, see also CAT BALLOU (1965).

2. Analyze a western film for the kinds of violence it presents. Besides counting how many people are killed, it is important to notice *how* this gunplay takes place. What is the attitude of the characters and the film maker toward this violence? Compare the treatment of violence in a particular western to that in an old gangster film and/or to BONNIE AND CLYDE. Recent films with western elements which could be considered here include THE PROFESSIONALS, FISTFUL OF DOLLARS and MACKENNA'S GOLD.

3. Compare Angela Douglas' take-off on Annie Oakley in CARRY ON, COWBOY (U.K. 1966) to Barbara Stanwyck's classic portrayal in ANNIE OAKLEY (1935), or Betty Hutton's in ANNIE GET YOUR GUN (1950). Could each of these diverse interpretations of a historical character be "correct"?

4. Compare the Japanese film SEVEN SAMURAI, directed by Akira Kurosawa, 1954, to THE MAGNIFICENT SEVEN, directed by John Sturges, 1960. For a complete study consider also THE RETURN OF THE SEVEN directed by Burt Kennedy, 1967.

5. What liberties with history are often taken by western film? See THE REAL WEST, NBC-TV documentary (March 29, 1961) or several books written on the real West in the library.

Seven

The Comedy

JAMES W. ARNOLD

The popular and artistic success of film comedy during the screen's silent era was the result of a happy collaboration between style and medium. The slapstick sketches and broad burlesque mannerisms that stage comedians like Charlie Chaplin brought with them to Hollywood proved ideal for a soundless medium in which visuals told everything and utter surface simplicity was a distinct asset. The pantomime and the sight gag, merely part of the tools of the trade in the music hall, became the essence in the cinema. What's more, the comedians found their sight gag skills enlarged by the possibilities of the new medium: because of the close-up, even small gestures could be funny; because of editing, the wildest improbabilities could be made to happen; because of the infinite expansiveness of film space, the comic chase could be deliriously broadened.

There was also the opportunity to work with objects, which could in film be given an importance and life of their own. Most providential of all, the obvious and easily identifiable characters they had begun to develop on stage proved ideally suited to the screen, where characterization usually had to be quick and visual. Chaplin, Keaton, Lloyd, Langdon were always the same character, down to the smallest item of costume and gesture, in film after film.

Today the basis of film comedy remains the same—the joke based on sight and movement, with the possibilities of sound (in terms of human speech, music and "noise") added. It is true that successful film comedies have been built solely on character situations and witty dia-

[59]

logue. In such cases the audience has been responding to a more or less artfully photographed stage play. PHILADELPHIA STORY (1940), STATE OF THE UNION (1948), MARY, MARY (1963) are good examples. Today most adapters of stage comedies make certain that in the film version the lead is given to the visual (THE KNACK AND HOW TO GET IT, A THOUSAND CLOWNS). Even largely verbal comedians like Bob Hope and Groucho Marx, in their films lean heavily on sight gags, often using their verbal wit to comment on or counterpoint what is seen. In recent years, in fact, many important movie comedies have returned to the broad techniques of the silent era or broken new comic ground by exploiting the possibilities of editing (THE GREAT RACE, THOSE MAGNIFICENT MEN IN THEIR FLYING MACHINES, THE RUSSIANS ARE COMING, BILLY LIAR, HELP!, etc.) Chapter Twelve, programs 9 and 34, recommends several comedy films.

SINGIN' IN THE RAIN (1952), a Technicolor musical made in Hollywood by the directorial team of Gene Kelly and Stanley Donen, is dearly regarded by movie buffs, partly because it is an affectionate spoof of the movie industry itself during the painful years of its transition from silents to sound. Its musical numbers are also brightly done, but it is primarily an intriguing example of "cinematic" comedy: most of its comic effects depend on sight gags, incongruous editing, or the skillfully ridiculous contrast between what we see on the screen and what we hear on the sound track.

RAIN is basically the story of a silent film idol (played by Gene Kelly) who begins to realize his acting talents will be inappropriate in the new sound era. So he talks his studio into converting his newest Douglas Fairbanks-type silent adventure into a singing-and-dancing musical romance. The main problem is that his longtime co-star (Jean Hagen) has no musical talent and talks like a high-pitched kewpie doll. To save Miss Hagen's career and the film, her voice and singing are dubbed by a young starlet (Debbie Reynolds). Eventually, of course, the mean and self-centered Miss Hagen is dumped entirely and Miss Reynolds justly gets both the role and the leading man.

The beauty of the technique is revealed in the opening sequence where Kelly describes his early career for the benefit of an enraptured preview audience. His words are contrasted with the flashback images as he speaks, for example, of his high society friends, and we see him in a poolroom. As he describes his important early film roles, we see that he was a stuntman: the humor in each scene depends, further, on the limited screen image. We see him, glamorously garbed, roaring off on a motorcycle; as the camera pulls back and pans, it becomes clear he is going

Stan Laurel and Oliver Hardy

SINGIN' IN THE RAIN, *1952, Gene Kelly and Donald O'Connor*

to drive it off a cliff into a lake. It is twice as funny, because we couldn't see that cliff in the first shot.

Then we are shown a segment of Kelly's silent movie, which is actually rather a straight-faced and expert imitation of the acrobatic Fairbanks derring-do. But it is made comic by the frequent insertion of exaggeratedly inane dialogue subtitles. This bit also helps the movie's main theme by showing how unimportant intelligent speech was to the silent film.

Later, at a party, Kelly's producer presents a demonstration film which shows off the new talking-picture process (this technique of a film-within-a-film is used with comic effect throughout the movie). The humor of the moment depends entirely on the exaggerated lip movements of the pompous fellow giving the demonstration, his obvious lack-of-ease before the camera, and the distortion of his face when he walks to the camera for a close-up.

Next we find Kelly and his buddy (Donald O'Connor) at the studio lot. As they discuss their problems, they walk by an assembly line of adjacent sets, each being used for a production absurdly typical of the time. But the main laugh is produced again by the limited screen image, the humor growing as each new and wildly different set comes into view. The scene could not easily be done on a stage; even if it could, we would have to see all the sets simultaneously.

Later, there is a marvelously edited montage of typical scenes from the over-elaborate musicals of the 1930's, complete with the hundreds of girls dancing in unison to Busby Berkeley-type choreography. Cinema can perhaps be spoofed in other media, but not through the deliberately over-ripe use of cutting, camera angles, movement, and optical illusions.

Perhaps the most famous sequences in RAIN are those describing the director's frustrating efforts to get his cast to use dialogue mikes for the first time. The hilarity depends on the contrast between what the actors are trying to do and the actual sound that comes over the mike, e.g., Miss Hagen keeps forgetting where the mike is and her tinny voice constantly fluctuates in volume. Finally, after the mike is hidden in her bosom, it picks up her heartbeats and the sound of Kelly gallantly smooching her arm comes across like a giant bowl of snapping Rice Krispies. Incidentally, this whole sequence is shot cleverly from both inside and outside the studio sound room for the sake of maximum comic contrast between image and sound. Later, of course, we go to a theater to see the film that results from this nonsense, and again the comedy originates in the unexpected sound, chiefly from Miss Hagen's nervous habit of twirling her beads.

Several scenes later in the movie either describe the dubbing process or work comedy off the confusion that results from it. And the very last shot is a typically virtuoso filmic transition, a dissolve from a close-up of the leads to their pictures on a billboard advertising the new movie. As the camera pulls back, we see them again, in the flesh, holding hands under the giant sign.

Good comedy, of course, must be funny. But in evaluating movie comedy, the chief question is: *how* is it funny? It should make its jokes in ways that are united to the nature of the medium, i.e., in ways that are predominantly filmic.

A SELECTED BIBLIOGRAPHY ON THE COMEDY

See the literature marked "7" in the Bibliography at the close of the book for complete data on these and other related readings.

Agee "Comedy's Greatest Era," *Life,* September 3, 1949.
Blesch *Keaton.*
Bowman *Charlie Chaplin, His Life and Art.*
Chaplin *My Autobiography.*
Chaplin, Charles, Jr. *My Father, Charlie Chaplin.*
Eyles *The Marx Brothers.*
Griffith *Cinema of Gene Kelly.*
Lahue *World of Laughter.*
McCabe *Mr. Laurel and Mr. Hardy.*
McDonald and Conway and Ricci *The Films of Charlie Chaplin.*
Montgomery *Comedy Films.*
Sennett *King of Comedy, As Told to Cameron Shipp.*

[SPIN-OFFS]

Discussion on SINGIN' IN THE RAIN

1. Which sight gags in SINGIN' IN THE RAIN could not have been produced on the stage; which could just as easily have been produced well on stage? (One of the key elements of the musical HAIR is the actor's involvement with the people in the audience—running up and down the aisles, etc. Is there any way which HAIR as a film could achieve a similar effect?)

2. What is "cinematic" about the way Donald O'Connor presents his idea for dubbing Debbie Reynold's voice?

3. Which elements in the long "Gotta Dance" ballet depend on

cinema techniques and which do not? Musical film expert Miles Kreuger claims that this ballet is one long gag. He claims that its only purpose is to lead up to the line which follows: "I don't like it." Did the ballet seem overdrawn and out-of-place to you?

4. Is there anything about the principals' final reunion on stage which is "out of tune" with the rest of the movie?

5. Why don't we feel sorry for Miss Hagen at the end? Or should we?

Discussion on Comedy in General

1. Some comic strips would make good films and others would not. Would your favorite comic strip make a good animated film, live actor film, or puppet film? Why are some jokes better in one media than others?

2. The television version of Charles Schulz's famous Peanuts was disappointing to some people who had already fixed in their "inner ear" how the voice of Charlie Brown, Lucy, Linus, etc., would or "should" sound. When they heard the television version their image was challenged. Is there any advantage in leaving something for the beholder to fill in for himself? Do author's often do this? How do you think the arms of the statue Venus de Milo were originally posed? Does it matter? Can you think of films which leave much to the imagination of the viewer?

3. Which jokes in this month's *Reader's Digest* would "come off" as visual gags? Which would fail? Which would make a good short film? What elements seem necessary for a successful sight gag?

4. You can probably recite several of the popular graffiti. Is there such a thing as "visual graffiti?" Could you imagine a film in which such graffiti would be an important element?

Projects

1. Analyze the script of a recent Broadway comedy with a view toward adapting its comic elements for the screen.

2. Consider a few currently popular comedians, and discuss whether their talents are potentially suited to film medium. Some radio comedians were never quite successful on film. What does a comedian have to look like?

3. Sometimes movies have titles which are very misleading. How many people probably intended to relax with a light-hearted comedy when they sat down to view the filmed version of Graham Greene's THE COMEDIANS? This was anything but a funny film. Can you think of other examples of misleading titles? Sometimes a film's title is itself a joke. Can you name some such titles?

4. An effective movie ad on television or in the newspapers can at-

tract an audience to a poor film. Sketch out an ad for a film which you like. Compare your ad to the ones the papers ran. Why do advertising campaigns often change their appeal and "pitch" to fit a certain locality? Can you find examples of this type of "localizing" a movie campaign? Obtain out-of-town newspapers and compare movie ads to the ones in your town.

Eight

Documentary: Film as Social Commentary

RICHARD B. BYRNE - SHARON FEYEN

The documentary film has been called by some critics and analysts a vital social statement. It is a type of film as record; in addition to recording, it sometimes organizes information in order to instruct or to move the public to action regarding a public issue. Thus it may be a kind of visual editorial as well as a report.

John Grierson called the documentary film the "creative treatment of actuality." By definition, the documentary is a nonfiction, concerned with the exposition of reality rather than the development of a fictional plot. It shows the real life events in such a way as to create understanding and clarify the social issues involved.

Paul Rotha has described four distinct "traditions" of the documentary film. 1.) The "Naturalist" tradition shows the primitive man pitted against his natural environment. Examples can be seen in the films of Robert Flaherty in which he shows the difficult life of the Eskimo (NANOOK OF THE NORTH, 1922) and the inhabitants of the Aran isles (MAN OF ARAN, 1934) or the traditions and daily activities of the South Seas (MOANA, 1926) and the southern bayou country (LOUISIANA STORY, 1948). Some Flaherty films are given in Chapter Twelve, program 43.

2.) The "Realist" tradition, or "Continental Impressionism," is focused on the hustle and bustle of city life. Using then avant-garde cutting techniques, the films showed a fascination with machinery and the machine-like quality of the daily life of city dwellers. Examples are Alberto Cavalcanti's RIEN QUE LES HEURES (1926), Walter Ruttmann's BERLIN, SYMPHONY OF A GREAT CITY (1927), and Joris Ivens' THE BRIDGE (1928).

[67]

The remaining two traditions, the "Newsreel" and the "Propagandist," can be seen in the types of films mentioned under Soviet montage in Chapter One. These films advocate a specific attitude toward issues, and urge the audience to take equally specific action about those issues after viewing the individual films. These categories, or traditions, are probably outdated today, and are no longer useful as a means of describing film types, but they indicate the directions film documentaries have taken.

There has always been a great deal of dispute over what deserves to be called documentary. Many seem to agree that fundamentally a documentary film is one that uses the materials of real life—people, things, locales—for the sake of either describing that reality or persuading us to react to it in a certain way, or possibly a little of both. The films listed as documentaries in Chapter Twelve follow this more liberal definition. However, Chapter Thirteen distinguishes between "documentaries" and "cinéma vérité".

There is argument over whether the camera should stick to what it literally "finds," and if so, whether it may give the material shape (like a news story) or allow it to find its own shape. (The latter is pure cinéma vérité style, in which the film maker simply observes and records what happens, whether it is dull or exciting or meaningful or not. Chapter Thirteen, Property 9, suggests examples of cinéma vérité.)

Others maintain that the important thing is to capture the "essence" of reality, and that to achieve this, you may have to re-create what does not fortuitously happen when the camera is present. Thus, the director can take a typical event and "stage" it for his cameras, as Flaherty frequently did and, as would obviously be necessary, if the film were dealing with historical rather than current reality. In this sense, Peter Watkins' brutal re-staging of the 18th century THE BATTLE OF CULLODEN (in the form of a TV documentary) or Keith Brownlow's IT HAPPENED HERE, which describes what probably would have happened if the Nazis had conquered England, could validly be called documentaries. This kind of documentary is not far removed from the "documentary style" fiction film, especially if the fiction film uses actual persons (rather than actors), real locales and a "true story".

The documentary impulse can be seen in commercial films, especially from 1930 to 1950, when many Hollywood films dealt with real social problems such as gangsterism, unionism, race relations, and the financial distress of the Depression. This documentary social concern became important enough for Warner Brothers to adopt "Good films, good citizenship" as their motto. Many crime-detective films of the 1940's used documentary techniques for added realism: BOOMERANG (1946), HOUSE

ON 92ND STREET (1945), CALL NORTHSIDE 777 (1947). See programs 44, 45 and 46 in Chapter Twelve.

As mentioned in Chapter One, the neo-realist movement in Italy can also be seen as an outgrowth of the documentary approach. Such films as ROME: AN OPEN CITY (1945), SHOESHINE (1947), THE BICYCLE THIEF (1948), and UMBERTO D (1952), were attempts to portray the real everyday problems of real people. By and large the actors were non-professionals, the locations were real, the stories essentially true, and the directors presented their material as objectively as possible. There was also an attempt to avoid the "final ending" or problem solution typical of fiction films but not of real life. See Chapter Twelve, program 37.

Today the most important style in documentary is cinéma vérité (or film truth), which means essentially that the film maker deals only with unstaged reality "found" by the camera, that he interferes with that reality as little as possible (either in shooting or editing), and the event itself, rather than any preconceived story or theme, dictates the film structure and what-to-look-at. Cinéma vérité is reality shot-from-the-hip.

This, of course, has always been the basic aim of the documentarist: to capture reality as it is, without somehow spoiling it by the presence of his crew and equipment. The cinéma vérité approach has been made possible by technical developments in equipment (fast film and lenses, directional mikes, portable cameras, and sound recorders) which render the film maker all but invisible. The style has tended to make even the traditional voice-over-narrative obsolete; now we simply figure out what is happening by listening to actual sounds and conversations.

The approach was fostered in France in the early 1960's by Jean Rouch (CHRONICLE OF A SUMMER), Chris Marker (LE JOLI MAI), and others, and in North America by the National Film Board of Canada (LONELY BOY, END OF SUMMER, STRAVINSKY) and the talented group of film makers gathered in New York by Robert Drew to make television documentaries. These included Albert and David Maysles (PRIMARY), Donn Pennebaker (DON'T LOOK BACK) and Richard Leacrock (CRISIS), who had been Flaherty's cameraman in LOUISIANA STORY.

Cinéma vérité style is easily identified by its characteristic hand-held camera, spontaneous panning and zooming, uneven sound and lighting quality, restless searching for better viewpoint, and general lack of the presence of a reporter or narrative voice. Currently, it is the dominant style in first-class TV documentaries, with such powerful examples as ABC's MARATHON, Jack Willis' EVERY SEVENTH CHILD, Allan King's WARRENDALE, and William Jersey's and Barbara Connell's A TIME FOR

BURNING. Drew-produced classics include THE CHAIR, NEHRU, SHOW-MAN, FOOTBALL, and JANE. The influence is noticeable in such widely divergent features as NOBODY WAVED GOODBYE (1965), THE PAWN-BROKER (1963), and THE GOSPEL ACCORDING TO ST. MATTHEW (1965).

One of the best traditional-style documentaries of recent years, and also an interesting example of a film that takes a stand and tries to influence its audience is HARVEST OF SHAME, which originally appeared on CBS REPORTS.

The film, called by critics "an editorial documentary in its frankest manner," was televised November 25, 1960. HARVEST OF SHAME, produced by David Lowe and narrated by Edward R. Murrow, was presented with a timely sense of irony, during the Thanksgiving holidays.

HARVEST OF SHAME exposes the extreme poverty of the migrant farm worker in America, and employs the actual environment, direct, on-the-spot interviews, and editing which emphasize the inhuman situations in which the reporter found the people.

Like most films, HARVEST would best be seen "cold" without much or any pre-discussion. The teacher or discussion leader would do well to simply state the data of time, producer and topic, and then screen the film.

A SELECTED BIBLIOGRAPHY ON THE DOCUMENTARY FILM

See the literature marked "8" in the Bibliography at the close of the book for complete data on these and other related readings.

Bluem *Documentary in American Television*. (Excellent bibliography.)

Calder and Marshall *The Innocent Eye*.

Hardy *Grierson on Documentary*.

Kuhns and Stanley "The Film as Fact: The Documentary." (Chapter Eleven in *Exploring the Film*.)

Rotha *Documentary Film*.

[SPIN-OFFS]

Discussion on Harvest of Shame

1. What was Murrow's main point? How did he make this point clear at the outset? From a cinematic standpoint?

2. Do you think the documentary "took a stand" or was it merely recording facts?

HARVEST OF SHAME, *CBS-TV Reports, Thanksgiving, 1960*

3. Which scenes or sequences were effective in emphasizing the main point of the film?

4. Do you think this film had an impact as forceful as the book, or the 1940 film THE GRAPES OF WRATH? (Finding reviews of the film and the book THE GRAPES OF WRATH, written at the time of their first appearance, might be worthwhile research.)

5. How did editing affect the film? Speed? Use of black and white as contrasted with color photography? Use of real people, in real situations, rather than the more dramatic elements of a Hollywood production?

Discussion on Documentaries in General

1. What subjects are vital and should be documented on film today? Are not newspapers and magazines and radio doing an adequate job keeping people informed? How would a film documentary be different from television coverage?

2. If you had to make a half-hour version of a particular current feature film, what scenes would you cut and which would be essential to keep. Does this mean that the scenes you decided not to keep should have been left out of the original? Have you kept the plot intact or did you decide to sacrifice the story-line for the spirit of the film? What does a director of a documentary often have to do in this regard?

3. A film maker in New York City is presently doing a documentary on one of the up-town streets. It is taking him several years as he begins on the East Side and records impressions of each block as he goes West. Is there a section of your town which could be similarly recorded and interpreted on film? What would be the purpose of such a documentary?

4. In what way are "home movies" often documentaries?

Projects

1. Film a day in your life, or a day the way you see it, or your impression of how other people see you.

2. Film a scene the way you think a child, a teenager, a college student, an adult and a senior citizen would see it—five different interpretations of the exact same scene. A good setting could be a department store, a busy park, or fans at a ball game.

3. Are some things "too hot to report"? Who determines what the public will see in matters that are very "touchy"? Sketch a screen script for a documentary on a current local event being reported in the newspapers or on television.

4. Collect a series of colored slides which you can arrange and a soundtrack in order to bring out a point: pollution, driving habits of

Willard Van Dyke's THE CITY, *1939*

adults and teens, injustice to minority groups, or any number of social situations. Can you "slant" your program either way by visual effects alone? Could you make two programs (one "for" and the other "against") using practically the same factual data, but changing only the visual impressions?

5. After screening HARVEST OF SHAME a second time, choose a topic on which to do research and prepare a shooting script. Remember that the main objective of your film will be, like the objective in HARVEST, to persuade through a powerful presentation of fact.

6. Live television can take a stand as much as a filmed documentary. During one of the particularly dull speeches of the 1968 National Democratic Convention, one editorializing television cameraman kept panning the convention hall showing rows and rows of empty seats. Make a list of the live television coverage you watch this week and observe when and if "loaded" camerawork editorialized on the event. With two television sets (or more) you could watch several different interpretations of the same live event, noting the "stand" taken by each.

Part Four

The Art of Film

Federico Fellini on the set of 8½, 1963

Nine

The Art of the Movie Director

PATRICK SAMWAY, S.J.

A movie director needs five eyes; one to scrutinize the story that he is about to film, another to look for the members of the cast, a third to visualize the dramatic patterns of the film as it will be acted out, a fourth to see how he can achieve certain moods and effects, and a fifth eye to foresee the relationships between the various actors as they react to one another's personalities. In other words, a movie director must be a man with vision. Such directors are difficult to find.

European films have gained popularity among American audiences mainly because of the directors who creatively attempt to interpret the energies of man, rather than to focus their attention on the box office appeal of famous actors. Federico Fellini is keenly aware of the process of directing a movie. As Anthony Quinn, a star of LA STRADA, said: "As soon as I started working for Fellini, I realized that he was far from crazy, that he was, in fact, the most talented, intelligent, sensitive and perceptive director I'd ever worked for." The problems which Fellini faces are indicative of the problems faced by all directors.

The initial problem, which all directors must face, is that they come to grips with their own personalities, backgrounds, and values in life. Without such knowledge, a director is incapable of communicating a vision of life to others. Fellini's genius has its roots in the people, smells, faces, towns, and roads of Italy. He left his native Rimini in 1937 when he was 17 and worked for a time in Florence and Rome as a free-lance artist and writer for a small magazine. In 1939, he traveled around Italy with a touring vaudeville show, acquiring a love for the circus which is reflected in a number of his films, especially LA STRADA. "As we went about the country from town to town, I discovered, in an almost mystic way, a sense of the mystery of the Italian character. I was overwhelmed by the variety of the country's physical landscape and, too, by the variety of its human landscapes." Like Ingmar Bergman in Sweden and François Truffaut in France, Fellini investigates and interprets what is closest to his own native experience.

When the Germans invaded Italy, Fellini helped to support himself by writing a number of movie scripts. In 1943, he married Giulietta (JULIET OF THE SPIRITS) Masina, who has acted in many of his films. Fellini's first notable film achievement was assisting Roberto Rossellini with the production of ROME: AN OPEN CITY, a neo-realistic film about the plight of the Romans during the difficult time of the Nazi occupation. He wrote the script and acted a major part in THE MIRACLE, a peasant folk tale which he transformed into a widely acclaimed, if often controversial, film.

With the success of LA STRADA (1954), NIGHTS OF CABIRIA (1957) (both won Oscars as best foreign films) and JULIET OF THE SPIRITS (1965), Fellini has shown that his prophecy is not accurate: "A writer can write for maybe fifty years, but a film director's creative life is, mysteriously, perhaps because success destroys him, much shorter. After 15 years or so, a director is burned out and finished." Fellini has not stopped maturing as a director: JULIET OF THE SPIRITS is a breakthrough in the use of color for an art film.

For Fellini, the process of directing a film resembles a structured "happening." "In creating a film, I most often begin with the slightest hint of an idea, a character, or a situation—it is a candle that magically lights itself in a vast, dark, and gusty room. One must walk softly about the room, closing all of the windows, so that the flame will not blow out in the winds." Fellini meets with his three co-writers, Tullio Finelli, Ennio Flaiano, and Brunello Rondi, and together they discuss the characters, scenes, faces, and movements of the film. Later, the four meet with Fellini's 30 assistants to arrange for the technical details. Once the film is under way, it is not unusual for Fellini to work for 18 hours a day.

Fellini is most conscious of the power of the film. He lets the matter shape the structure of the film: "If I first carefully wrote out a completed scenario, I'd feel that the thing had already been accomplished in the writing—I'd have no interest in trying to film it." He usually works on a film in sequence with little or no dialogue. This allows him to add spontaneously to the film whenever it is thought necessary. "I love to improvise while filming—something unexpected in one scene suddenly leads perhaps to another scene I'd never dreamed of, and then to another." Fellini firmly believes that one cannot paint a picture by following a number code.

Thus, Fellini is not a slave to a typed script; he is able to see the deficiencies of any script and to let his own creative genius re-work, reshape, recreate what is lacking in the script.

In addition to creating a suitable story, a director must concern himself with the selection of the actors. Unless a story has a strong cast, it will dry up and wilt, and the film will never come to maturity. When Fellini wanted an actress to play the lead in LA STRADA, he went to an Umbrian olive merchant who suggested his girl friend. This was unthinkable. So Fellini began to interview 5,000 girls. After hours of interviewing and searching through endless files of photographs, he finally decided on Giulietta Masina, who possessed the elusive and captivating features of Gelsomina. It was her face, with its smile, grimaces, tears, and charm that made successful what G. B. Cavallaro called "the fantastic history of a sad honeymoon with a posthumous declaration of love."

Once the director has chosen the story and the actors, it is imperative that he try to visualize a dramatic pattern, to give the story a mood, an emphasis, a setting. The story of LA STRADA is more than a series of episodes centering in a witless peasant girl who, after being sold to Zampano, a traveling circus strong-man, accompanies him along the roads of Italy. The story is replete with nuances and overtones to give it an interior unity and visual coherence. Gelsomina's charming simplicity is emphasized by her tooting a horn and banging a drum. Any attempt at a personal act of self-expression by Gelsomina is quickly rebuffed by Zampano. But Zampano is not the only man in her life: the Fool, Matto, gives Gelsomina an inkling of what it means to be human and to find a place in the world. Zampano's anger and impatience, however, kill Matto. Later, after Zampano has abandoned Gelsomina, he learns that she died by the sea. Somehow, Zampano must learn to reconcile his lonely existence, the dunes, the melancholy, the long roads, with the warmth and vitality he once knew with Gelsomina.

Unlike some of his later films, Fellini's camera technique in LA STRADA is not flamboyant. He prefers to use a natural setting with available light to create his desired mood. One important effect which he used in this film is what Edouard de Laurot calls a "feint." When Gelsomina arrives a strange locale, she questions the circus owner's wife:

Gelsomina: "Oh! Where are we?"

The circus owner's wife: "In Rome. St. Paul's Cathedral is over there." (She points off frame.) [Rome is never seen because it remains "off frame." The next shot is not what would be normally expected, St. Paul's Cathedral, with Zampano and the circus manager under the tent. The viewer's imagination anticipates one scene, but in reality, he is directed towards a different object or event. The result is a creative fusion of both scenes in the mind of the viewer. This is one way a director like Fellini can achieve a synthesis of two related ideas or events.]

One final area which is an important part of the director's job is to visualize how the various actors will react to one another. Even if a director employs a number of excellent actors, the film will not succeed unless these actors communicate with one another. The actor is required to do much more than merely to recite a certain number of lines. In the following sequence, we are able to enter Fellini's mind and see how he structured the encounter between Gelsomina and Matto:

Country road. Gelsomina following three musicians, in step with the music. Dissolve.

Scene in a small town. A procession is passing. Dusk. Voices chanting religious music.

Long Shot: Details of the procession: crucifix, holy images, saints, a priest blessing the crowd.

Medium Shot: Gelsomina in the crowd, her eyes wide open in admiration of the religious insignia.

Long Shot: Entire piazza.

Long Shot: Interior of the church. Church bells. Dissolve exterior. Night. Man on rope. Piazza in town at night.

Rain of applause.

Close-up: Announcer (through loudspeaker): "In a moment Matto will perform the most dangerous stunts. Walking 40 metres above the ground, he will eat a dish of spaghetti . . . ." [In this way, Gelsomina is psychologically prepared to meet Matto as an angel-acrobat who is a link between the church and the circus. Such careful preparation for the encounter between Gelsomina and Matto will make the future scenes where they are together all the more successful.]

The secret of Fellini's success as a director is that he is able to focus all of his talents into one unified vision. As Anne Sullivan helped Helen Keller to see, so too, Fellini helps his audiences to achieve a new perspective on life. The viewer is able to fuse his own vision to that of Fellini's and thereby become a richer person. In no way has Fellini given us answers about the meaning of life, but he has asked and dramatized the most basic questions which face men today. This is perhaps the more difficult task.

Fellini's La Strada, *1956, Anthony Quinn and Giulietta Masina*

A SELECTED BIBLIOGRAPHY ON THE MOVIE DIRECTOR

See the literature marked "9" in the Bibliography at the close of the book for complete data on these and other related readings.

Antonioni *Screenplays.*

Barry *D. W. Griffith, American Film Master.*

Bergman *Four Screenplays.*

Bogdanovich *Cinema of Alfred Hitchcock.*

Bogdanovich *Cinema of Howard Hawks.*

Bogdanovich *Cinema of Orson Welles.*

Budgen *Fellini.*

Cowie *Antonioni, Bergman, Resnais.*

Donner *The Personal Vision of Ingmar Bergman.*

Fellini *Juliet of the Spirits.*

Harcourt "The Secret Life of Federico Fellini," *Film Quarterly,* XIX (Spring, 1966), pp. 4-19.

Kyrou *Luis Buñuel.*

Nizhnii *Lessons With Eisenstein.*

Perry *The Films of Alfred Hitchcock.*

Richie *The Films of Akira Kurosawa.*

Sarris *The Films of Josef Von Sternberg.*

Stevenson and Debriz *The Cinema As An Art.*

Taylor *Cinema Eye, Cinema Ear.* (Fellini, Antonioni, Bresson, Buñuel, Hitchcock, Bergman, Truffaut, Godard and Resnais.)

Williams "Fellini's Voices," *Film Quarterly* (Spring, 1968), pp. 21-25.

[SPIN-OFFS]

Discussion on LA STRADA

Read the following critiques of LA STRADA and try to select the one which best suits and summarizes your reaction and understanding of the film (If none does, draft your own review):

> What we see for the most part are film versions of work done for other purposes and translated to the screen by teams of skilled technicians. The result may have entertainment value, but it is almost always a frustrated movie. LA STRADA, by contrast, is pure movie—it could not be done in any other form.
> Robert Hatch, THE NATION, August 4, 1956. Reprinted by Permission of THE NATION, Nation Co., Inc.

On one level the theme is the eternal one of the conflict between body (the strong man), mind (the clown), and spirit (the girl); but on another and perhaps more pertinent level the strongman may represent the brutish forces that have been unleashed in all the Western world by the success of democracy; the girl represents the simple verity in the hearts of ordinary people assumed by democratic sentiment; and the clown the intellectuals who have risen on the tide of democracy, yet owe an allegiance to the culture of a class-structured past.

James Reichley, THE NEW REPUBLIC, December 31, 1956. Reprinted by Permission of THE NEW REPUBLIC, Copyright 1956, Harrison-Blaine of New Jersey, Inc.

From start to finish LA STRADA has been shaped with a sure feeling for overtone, for symbol, for a sensory rather than a literal form of perception. And what makes it completely extraordinary is the way its poetry, its symbols, its modest philosophy all flow from incidents so commonplace that only in their justapositions do they begin to acquire significance. It is like a modern morality play, set along the fringes of our urban society.

Arthur Knight, "Italian Realism Refreshed", SATURDAY REVIEW, June 30, 1956. Copyright 1956, The Saturday Review Associates, Inc.

A more recent review by John M. Culkin, S.J., (MOTIVE XXVII, No. 2, November, 1966) stresses the fact that Fellini's films incarnate a visceral, tactile, and emotional approach to questions which in our culture are treated in a rational style which is uninvolved and antiseptic. Culkin also notes that LA STRADA begins and ends by the sea. Fellini has said that for him the sea "is a comforting mystery, conveying the idea of permanence, of eternity, of the primal element." In addition, because of Fellini's love and respect for people, he is desperately aware of the need for communication among people. The theme recurs in all his films, as indeed it does in most serious films today. History of a closed person who would like to communicate with others, LA STRADA centers around a woman who would "like to speak to a man who doesn't want to understand."

Discussion on Directing in General

1. Invite the director of the school play and the music director into the group and ask them to explain their job in terms of directing, and to show how their work differs from that of a movie director.

2. Chapter Three mentioned the soundtrack of the film THE DIARY OF ANNE FRANK. The audio effects achieved in that film were mainly due to the masterful direction of George Stevens. SHANE, also directed by Stevens, is discussed in Chapter Six. A comparison of the two films

would illustrate the role of a director in "conducting" a soundtrack. What are the comparisons between the director of a film and the conductor of a symphonic orchestra?

3. What advantages or disadvantages does a director have when he composes his own script rather than working from a script based on a novel or short story? (A review of Budd Schulberg's comments at the end of Chapter Four, might be helpful here.)

4. Compare the style of Bergman or another accomplished director, with the style of Fellini. How is each one's background and personality revealed in his style of directing? The lists of directors and their films in Chapter Twelve, program 36 to 47 will help in picking directors to compare.

5. What norms would a director use when deciding to use color in film? Why did Fellini do JULIET OF THE SPIRITS in color? Why did Antonioni do THE RED DESERT in color? Did these two masters pick good subjects for their first color films?

6. Is it valid to ask how Picasso would have painted the Mona Lisa, or how Frank Lloyd Wright would have built the Empire State Building? How would Fellini have directed BLOW-UP, or Hitchcock have done CLOSELY WATCHED TRAINS, Huston with LA STRADA, etc.

7. Even the Swedes say that Bergman has captured the spirit of Sweden in his films. Has any American director captured the spirit of America?

8. Was Alfred Hitchcock unable to give the episodes in his television series the same suspenseful treatment which he could employ in a full length feature? Is time necessary for the effect of suspense? Have you seen a television commercial which achieves suspense in a few short seconds? How does the direction of a suspense film differ from the direction of other types of film?

9. What is the relationship between editing a film and the direction of the same film? This discussion leads into Chapter Ten on Editing.

Projects

1. What different interpretations of an object or person do you get by viewing the subject from a second floor window, from eye-level, or from below? What differences result from viewing the same subject from a distance, through a window, in a mirror, etc. When action takes place in a room (two men shooting pool, for example) different views could be taken of the scene, each having a particular value. With a camera alone, how could you make the scene very serious, humorous, sad, etc., without changing what the subjects are actually doing?

2. Pan a scene through a square opening cut in the middle of a card. Pause for a longer look at certain objects and pass quickly over others. The second time pause at the objects you skipped the first time. What can a camera do which your eyes cannot? How could the same scene be panned with entirely different results? How could a storage attic or a family kitchen be filmed in such a way that either nostalgia, mystery, humor or sadness could be the visual effect? Make a film of such a scene, giving it various interpretations.

3. Play the role of director. How do you get your actors to portray a particular part? Role play how Bergman, Welles, Chaplin, Fellini or Hitchcock would direct the same scene. Such a scene could be the return of a soldier from Vietnam to his home town, the first date of a young girl, etc.

4. Write a screen play for "The Prom", a short film showing only objects as symbols of preparing for and attending the Junior dance. Do a version with dialogue and a version with music only. Can objects alone tell a story?

5. A charade game can be played by describing a film you would like to make of a certain book, play, poem, song or comic strip. Describe how the film would open, who would play in it, what the major scenes would be, etc. You can also combine characters and plots from various sources, making a mad, mad, mad, mad film.

6. Introduce your group to a new film in town with a festival of older films by the same director or major actor. Are there several films presently being shown in your area which have the same director, actor or other similarity? The managers of these movie houses might cooperate with your group in a "Rod Steiger Field Trip," or a "Fellini Weekend," or a "Peter Sellers Festival".

Sergei Eisenstein, 1898-1948

Ten

The Fine Art of Editing

MICHAEL M. DORCY, S.J.

"The foundation of film art," observed Vsevolod Pudovkin, the famous Russian film director and theorist, "is editing." One does not "shoot" a film, he insisted; one builds a movie as one does a building, brick by brick. The bricks in this case are so many small strips of celluloid, or an equivalent, which bear some resemblance to reality.

Sergei Eisenstein wished to qualify Pudovkin's observation about building films out of so many "bricks." Eisenstein, Pudovkin's equally famous contemporary, observed that shots are not placed side by side; rather, they collide with one another and, fusing, form a third reality, some reality not contained in either of the two shots when taken separately, nor properly explained as merely the sum total of the two separate shots. It is a kind of chemical reaction, if you will—the sort of thing that takes place when the substances of Na and Cl, neither one the kind of thing one would want to sprinkle on a hamburger, are put together to form the totally new reality we know as common table salt.

Eisenstein borrowed from the oriental ideogram further to explain this remarkable quality which editing was capable of. In oriental ideographic writing, where a picture stands directly for an idea and not a sound, the reality expressed by a combination of two of these "word-pictures" is not simply a matter of simple addition. Putting two word-pictures together starts all sorts of things happening. The pictures react on one another, dramatically.

For example, in Chinese the word-picture or hieroglyph for "eye" is combined with the word-picture for "water" to create the abstract idea

[87]

of "sorrow." The notion "to bark" is formed by combining the hiero-glyphs of "dog" and "mouth". The same "mouth" with the word-picture for "bird" adds up to "singing". With the word-pictures for a "child" that same "mouth" starts "screaming".

Thus it is not the *content* of the parts as much as the *order* of the parts which is important. To illustrate this fact in the film, Pudovkin referred to the following sequence of shots:

1.) a man's smiling face;
2.) a revolver is pointed at the man;
3.) the same face showing dismay or fright.

If one were to reverse the first and third shots, Pudovkin observed, the effect would be changed completely. The man at whom the gun is pointed—if not a coward, certainly an ordinary man—suddenly becomes superior to his situation. He becomes a brave or a foolish man.

Eisenstein pointed to the classic experiments of another Russian film director to illustrate the power of editing. Lev Kuleshov, the director, had clipped some close-ups of the actor Ivan Mozhuknin from an old film. The close-ups were of a face rather devoid of any significant ex-pression at all. He inserted these clips within another film: once next to a shot of a bowl of soup, once next to a young child, playing, and once next to a shot of a woman lying in a coffin. The audience which saw the film remarked that at the first point the actor had hunger written all over his face; at the second point that face showed affection and paternal love; at the third point, sorrow. Kuleshov pointed out that it was the same expressionless face in each instance. The same phe-nomenon had taken place as in the oriental ideogram: the emergence of a new concept, contained in neither of the independent elements.

In Pare Lorentz's classic American documentary, THE RIVER (1937), we find the following sequence of shots:

1.) from a distance, a hillside covered with trees;
2.) closer, until one tree becomes predominant;
3.) the trunk of one tree fills the screen; an ax begins to cut into the tree;
4.) a series of shots of trees falling (we only see a single tree through part of its fall; each time, before the tree hits, we cut to another tree starting to fall);
5.) finally, one tree falls into the river with a splash.

Without a word from the narrator, the meaning is clear: eventually all the trees get down to the river.

Like every paragraph or sentence in a written composition, every shot in a film is related to the ones immediately before and after. The linkage may be unifying or contrasting; this is one way in which, in very simple terms, the film makers play on our sensitivities.

SYMBOLISM

Art in any form has always dealt with the very real world that lies at our fingertips in order to communicate something of that just-as-real world which lies within. Through editing, through juxtaposition of people and things, the film maker can suggest that one item is to be identified with another in a symbolic way.

For example, the Chaplin film, MODERN TIMES (1936), opens with the following shots:

1.) a flock of sheep are being driven through the gate of a sheep pen;
2.) a crowd of workers emerge from a subway exit.

Each shot is intelligible in itself, but in juxtaposition the two shots take on a meaning completely beyond the potential of either shot taken separately. The shot of the people leaving the subway is warped by the preceding shot, creating an entirely new world of social comment. Shot may be juxtaposed with shot, or perhaps with sound, as in the famous scene in Carl Foreman's THE VICTORS (1962), where a young deserter is shot while we hear the Sinatra recording of "Have Yourself a Merry Little Christmas." See examples given with Property 13 in Chapter Thirteen.

THE MANIPULATION OF TIME

In Orson Welles' masterpiece, CITIZEN KANE, one quick sequence of shots conveys the gradual ruin of Kane's marriage to Emily. A series of conversations across the breakfast table, scenes which, in reality, would be separated by considerable lapses of time, are melted into one time sequence by swish-pans across to the table. The characters, and their love for each other, age before our eyes. All the dimensions of the couple's life together are mirrored in that one setting. We see Charles Foster Kane and his wife, Emily, gradually drawing away from each other. We watch the marriage, as it literally fades from newlywed warmth to coldness and indifference.

The "Diving Sequence" from Leni Riefenstahl's OLYMPIC GAMES 1936, combines slow-motion and reverse action photography with angle changes to extend an individual action; via editing it also eliminates the time that normally would elapse between the actions and further illustrates the film's ability to create a totally new time-space continuum, a feat unique to the art of the film. See examples given with Property 7 in Chapter Thirteen.

POINT OF VIEW

The short study, THE CRITIC AND GREAT EXPECTATIONS, shows the opening sequence of David Lean's 1946 adaptation of Dickens' novel and illustrates how the director's choice of a particular series of angles for shots makes the audience momentarily share young Pip's point of view, creating a sense of surprise rather than the feeling of suspense that a slight alteration in the editing could have achieved. See examples given with Nos. 10 and 11, Chapter Thirteen.

TEMPO AND RHYTHM

GLASS, a short Dutch film by Bert Haanstra, harmonizes editing with a jazz composition and sets up a sharp but delightful visual and aural contrast which, without the aid of any commentator, stresses the value of human over machine labor. The final sequence in Basil Wright and Harry Watt's NIGHT MAIL, is an interesting harmony of the visual with a musical score by Benjamin Britten and a poetic commentary by W. H. Auden. Another train ride is the content of PACIFIC 231, a virtuoso display of editing to a musical composition by Arthur Honegger. The effectiveness of a particular choice of tempo and rhythm in editing can be seen easily in the rapid cutting of the lunch-hour sequence in THE CITY (1939) where film makers R. Steiner and Willard Van Dyke humorously capture the absurdities and hectic pace of big-city living.

Through the fine art of editing the film maker suggests values, creates point of view, rhythm and the manipulation of time and space which is unique to movies. Ultimately, to become sensitive to film means to become sensitive to the techniques and effects of editing.

A SELECTED BIBLIOGRAPHY ON FILM EDITING

See the literature marked "10" in the Bibliography at the close of the book for complete data on these and other related readings.

Eisenstein *Film Form and the Film Sense.*
Knight *The Liveliest Art.*
Lindgren *The Art of the Film.*
Manoogian *The Film-Maker's Art.*
Pudovkin *Film Techniques and Film Acting.*
Reisz *The Technique of Film Editing.*
Stevenson and Debrix *The Cinema as Art.*

[SPIN-OFFS]

Discussion

1. You have most likely seen foreign language films presented in at least one of three ways. They can be in their original form, entirely without English. They can be adapted to English by adding subtitles, usually at the bottom of the screen, and at the same time keeping the original sound track. Or, they can be "dubbed", adding a new sound track which attempts to match the lip movements of the actors to English words. Which way do you prefer? Or, does it depend on the particular film? Imagine the distinctive voice of your favorite actor/actress being erased and a foreign language synchronized in its place. (The film SINGIN' IN THE RAIN, discussed in Chapter Seven, has some appropriate scenes about dubbing.) Or, imagine trying to read subtitles during a very active scene in which watching the action is essential. Can you appreciate an opera sung in a language you do not understand? How were subtitles used in THOROUGHLY MODERN MILLIE? When do television commercials often use subtitles? (See Gerald Pratley's essay "Now Entirely in English!" in TAKE ONE, I, 10, p. 8-9.)

2. Some of the stills in this book were chosen because they seem to capture the whole spirit of a particular movie. See especially the pictures from STALAG 17 and THE GRADUATE. Do you agree that these scenes help to recall the entire film? Can you think of a scene which would symbolize the entirety of your favorite film. Would everyone pick the same scene?

3. Just as a particular scene can capture a whole film, one particular line from the script can be a similar microcosm of a movie. For many filmgoers the key-line from MARTY is "What do you wanna do tonight, Marty?" (More specifically, it is the long pause after this question which tells Marty's story.) Is there a single line that would seem to say nearly everything about the films SHANE and ALFIE?

4. Compare the endings of THE 400 BLOWS, THE LONELINESS OF THE LONG DISTANCE RUNNER, NO REASON TO STAY and A THOUSAND CLOWNS. Do the plots and the main characters of these films have any common ground which would lead to such similar endings?

5. This chapter mentioned the effect when a film's visual image is in direct contrast to its soundtrack. In THE VICTORS a man is killed while a song about peace is sung. This scene could have been presented several different ways: the sound of the gunshot could have been heard as well as the song being sung; the song alone could have been recorded and only the effect of the shot seen; or, the song could have paused as the shot

rang out. What effect would each way have? Is one way better than another? How was a similar audio-visual contrast used very effectively during the closing scene of ELVIRA MADIGAN? Do you recall other films which employ this contrast of sound and sight? Jack Kupa's five and one-half minute film OFFSPRING juxtaposes the sound of an eight-year-old girl singing Pete Seeger's "Where Have All the Flowers Gone?" against scenes of bombings and burnings in Vietnam (see VARIETY, August 21, 1968). It seems that ever since Eisenstein's BATTLESHIP POTEMKIN this sort of contrast-montage often deals with the subject of war versus peace. Usually a contrast between "what is" and "what should be" brings about a humorous response. What keeps the peace-war contrast from being humorous?

Projects

1. As a follow-up from the above discussion, put contrasting sound to a series of slides or a movie showing the busy rush hour traffic, or put contrasting pictures to the song "We Shall Overcome". What subtle changes could be made in such juxtapositions to make them either humorous or tragic?

2. What makes any collage or montage effective? What is our reaction to juxtapositioning in our own lives? For example, why don't we have a celebration in one room when someone is sick in the next room? And if we do, what is that usually interpreted as saying? Collect pictures which can be juxtaposed and others which should not be.

3. Take polaroid shots of a brief sequence. Write a script of captions. Re-arrange the photos and the captions for various effects. If you were dealing with motion pictures what added difficulties and possibilities would you have?

4. Write an original short sketch as a stage drama, then film the same action, using the fullest possibilities of camera movement. What differences will result?

5. You have noticed short and longer versions of certain television commercials. What is usually cut from the longer form? What is always kept? What short films do you think could be expanded to feature length? What would you add which would not be merely padding, but would be integrated to the new form? Add a new character and a subplot to YOU'RE NO GOOD. For example, add a boy who owns the stolen motorcycle and who is also in love with the girl. Or, in NO REASON TO STAY, add a teacher who also wants to "drop out" of the academic scene and—if you want to complicate the picture—is the father of the girl. Will these expansions make these shorts better films? In their present

form could they be cut down to even briefer form and keep their basic "message" and spirit?

6. The rather unsuccessful 1961 comedy ZOTZ! employs slow motion very cleverly. A professor finds an old coin which apparently has the power to make people move in slow motion. Write a scene from a more plausible plot and act it out, employing slow motion, fast motion and stop motion.

7. Some symbols appear often in films, each time with slightly different meaning. Recall the role of the fish symbol at the end of THE OLD MAN AND THE SEA and at the end of LA DOLCE VITA. What does the fish symbolize in each of these closing scenes? What meaning does the fish have in the short film THE GOLDEN FISH? Is there always something in common with these fish symbols? How is the clock symbol used in HIGH NOON, DAVID AND LISA and OF TIME, WORK AND LEISURE? Can you recall films which use water, fire or flowers as a key symbol? What other symbols often appear in films? Some symbols are heard instead of seen. How is this true in ASSEMBLY LINE, THE THIRD MAN and A TIME OUT OF WAR?

Part Five

Film Programming

THE PRESIDENT'S ANALYST, *1967, James Coburn*

Eleven

Suggestions for a Film Series

FRANCES BOCK

How do you start a film series? With fervor, small numbers, limited facilities. Fervor is *almost* enough to get a program off the ground. Small numbers provide a more workable situation to anneal interest, to try formats, to carry on discussions. Limited facilities have their own challenge to be met and overcome with a bit of strain, a bit of strategy. The main thing is to get started and to keep learning from the group experience.

For instance, one school that could not introduce film study into the curriculum started a monthly film study club which met, as the other school clubs did, on Monday after school. Another school concentrated on a weekend film seminar each semester. Still another, believing in film as a generation-gap jumper, ran a monthly series for students and their parents. Another, with an honors reading seminar as a nucleus, invited all school comers to a Thursday evening film series. Three neighboring (and neighborly) schools, having introduced film study via short films in the English curriculum, combined forces for a monthly feature series for students in these courses.

Probably the best single answer to how to start a film series, then, is that there is no single answer. However, there are other questions before you arrive at your own answer: how wide is the interest, how extensive are funds, how available are time and space and facilities, and how ready is your audience? Each of these situations suggests a difference in film choices.

[97]

In the matter of film choice there are many suggestions but no "musts." The school, starting fresh, will probably choose films of sure-fire interest, good basic film technique, enough familiarity for identification and enough unfamiliarity so that the program is left untouched by the local TV offerings. The film group narrowing the generation gap may want to choose films with themes close to that purpose. The combined schools, which have done groundwork in class, may set up a series on the basis of increasingly complex films over a year's time. You may want to check with those who have run series for good films that have "taken" with young audiences, but there is no canonized list.

While a number of bases for film choices can be valid, one thing seems a *must:* introduction to basic film language and technique. Here several possibilities suggest themselves. Perhaps two short films on the same subject, one mediocre-to-awful and one well made. The audience, without getting entangled in subject matter *per se* and with some direction, can arrive at basic film techniques inductively by trying to account for the differences in the films.

There are several other suggestions. Perhaps a short film with the sound track cut off and a running commentary provided. Perhaps a slide lecture with selected still photos illustrating camera angle, distance, etc. Perhaps a TV-station-loaned ad clip showing shot, pace, editing, sound, color. The choice of the feature film to follow can be based on related themes, important directors, important films of increasing complexity, genre: musical, documentary, Western, satire, novel adaptation, etc. See Chapter Twelve for suggested film groups and programs.

Again, though suggestions from others may be helpful, the most important thing is to know the people in your own audience, grab them where they are, and go on from there.

Actual format of the film evening or afternoon should include some introduction to the film, the viewing itself, and its discussion. The introduction can be but need not be boring. Over talk preceding the film can condition the audience into knot-hole viewing or dull them into academic tune-off. Undertalk can lead to mindless viewing and meaningless discussion. Both the film itself and the seeing-stage of the audience will suggest how much and what backgrounding is helpful. Some background on the director may or may not be necessary. One or two open-ended questions or a point of controversy about the film may suffice. Ray Sanders, author of Chapter Five, suggests ways of varying introductions, including debate, role playing, student readings *(Catholic School Journal,* April, 1968). In any event, the introduction should prepare for, not block, more sensitized viewing. If you do not feel competent enough to handle it at the start, you may want to call in local help from other high schools or the nearby college. One realistic film series director had a different guest teacher each month, with no harm to his own position and great help to both the series audience and to the adult guests.

But again, the group, as it develops, will discover what film viewing is about and will have its own suggestions. Herein lies a solid working principle: the students should become increasingly involved in *all* aspects of the program. Discussion following the film can take a variety of forms, and the series director should have an ear to play it by. At times, a general audience discussion, with roving mikes, will be best. At other times, you may want to move into smaller groups so everyone gets his chance. In either case, if you find a compatible pair, two adults or an adult and a student can lead the discussion *a la* Huntley-Brinkley. Somehow the group must get the message that the discussion extends beyond the viewing experience. In the beginning, the adults can lead the discussions, later co-lead them with students, and not too much later, sit by as resource persons for student leaders.

Film series experience suggests some other good working principles for discussions. Discussion leaders should preview the film, preferably together, and work out a few incisive lead questions.

The discussion should be just that, not a lecture or question-and-answer period. This is a time to increase viewing capacity. Everyone's reflections are to be heard, considered, shared. Sometimes questions will be superfluous. An immediate reaction—"What a weird ending!"—can be enough to get everyone off the ground. Discussion should be a matter of shared insights on the film, un-academic, but based on what is in the film.

You will discover that progressive viewing and discussing will lead to an expansion of the audience's sensitivity to an increasingly wide variety of films and to the whole world of think-feel. One boys' school started with a weekly session of very different films, both short and feature-length, having a short full-audience discussion after the screening. The open-endedness of the discussions soon led them to a tradition of a smaller group's continuing the talk over Cokes in the home of one of the faculty members. As the school year ended, the boys agitated for a summer film series and got it, although it wasn't in the original plan.

The film series will thus begin taking its own shape, expanding as the word gets around to other students and to other adults. You could run a "bring-a-friend" or a "bring-a-parent" night. Generally, though, the same group should carry through the series, growing together in viewing and reflecting, and building a common experience for contrast and comparison. The sales of series tickets helps insure the carry-through of the group and also helps the series director plan money and movies early enough to insure prompt deliveries of first choices and economically enough to break even.

Which brings us to other practical matters.

Probably it would be a good idea to make interest the only basis for selection of students for the series. Or it would be a good idea to introduce the series and its purpose and plan to the parents and other members of the faculty via letter or open meetings or whatever medium fits your situation. You should also lessen the irritation elements that can discourage attendance and involvement by providing functional projectors, good viewing and hearing situation, room and reasonable time for discussion, punctual starting, advance and regular dates, and reasonable ending times. No good discussion ever really ends and no really good film is ever talked out.

The point therefore, is to get started with your fervor, your small group, your limited facilities. Then, as your series progresses, watch all three grow.

Twelve

Suggested Film
Program Groupings

DONALD WIGAL

The following programs are arranged around the patterns which films
have formed. A film usually has some similarity to another film and
therefore a certain "category" begins to form. Likewise, a film will
probably have a theme similar to a theme of another film. In doing
so the film does not lose its identity. A major contributor to this film's
uniqueness is its director. The following programs are based on these
three important elements: categories, themes, and directors of films.

Programs   1-10: Categories of films
            11-25: Themes of films
            26-35: Themes in each category of films
            36-42: Foreign directors and their films
            43-47: American directors and their films

In each program there are film groups, each listed in chronological
order so as to illustrate whatever evolution may have taken place in that
particular type of film.

Americans see more film on television than in movie houses or class-
rooms. Therefore, these programs include examples which are presently
available only on 35mm or video-tape. We may expect some of these
to be available eventually also on 16mm. Films which are indicated
(*) are already on 16mm and most of these are listed in Appendix I
with additional information on their availability. All the films in programs 36–47 are now on 16mm.

The suggested readings following most of these programs are intended primarily for the adult and/or teacher of film. Students could study the literary source for one of the film adaptations mentioned in each program. Many of these are available in paperback. Other readings recommended for high school students are indicated (with the number 18) in the Bibliography.

The following categories are "broad" and do not intend to be strict academic distinctions. Some of the films listed as "Westerns," for example, would be considered as merely having "Western elements" by Allen Eyles *(The Western)*. Some of the listings under documentaries would not fulfill A. William Bluem's description of a documentary *(Documentary in American Television).*

PROGRAM ONE: Directing/Editing

Film group

1. Short Films	*Olympic Games, 1936 *The River (37) *The City (39) *The Red Balloon (France 56) *N.Y., N.Y. (57) *The Parable (64)
2. Comedies	*A Night at the Opera (35) The Mouse That Roared (U.K. 59) *Tom Jones (U.K. 63) *Dr. Strangelove (U.K. 64) *The Knack . . . And How to Get It (U.K. 65) The Party (U.K. 68)
3. Musicals	*An American in Paris (51) *Singin' In the Rain (52) Sound of Music (64) Hard Day's Night (U.K. 64) My Fair Lady (65) Finian's Rainbow (68)
4. Romances	*David and Lisa (62) *Jules et Jim (France 62) *Love With the Proper Stranger (63) A Man and a Woman (France 66) Elvira Madigan (Sweden 67)

5. Mysteries	*The Big Sleep (46) M. (50) *Psycho (60) *The Innocents (61) *The Birds (63) *The Haunting (63) *Arabesque (U.K. 66)
6. Westerns	The Covered Wagon (23) *High Noon (52) *Shane (53) *Lonely Are the Brave (62)
7. Documentaries	*Birth of a Nation (15) *Nanook of the North (22) *Potemkin (U.S.S.R. 25) Song of Ceylon (34) *Night Mail (36) *Grapes of Wrath (40) *The True Glory (45) Africa (ABC-TV, 9/10/68)
8. Adaptations	*Birth of a Nation (15) *The Magnificent Ambersons (42) *All the King's Men (49) *Home of the Brave (49) *Death of a Salesman (51) *Twelve Angry Men (54) *East of Eden (55) *To Kill a Mockingbird (62) *Dr. Strangelove (64) *Fahrenheit 451 (U.K. 66)
9. Foreign Films	See Programs 36-42: Foreign Directors.

SUGGESTED READINGS

Chapters Nine and Ten.
Books marked 9 and 10 in the Bibliography.

PROGRAM TWO: Foreign Films

Film group

10. Short Films	*The Red Balloon (France 56)

*Children Adrift (France 58)
*Glass (Holland 59)
*The Golden Fish (France 59)
*The Colt (Russia 60)
*The House (Holland 61)
*The Pusher (Yugoslavia 62)
*The Magician (Poland 64)
*The Daisy (Bulgaria 65)
*The Wall (Yugoslavia 65)

11. Comedies

Captain of Koepenick (Austria 41)
Caesar and Cleopatra (U.K. 46)
Edouard et Caroline (France 51)
*My Uncle (France 58)

12. Musicals

The Beggar's Opera (U.K. 53)
Rosemary (Germany 58)
*The Umbrellas of Cherbourg
(France 64)

13. Romances

Brief Encounter (U.K. 45)
Romeo and Juliet (Italy 54)
*Jules et Jim (France 62)
*Sundays and Cybele (France 62)
Elvira Madigan (Sweden 67)

14. Mysteries

Day of Wrath (Denmark 43)
Les Diaboliques (France 54)
Ashes and Diamonds (Poland 58)

15. Westerns

Rashomon (Japan 50)
*Seven Samurai (Japan 54)
The Americano (Brazil 55)
The Treasure of Pancho Villa
(Mexico 55)

16. Documentaries

*Desert Victory (U.K. 42)
*Rome: An Open City (Italy 46)
*Night and Fog (France 55)

17. Adaptations

*Henry V (U.K. 45)
*Gate of Hell (Japan 54)
*Billy Budd (U.K. 62)
*Tom Jones (U.K. 63)
*The Gospel According to St. Mat-
thew (Italy 65)

| Directing and | See Programs 36-42: Foreign |
| Editing | Directors. |

SUGGESTED READINGS

Chapter One.
Books marked 14 and 15 in the Bibliography.

PROGRAM THREE: Adaptations

Film group

18. Short Films
*A Unicorn in the Garden (53)
*An Occurrence at Owl Creek Bridge (France 62)
*The Nose (France 63)
*Hangman (64)
*I Wonder Why (65)

19. Comedies
*Tom Jones (U.K. 63)
*Dr. Strangelove (U.K. 64)
The Loved One (U.K. 64)
*The Knack . . . And How to Get It (U.K. 65)
*A Thousand Clowns (65)

20. Musicals
Abie's Irish Rose (46)
In the Good Old Summertime (49)
Alice in Wonderland (51)
Kiss Me Kate (53)
*Seven Brides for Seven Brothers (54)
*Guys and Dolls (55)
*Oklahoma (55)
*The King and I (56)
*West Side Story (61)
Inside Daisy Clover (67)

21. Romances
*Cyrano de Bergerac (50)
*The African Queen (U.K. 51)
Kiss Me Kate (53)
Brief Encounter (U.K. 54)
Romeo and Juliet (Italy 54)
*East of Eden (55)

22. Mysteries	*Dr. Jekyll and Mister Hyde (41) *The Big Sleep (46) *Detective Story (51) *Night of the Hunter (55) The Innocents (61) *The Haunting (63)
23. Westerns	Destry Rides Again (39) *The Ox-Bow Incident (43) *Shane (53) The Deerslayer (57)
24. Documentaries	The Plow that Broke the Plains (36) *Night and Fog (France 55) *No Hiding Place (63)
Foreign Films	See film group 17.
Directing and Editing	See film group 8.

SUGGESTED READING

Chapters Three and Four.
Books marked 3 and 4 in the Bibliography.

PROGRAM FOUR: Documentaries

Film group

25. Short Films	*The City (39) *Night and Fog (France 55) *Harvest of Shame (61) *Runner (62) *Conformity (63) *The Detached Americans (64) *The Inheritance (64) *Memorandum (Canada 66)
26. Comedies	*Buster Keaton Rides Again (Canada 65) Laughter, U.S.A. (NBC-TV, Project XX 61) The Golden Age of Comedy When Comedy Was King

27. Musicals	*Lonely Boy (Canada 62)
	Regards to George M. Cohan (NBC-TV, Project XX 62)
	Don't Look Back (U.K. 65)
28. Romances	Vincent Van Gogh: A Self-Portrait (NBC-TV, 11/17/61)
	*End of Summer (Canada 64)
29. Mysteries	*A Night at the Opera (35)
	The Man Who Knew Too Much (56)
30. Westerns	The Cowboy (54)
	The Real West (NBC-TV, Project XX, 3/29/61)
Adaptations	See film group 24.
Foreign Films	See film group 17.
Directing and Editing	See film group 9.

SUGGESTED READING

Chapter Eight.
Books marked 8 in the Bibliography.

PROGRAM FIVE: Westerns

Film group

31. Short Films	Many serials, from the 1911 Broncho Billy cowboy series and the Tom Mix, Gene Autry, Roy Rogers, Lone Ranger serials to the many current TV shows.
32. Comedies	Destry Rides Again (39)
	My Little Chickadee (40)
	Saratoga Trunk (43)
	Pardners (56)
	*Lonely Are the Brave (62)
	Cat Ballou (65)

33. Musicals	Rose Marie (36) Annie Get Your Gun (50) Calamity Jane (53) Red Garters (53) *Seven Brides for Seven Brothers (54) The Second Greatest Sex (55)
34. Romances	The Virginian (29) Destry Rides Again (39) The Last Frontier (56) Run of the Arrow (57) Waco (66)
35. Mysteries	Pursued (47) *Bad Day at Black Rock (54) The Professionals (66)
Documentaries	See film group 30.
Adaptations	See film group 23.
Foreign Films	See film group 15.
Directing and Editing	See film group 6.

SUGGESTED READING

Chapter Six.
Books marked 6 in the Bibliography.

PROGRAM SIX: Mysteries

Film group

36. Short films	*The Golden Fish (France 59) *Moonbird (59)
37. Comedies	*Duck Soup (33) The Trouble With Harry (56) *That Man From Rio (France 64)
38. Musicals	Carousel (56) Porgy and Bess (59)

39. Romances	The Thirty-Nine Steps (35) Key Largo (48) The Key (58) *North by Northwest (59)
Westerns	See film group 35.
Documentaries	See film group 29.
Adaptations	See film group 22.
Foreign Films	See film group 14.
Directing and Editing	See film group 5.

SUGGESTED READING

Bogdanovich, *Cinema of Alfred Hitchcock.*
Clarens, *An Illustrated History of the Horror Film.*
Hall, "The Fantasy Makers" from *Psychology Today.*
Perry, *The Films of Alfred Hitchcock.*
Wood, *Hitchcock's Films.*

PROGRAM SEVEN: Romances

Film group

40. Short Films	*The Adventures of * (57) *The Tender Game (62) *You're No Good (Canada 62) *Phoebe (Canada 64) *The Game (Canada 66) Skater-Dater (67)
41. Comedies	Adam's Rib (49) *All About Eve (50) Born Yesterday (50) Summer Magic (62)
42. Musicals	Meet Me in St. Louis (44) *The King and I (56)

	*The Umbrellas of Cherbourg (France 64) Finian's Rainbow (68)
Mysteries	See film group 39.
Westerns	See film group 34.
Documentaries	See film group 28.
Adaptations	See film group 21.
Foreign Films	See film group 13.
Directing and Editing	See film group 4.

SUGGESTED READING

Hall, "The Fantasy Makers" from *Psychology Today.*
Mayer, *Foreign Films on American Screens.*
Wood, *The Fabulous Films of the Twenties.*

PROGRAM EIGHT: Musicals

Film group

43. Short Films	Silly Symphonies (29) Fantasia (41) (Excerpts, e.g. "The Rite of Spring" sequence) Gay Purr-ee (61) *Tender Game (62) *New Born Again (66)
44. Comedies	State Fair (45) *Oklahoma (55) State Fair (61) Bye Bye Birdie (62) The Unsinkable Molly Brown (63)
Romances	See film group 42.
Mysteries	See film group 38.

Westerns	See film group 33.
Documentaries	See film group 27.
Adaptations	See film group 20.
Foreign Films	See film group 12.
Directing and Editing	See film group 3.

SUGGESTED READING

Chapter Seven.
Books marked 7 in the Bibliography.

PROGRAM NINE: Comedies

Film group

45. Short Films	*Fiddle-de-dee (47) *The Chicken (France 63) *The Critic (63) *Automania 2000 (U.K. 64) *That's Me (64) When Comedy Was King
Musicals	See film group 44.
Romances	See film group 41.
Mysteries	See film group 37.
Westerns	See film group 32.
Documentaries	See film group 26.
Adaptations	See film group 19.
Foreign Films	See film group 11.
Directing and Editing	See film group 2.

SUGGESTED READING

Chapter Seven.
Books marked 7 in the Bibliography.

PROGRAM TEN: Short Films

Film group

Comedies	See film group 45.
Musicals	See film group 43.
Romances	See film group 40.
Mysteries	See film group 36.
Westerns	See film group 31.
Documentaries	See film group 25.
Adaptations	See film group 18.
Foreign Films	See film group 10.
Directing and Editing	See film group 1.

SUGGESTED READING

Chapter Five.
Books marked 5 in the Bibliography.

PROGRAM ELEVEN: Prejudice as It Limits Man

Film group

46. Directing and Editing
　　　　　　　　　　*Intolerance (16)
　　　　　　　　　　Life Boat (43)
　　　　　　　　　　The Defiant Ones (58)

*Judgment at Nuremberg (61)
*To Kill a Mockingbird (62)

47. Foreign Films

Romeo and Juliet (Italy 54)
Nazarin (Mexico 58)
The Shop on Main Street (Czech 64)

48. Adaptations

*Home of the Brave (49)
*Intruder in the Dust (49)
Asphalt Jungle (50)
*A Raisin in the Sun (61)
*The Pawnbroker (64)
*Othello (66)
*To Sir with Love (67)
The Heart is a Lonely Hunter (68)

49. Documentaries

*Intolerance (16)
*Potemkin (U.S.S.R. 25)
*Harvest of Shame (61)
*Let My People Go (65)
*Nothing But a Man (65)
*A Time for Burning (66)

50. Westerns

Broken Arrow (50)
*Bad Day at Black Rock (54)
Duel at Diablo (65)
Hombre (67)

51. Mysteries

*The Informer (35)
*The House on 92nd Street (45)
Crossfire (47)
In the Heat of the Night (67)

52. Romances

Pinky (49)
*A Taste of Honey (U.K. 62)
Patch of Blue (66)
The L-Shaped Room (63)

53. Musicals

Porgy and Bess (42)
Carmen Jones (54)
*The King and I (56)
South Pacific (58)
Flower Drum Song (61)
*West Side Story (61)

A Patch of Blue, *1965, Sidney Poitier and Elizabeth Hartman*

54. Comedies	*The Overcoat (U.S.S.R. 53) Guess Who's Coming To Dinner (67)
55. Short Films .	*Boundary Lines (47) *The Quiet One (48) *The Toymaker (52) *The Critic (63) *No Hiding Place (63) *I Wonder Why (65) An Interview with Bruce Gordon (67) Little Yellow, Little Blue (67) *Willie Catches On (Canada 67)

SUGGESTED READING

Haselden, *Morality and the Mass Media.*
Huaco, *The Sociology of Film Art.*
Kuhns, *Environmental Man.*
McCann, *Film and Society.*
Schillaci, *Movies and Morals.*
Sugy, "Black Men or Good Niggers?" from *Take One.*
Wright, *Mass Communications.*

PROGRAM TWELVE: Finding One's Place in the World

Film group

56. Direction and Editing	*The Quiet One (48) *Marty (55) *Lust for Life (56) *Days of Wine and Roses (62) *The Loneliness of the Long Distance Runner (U.K. 62) *Nobody Waved Goodbye (Canada 64) Alfie (66)
57. Foreign Films	The Burmese Harp (Japan 56) *The 400 Blows (France 59) Room at the Top (U.K. 59) *La Dolce Vita (Italy 61)

The Pumpkin Eater (U.K. 63)
*Persona (Sweden 65)

58. Adaptations

*David Copperfield (34)
*Hamlet (U.K. 48)
*Animal Farm (U.K. 54)
*East of Eden (55)
*Rebel Without a Cause (55)
*The Nun's Story (59)
*West Side Story (61)
*Requiem for a Heavyweight (62)
*Sundays and Cybele (France 62)
Ulysses (67)

59. Documentaries

*The Quiet One (48)
On the Bowery (54)
*Lonely Boy (Canada 62)
*End of Summer (Canada 64)

60. Westerns

The Hanging Tree (59)
Hud (63)

61. Mysteries

M. (Germany 31)
The Maltese Falcon (41)

62. Romances

*Marty (55)
Cat on a Hot Tin Roof (58)
*Sundays and Cybele (France 62)

63. Musicals

Carousel (56)
*West Side Story (61)
Sound of Music (63)

64. Comedies

Bringing Up Baby (38)
Caesar and Cleopatra (U.K. 45)
The Seven Year Itch (55)

65. Short Films

*The Adventures of * (57)
*Assembly Line (61)
*Of Stars and Men (61)
*Blind Gary Davis (62)
*Good Night, Socrates (62)
*Run! (62)
*Conformity (63)
*Runner (63)

The Pawnbroker, *Rod Steiger, 1965*

*Cornet at Night (64)
*Phoebe (64)
*Hey! Stop That (65)

SUGGESTED READING

Fairlie, "The Unreal World of Television News" from White-Averson's *Sight, Sound and Society*.
Fellini, *La Dolce Vita*.
Hall, "The Fantasy Makers" from *Psychology Today*.
Kuhns, *Environmental Man*.

PROGRAM THIRTEEN: Men at War

Film group

66. Directing and Editing	*Desert Victory (U.K. 42) *The Bridge on the River Kwai (U.K. 57) Question 7 (61) The Longest Day (62) *The Manchurian Candidate (62) The Victors (62)
67. Foreign Films	Arsenal (U.S.S.R. 29)† Westfront 1918 (Germany 30)† *Rome: An Open City (Italy 46) Children of Hiroshima (Japan 52) The Forty-First (U.S.S.R. 56)† *The Bridge (Germany 60)† The Good Soldier Schweik (Germany 60)† General Della Rovere (Italy 60)† *La Guerre est Finie (France 65) *The War Game (U.K. 67)
68. Adaptations	All Quiet on the Western Front (30)† The Red Badge of Courage (51) *Stalag 17 (52) See Chapter Four. *Caine Mutiny (54) *The Diary of Anne Frank (59)

THE GUNS OF NAVARONE, *1961, Gregory Peck and David Niven*

*Occurrence at Owl Creek Bridge (France 62) See Chapter Three.
*The Great Escape (63)
*Fail Safe (64)

69. Documentaries

*Potemkin (U.S.S.R. 25)
Ten Days that Shook the World (U.S.S.R. 28)
The Battle of San Pietro (44)
A Diary for Timothy (45)
*The True Glory (45)
*Night and Fog (France 55)
*Judgment at Nuremberg (61)
Over There, 1914-1918 (France 63)†
*The War Game (U.K. 67)

70. Westerns

Yellow Rose of Texas (44)
The Red Badge of Courage (51)
The Alamo (60)

71. Mysteries

*A Man Escaped (France 57)
Man Hunt (58)
The Spy Who Came In From the Cold (65)
*The Train (65)

72. Romances

Gone With the Wind (39)
The Last Bridge (Yugoslavia 53)†
*The Cranes Are Flying (U.S.S.R. 57)
Until They Sail (57)
*Ballad of a Soldier (U.S.S.R. 59)†
*Hiroshima, Mon Amour (France 59)
The Way of Youth (France 62)

73. Musicals

Thousands Cheer (43)
Anchors Aweigh (45)
South Pacific (58)
West Point Story (61)

74. Comedies

Behind the Front (26)
The General (26)
*Duck Soup (33)
To Be or Not To Be (42)
*The Best Years of Our Lives (46)
Mister Roberts (55)
Dr. Strangelove (63)

75. Short Films	The Bond (18)
	*A Time Out of War (54)
	*Night and Fog (France 55)
	*Vivre! (France 59)
	*The Colt (Russia 60)
	*The Hole (62)
	*The Magician (Poland 64)
	*Memorandum (Canada 66)
	*Time of the Locust (66)

SUGGESTED READING

†These films are discussed at length in the booklet *War and Peace* of the *Study of the Film* series published by Argus Communications, 1967, in cooperation with The Catholic Adult Education Center, 1307 South Wabash Avenue, Chicago, Illinois, 60605.

Capa, *Images of War.*

French, "Violence in the Cinema" from White-Averson's *Sight, Sound and Society.*

Gallez, "Patterns in Wartime Documentaries," from *The Quarterly of Film, Radio and Television.*

Huaco, *The Sociology of Film Art.*

Hughes, "Films of Peace and War," Volume Two of *Film.*

Kael, "Bonnie and Clyde," from *Kiss Kiss Bang Bang.*

Ross, *Picture* (on the film *Red Badge of Courage*).

PROGRAM FOURTEEN: Individual Conscience in an Indifferent World

Film group

76. Directing and Editing	The Life of Emile Zola (37)
	*Citizen Kane (41)
	*Boomerang (46)
	*On the Waterfront (54)
	*The Hustler (61)
	*Days of Wine and Roses (62)
	*Requiem for a Heavyweight (62)
	*The Pawnbroker (64)
77. Foreign Films	The Bicycle Thief (Italy 49)
	*Umberto D (Italy 52)
	*Two Men and a Wardrobe (Poland 57)

PLANET OF THE APES, *1968*

*The 400 Blows (France 59)
*Zorba the Greek (Greece 64)

78. Adaptations

Of Mice and Men (39)
*Caine Mutiny (54)
*Twelve Angry Men (54)
Court-Martial of Billy Mitchell (55)
*The Bridge on the River Kwai (U.K. 57)
*I Want to Live (59)
On the Beach (59)
Exodus (60)
*Lonely Are the Brave (62)
The Heart Is a Lonely Hunter (68)

79. Documentaries

*The Triumph of the Will (Germany 34-36)
*Harvest of Shame (61)
Freud (62)
*Conformity (63)
*The Detached Americans (64)
Don't Look Back (U.K. 65)

80. Westerns

*Northwest Passage (40)
*The Ox-Bow Incident (43)
*High Noon (52)
*Shane (53)
Left-Handed Gun (58)

81. Mysteries

Rear Window (54)
The Man Who Knew Too Much (56)
*Psycho (60)
*Blow-Up (Italy 66)

82. Romances

*Marty (55)
*Nights of Cabiria (Italy 57)
*Days of Wine and Roses (62)
*Zorba the Greek (Greece 64)

83. Musicals

Picnic (55)
The Unsinkable Molly Brown (63)
Stop the World I Want to Get Off (65)

84. Comedies

*Roman Holiday (53)

                                          *My Uncle (France 58)
                                          Divorce Italian Style (61)

85. Short Films

                                          *Boundary Lines (47)
                                          *Very Nice, Very Nice (Canada 61)
                                          *Good Night, Socrates (62)
                                          *The Detached Americans (64)
                                          *Hangman (64)
                                          *The Wall (Yugoslavia 65)

PROGRAM FIFTEEN: Growing Towards Maturity

Film group

**86. Directing and
      Editing**

                                          *Days of Wine and Roses (62)
                                          *A Taste of Honey (U.K. 62)
                                          *Nobody Waved Goodbye (Canada
                                          64)

87. Foreign Films

                                          The Bicycle Thief (Italy 49)
                                          The Great Adventure (Sweden 53)
                                          *Wild Strawberries (Sweden 57)
                                          *Lord of the Flies (U.K. 63)
                                          *Blow-Up (Italy 66)
                                          *Closely Watched Trains (Czech 67)
                                          *To Be a Crook (France 67)

88. Adaptations

                                          *Great Expectations (U.K. 47)
                                          *Hamlet (U.K. 48)
                                          *All the King's Men (49)
                                          *Intruder in the Dust (49)
                                          The Red Badge of Courage (51)
                                          *On the Waterfront (54)
                                          *The Diary of Anne Frank (59)
                                          *To Kill a Mockingbird (62)

89. Documentaries

                                          *The Quiet One (48)
                                          *The World of Apu (59)
                                          *Lonely Boy (Canada 62)
                                          *End of Summer (Canada 64)

90. Westerns

                                          Young Daniel Boone (50)

	*Lonely Are the Brave (62) Hud (63) The Sons of Katie Elder (65)
91. Mysteries	The Bad Seed (56) The Moonspinners (64)
92. Romances	Romeo and Juliet (Italy 54) *Ballad of a Soldier (U.S.S.R. 59) *David and Lisa (62) A Man and a Woman (France 66)
93. Musicals	*Singin' in the Rain (52) *Guys and Dolls (55) *West Side Story (61) Sound of Music (64)
94. Comedies	The Kidnapper (58) *Dr. Strangelove (64) Daisies (Sedmikrasky) (Czech 68) Life's Just Great (Livet ar Stenkul) (Sweden 68) You're a Big Boy Now (68)
95. Short Films	*The Tender Game (62) *End of Summer (Canada 64) *Phoebe (Canada 64) *No Reason to Stay (Canada 65) *You're No Good (Canada 65) Skater Dater (67)

PROGRAM SIXTEEN: What Really is Truth, Honor, Virtue . . .?

Film group

96. Directing and Editing	*La Dolce Vita (Italy 61) *David and Lisa (62) *The Gospel According to St. Matthew (Italy 65) *A Man for All Seasons (66)
97. Foreign Films	*The Virgin Spring (59)

A Man For All Seasons, *1966, Paul Scofield*

*The Trial of Joan of Arc (France 62)
*Persona (Sweden 65)

98. Adaptations

The Heart of the Matter (54)
*Twelve Angry Men (54)
The Court-Martial of Billy Mitchell (55)
*Lord of the Flies (U.K. 63)
*Tom Jones (U.K. 63)
The Comedians (67)
*In Cold Blood (67)

99. Documentaries

*Helen Keller in Her Story (53)
*The Loneliness of the Long Distance Runner (U.K. 62)
*Of Time, Work and Leisure (63)

100. Westerns

*The Ox-Bow Incident (43)
Rashomon (Japan 50)
*Shane (53)
The Professionals (66)

101. Mysteries

*Rififi (56)
*North by Northwest (59)
*The Innocents (61)
Rosemary's Baby (68)

102. Romances

*Marty (55)
*David and Lisa (62)
Elvira Madigan (Sweden 67)

103. Musicals

Peter Pan (52)
Mary Poppins (64)
*The Umbrellas of Cherbourg (France 64)

104. Comedies

Never on Sunday (Greece 60)
What Did You Do in the War, Daddy? (67)

105. Short Films

*Violinist (59)
*The Critic (63)
*Parable (64)
*The Top (65)
*Time of the Locust (66)

PROGRAM SEVENTEEN: An Individual's Fight for Integrity

Film group

106. Directing and Editing	*Great Expectations (U.K. 47) *Caine Mutiny (54) *Nights of Cabiria (Italy 57) *The Hustler (61) *David and Lisa (62) *The Loneliness of the Long Distance Runner (U.K. 62)
107. Foreign Films	*Triumph of the Will (Germany 34-36) The Heart of the Matter (54) *La Strada (Italy 54)
108. Adaptations	All that Money Can Buy (41) The Rose Tattoo (55) *Anastasia (56) *The Bridge on the River Kwai (U.K. 57) *The Miracle Worker (62) *Becket (U.K. 64) Night of the Iguana (64) *A Man For All Seasons (66)
109. Documentaries	*Nanook of the North (22) *Lonely Boy (Canada 62) *Nahanni (Canada 62)
110. Westerns	Destry Rides Again (39) Jim Thorpe—All American (51) *High Noon (52)
111. Mysteries	Rear Window (54) The Children's Hour (62) What Ever Happened to Baby Jane? (63)
112. Romances	Summer Interlude (Sweden 50) The Key (59) The Fox (68)
113. Musicals	*The King and I (56)

In the title role of RACHEL, RACHEL, *1968 Joanne Woodward runs off in panic after attending a tabernacle meeting*

*West Side Story (61)
My Fair Lady (65)

114. Comedies

Mister Roberts (55)
Heaven Knows, Mister Allison (56)
*My Uncle (France 58)
*A Thousand Clowns (65)

115. Short Films

*The Red Balloon (France 56)
*The Golden Fish (France 59)
*End of Summer (Canada 64)
*That's Me (64)
*No Reason to Stay (65)
*You're No Good (Canada 65)
The Last of the Mohicans (66)
The Last Pilgrim (68)

PROGRAM EIGHTEEN: Homo Viator

Film group

**116. Directing and
   Editing**

*On the Waterfront (54)
*Nights of Cabiria (Italy 57)
*Birdman of Alcatraz (62)
*The Miracle Worker (62)
*Nobody Waved Goodbye (Canada 64)
*Darling (U.K. 65)

117. Foreign Films

*Man of Aran (U.K. 34)
The Citadel (38)
*Ikiru (Japan 52)
*La Strada (Italy 54)
*The Seventh Seal (Sweden 56)
The Mark (61)
*Zorba the Greek (Greece 64)

118. Adaptations

*The Grapes of Wrath (40)
*Citizen Kane (41)
*Diary of a Country Priest (France 50)
*The Diary of Anne Frank (59)
*A Man for All Seasons (66)

119. Documentaries	*Nanook of the North (22) *Nahanni (Canada 62) *A Thousand Days (65) The Tunnel (NBC-TV)
120. Westerns	The Sheepman (58) One-Eyed Jacks (61) The Misfits (61)
121. Mysteries	Life Boat (43) The Third Man (U.K. 49) Rear Window (54) *North by Northwest (59) Night of the Iguana (64)
122. Romances	*A Place in the Sun (51) *Marty (55) *Closely Watched Trains (Czech 67)
123. Musicals	Picnic (55) *The King and I (56) *West Side Story (61)
124. Comedies	Never Give a Sucker an Even Break (41) Hans Christian Andersen (52) The Errand Boy (62) *That Man From Rio (France 64) *A Thousand Clowns (65)
125. Short Films	*Thursday's Children (U.K. 52) *Nahanni (Canada 62) *Blindness (64) *The Wall (Yugoslavia 65) The Antkeeper (68)

PROGRAM NINETEEN: Accent on the Family

Film group

126. Directing and Editing	*The Magnificent Ambersons (42) The Bicycle Thief (Italy 49) *A Raisin in the Sun (61)

BIRD MAN OF ALCATRAZ, *1962, Burt Lancaster and Thelma Ritter*

*Nobody Waved Goodbye (Canada 64)

127. Foreign Films

*The 400 Blows (France 59)
Edouard et Caroline (France 61)
Le Bonheur (France 65)

128. Adaptations

*The Grapes of Wrath (40)
*Intruder in the Dust (49)
*A Raisin in the Sun (61)

129. Documentaries

*The Diary of Anne Frank (59)
*The Detached Americans (64)
*Years of Lightning, Day of Drums (66)
The Population Explosion (CBS-TV)

130. Westerns

The Covered Wagon (23)
*Shane (53)
*Bad Day at Black Rock (54)
Cimarron (60)
Two Rode Together (61)

131. Mysteries

Les Parents Terribles (France 49)
*Hush, Hush Sweet Charlotte (61)
*In Cold Blood (67)

132. Romances

*The Best Years of our Lives (46)
Romeo and Juliet (Italy 54)
Through a Glass Darkly (Sweden 61)

133. Musicals

Meet Me in Saint Louis (44)
*Seven Brides for Seven Brothers (54)
I Could Go On Singing (62)
The Sound of Music (62)

134. Comedies

Please Don't Eat the Daisies (60)
Guess Who's Coming to Dinner (67)

135. Short Films

*Neighbors (Canada 52)
*Have I Told You Lately That I Love You? (58)
*The Colt (Russia 60)

PROGRAM TWENTY: It's a Woman's World

Film group

136. Directing and Editing	Diary of a Chambermaid (France 46) *Night of Cabiria (Italy 57) Diary of a Chambermaid (France 63) *Darling (U.K. 65) *Georgy Girl (66)
137. Foreign Films	*Never on Sunday (Greece 60) Two Women (Italy 60) *A Taste of Honey (U.K. 62) The Pumpkin Eater (U.K. 63)
138. Adaptations	*All About Eve (50) *Anastasia (56) *The Diary of Anne Frank (59) *The Nun's Story (59) *The Miracle Worker (62) *Darling (U.K. 65)
139. Documentaries	*Helen Keller in Her Story (53) *The Trial of Joan of Arc (62) The Beauty of Women (NBC-TV) The Soviet Woman (ABC-TV) The World of Jacqueline Kennedy (NBC-TV)
140. Westerns	Saratoga Trunk (43) *My Darling Clementine (46) Calamity Jane (53) McLintock! (63) The Scalphunters (67)
141. Mysteries	Rebecca (40) Laura (44) *The Lady from Shanghai (47) The Portrait of Jennie (47) The Children's Hour (62)
142. Romances	Ruby Gentry (52) The Fox (68)

Fellini's LA DOLCE VITA, *1959, Anita Ekberg*

143. Musicals	Annie Get Your Gun (50) *The King and I (56) Rosemary (Germany 58) Mary Poppins (64) My Fair Lady (65)
144. Comedies	The Desk Set (57) Lolita (62) Thoroughly Modern Millie (67)
145. Short Films	*Helen Keller in Her Story (53) *End of Summer (Canada 64) *Phoebe (64) *Sunday Lark (64)

PROGRAM TWENTY-ONE: Ask Any Man

Film group

146. Directing and Editing	Jim Thorpe—All American (51) *On the Waterfront (54) *The Hustler (61) *Billy Budd (U.K. 62) *Requiem for a Heavyweight (62)
147. Foreign Films	*Ballad of a Soldier (U.S.S.R. 59) *Knife in the Water (Poland 62) *Lawrence of Arabia (U.K. 62) *Whistle Down the Wind (U.K. 62)
148. Adaptations	*Henry V (U.K. 45) *Diary of a Country Priest (France 50) *Death of a Salesman (51) *The Old Man and the Sea (58) *A View From the Bridge (61) Mutiny on the Bounty (62) The Rafer Johnson Story (62) The Agony and the Ecstasy (U.K. 64) *Dr. Zhivago (U.K. 65)

*The Gospel According to St. Matthew (Italy 65)
*A Man For All Seasons (66)
The Heart Is a Lonely Hunter (68)

149. Documentaries

*Nanook of the North (22)
*That's Me (64)

150. Westerns

*The Treasure of Sierra Madre (47)
*High Noon (52)
*Shane (53)
Hud (63)
Mackenna's Gold (68)

151. Mysteries

Spellbound (45)
Key Largo (48)
The Third Man (49)
Rear Window (54)

152. Romances

*Marty (55)
*Zorba the Greek (Greece 64)
Alfie (66)
*Who's Afraid of Virginia Woolf? (66)

153. Musicals

The Glenn Miller Story (53)
The Music Man (62)
Don't Look Back (U.K. 67)

154. Comedies

*My Uncle (France 58)
Man's Favorite Sport (63)
*Tom Jones (U.K. 63)
The Odd Couple (68)

155. Short Films

*Nahanni (Canada 62)
*The Tender Game (62)
*The Game (Canada 66)
*No Reason to Stay (Canada 66)

PROGRAM TWENTY-TWO: Days of Youth

Film group

156. Directing and Editing

*Rebel Without a Cause (55)

A Taste of Honey, *1962*

	*The Loneliness of the Long Distance Runner (U.K. 62)
	*Nobody Waved Goodbye (Canada 64)
157. Foreign Films	Brighton Rock (U.K. 46) The Great Adventure (Sweden 53) Vitelloni (Italy 53) *The 400 Blows (France 59) *The Bridge (Germany 60)
158. Adaptations	A Tree Grows in Brooklyn (44) O. Henry's Full House (52) *Lord of the Flies (U.K. 53) So Big (53) *The Diary of Anne Frank (59) *To Kill a Mockingbird (62)
159. Documentaries	Meet Comrade Student (ABC-TV 9/28/62) *Sixteen in Webster Groves (66) *Satan's Choice (Canada 67)
160. Westerns	*Shane (53) *The Magnificent Seven (60) Young Jesse James (60)
161. Mysteries	The Boy With the Green Hair (48) The Kidnapper (58) *The Innocents (61)
162. Romances	Romeo and Juliet (Italy 54) *David and Lisa (62) *Jules and Jim (France 62)
163. Musicals	*West Side Story (61) Bye, Bye Birdie (62) *Help! (U.K. 65) Inside Daisy Clover (65)
164. Comedies	The Happiest Days of Your Life (U.K. 50) Mr. Hulot's Holiday (France 53) *The Knack . . . (U.K. 65)
165. Short Films	*The Mischief Makers (57)

*End of Summer (Canada 64)
*Phoebe (64)
*You're No Good (Canada 65)
*The Game (Canada 66)
*The Merry-Go-Round (Canada 66)
*Sixteen in Webster Groves (66)
Skater-Dater (66)

PROGRAM TWENTY-THREE:
"Your Young Men Will See Visions . . ."

Film group

166. Directing and Editing

*Louisiana Story (48)
*A Place in the Sun (51)
*On the Waterfront (54)
*Rebel Without a Cause (55)
Cléo de 5 à 7 (France 61)
*The Hustler (61)
*A Raisin in the Sun (61)

167. Foreign Films

*Ikiru (Japan 52)
The Great Adventure (Sweden 53)
*La Strada (Italy 54)
The Burmese Harp (Japan 56)
*The Seventh Seal (Sweden 56)
Room at the Top (U.K. 59)
*La Dolce Vita (Italy 61)
*8½ (Italy 62)
*Whistle Down the Wind (U.K. 62)

168. Adaptations

All Quiet on the Western Front (30)
*Great Expectations (U.K. 47)
*Hamlet (U.K. 48)
*Intruder in the Dust (49)
*A View from the Bridge (61)

169. Documentaries

A Diary for Timothy (45)
*Lonely Boy (Canada 62)
*Runner (62)
*That's Me (64)

170. Westerns

Vengeance Valley (51)

Franco Zeffirelli's ROMEO AND JULIET, *1968*

*Shane (53)
Hud (63)

171. Mysteries

The Boy With Green Hair (48)
The Children's Hour (62)
The Moonspinners (64)

172. Romances

*Marty (55)
*Wild Strawberries (Sweden 57)
*Ballad of a Soldier (U.S.S.R. 59)
*Love With the Proper Stranger (63)

173. Musicals

Alice in Wonderland (33)
The Wizard of Oz (39)
Peter Pan (52)
*West Side Story (61)

174. Comedies

Angels With Dirty Faces (38)
The Secret Life of Walter Mitty (47)
*My Uncle (France 58)

175. Short Films

*The Adventures of * (57)
*The Red Balloon (France 57)
*Time Piece (65)

PROGRAM TWENTY-FOUR: ". . . and Your Old Men Will Dream Dreams."

Film group

176. Directing and Editing

Boys Town (38)
*Citizen Kane (41)
Life Boat (43)
*The Treasure of Sierra Madre (48)
*Cyrano de Bergerac (50)
*Wild Strawberries (Sweden 57)

177. Foreign Films

*Man of Aran (U.K. 34)
Miracle in Milan (Italy 51)
*Umberto D (Italy 52)
*Wild Strawberries (Sweden 57)

178. Adaptations

Gone With the Wind (39)
Goodbye, Mister Chips (39)

*All the King's Men (49)
*Cyrano de Bergerac (50)
*Death of a Salesman (51)
*A Unicorn in the Garden (53)
 Moby Dick (56)
*The Old Man and the Sea (58)
*To Kill a Mockingbird (62)
*Fail Safe (64)

179. Documentaries

*Nanook of the North (22)
Meet Mr. Lincoln (NBC-TV
    2/11/59)

180. Westerns

*Treasure of Sierra Madre (48)
Hud (63)

181. Mysteries

*Night of the Hunter (55)
*The Innocents (61)
*The Pawnbroker (64)

182. Romances

Brief Encounter (U.K. 46)
*Wild Strawberries (Sweden 57)
Lolita (62)

183. Musicals

Pinocchio (40)
*The King and I (56)
Gigi (58)

184. Comedies

The Man Who Came to Dinner (42)
The Father of the Bride (50)
*Sunset Boulevard (50)

185. Short Films

*A Unicorn in the Garden (53)
*The Smile (France 60)
*The House (Holland 61)
*Nahanni (Canada 62)
*Help! My Snowman's Burning Down
    (64)
*The String Bean (France 64)

PROGRAM TWENTY-FIVE: Social Problems

Film group

**186. Directing and
    Editing**

Shoeshine (Italy 46)

*Intruder in the Dust (49)
*A Place in the Sun (51)
The Savage Eye (59)
*Requiem for a Heavyweight (62)
*2001: A Space Odyssey (68)

187. Foreign Films

*Umberto D (Italy 52)
*The Seventh Seal (Sweden 56)
*He Who Must Die (Greece 57)
We Are All Murderers (France 57)

188. Adaptations

*Greed (24)
*The Grapes of Wrath (40)
*Who's Afraid of Virginia Woolf?
    (66)

189. Documentaries

The Plow That Broke the Plains
    (36)
111th Street (62)
The Miner's Lament (ABC-TV
    4/19/63)
*The Inheritance (64)
*That's Me (64)

190. Westerns

*The Ox-Bow Incident (43)
*The Magnificent Seven (60)

191. Mysteries

*The Birds (63)

192. Romances

Bus Stop (56)
*Have I Told You Lately That I Love
    You? (58)
*The Key (59)
*Days of Wine and Roses (63)
The Comedians (67)

193. Musicals

Cabin in the Sky (43)
Carmen Jones (54)
*West Side Story (61)

194. Comedies

The Miracle of Morgan's Creek (44)
*The Overcoat (U.S.S.R. 53)
The Seven Year Itch (55)
The Wrong Box (67)

195. Short Films

*Neighbors (Canada 52)

*I Was A Ninety-Pound Weakling
  (60)
*Good Night, Socrates (62)
*The Pusher (Yugoslavia 62)
*Automania 2000 (U.K. 64)
*The Detached Americans (64)
*Smoking and You (U.K. 65)

Suggested Readings are given with Program 11.

PROGRAM TWENTY-SIX: Directors Treat Basic Themes

See film groups 46 56 66 76 86 96 106 116 126 136 146
  156 166 176 186

PROGRAM TWENTY-SEVEN: Foreign Films on Basic Themes

See film groups 47 57 67 77 87 97 107 117 127 137 147
  157 167 177 187

PROGRAM TWENTY-EIGHT: Film Adaptations of Basic Themes in Literature

See film groups 48 58 68 78 88 98 108 118 128 138 148
  158 168 178 188

PROGRAM TWENTY-NINE: Basic Themes in Documentaries

See film groups 49 59 69 79 89 99 109 119 129 139 149
  159 169 179 189

PROGRAM THIRTY: Basic Themes in Westerns

See film groups 50 60 70 80 90 100 110 120 130 140 150
  160 170 180 190

PROGRAM THIRTY-ONE: Basic Themes in Mysteries

See film groups 51 61 71 81 91 101 111 121 131 141 151
  161 171 181 191

PROGRAM THIRTY-TWO: Basic Themes in Romances

See film groups 52 62 72 82 92 102 112 122 132 142 152
  162 172 182 192

PROGRAM THIRTY-THREE: Basic Themes in Musicals

See film groups 53 63 73 83 93 103 113 123 133 143 153 163 173 183 193

PROGRAM THIRTY-FOUR: Basic Themes in Comedies

See film groups 54 64 74 84 94 104 114 124 134 144 154 164 174 184 194

PROGRAM THIRTY-FIVE: Basic Themes in Short Films

See film groups 55 65 75 85 95 105 115 125 135 145 155 165 175 185 195

PROGRAMS 36 to 42: FOREIGN DIRECTORS*

PROGRAM THIRTY-SIX: Russian Directors and Their Films

1924	Strike	Sergei M. Eisenstein (1899-1948)
1925	Potemkin	Eisenstein
1925-26	The Mechanics of the Brain (documentary)	Vsevold I. Pudovkin (1893-1953)
1926	Mother	Pudovkin
1927	The End of St. Petersburg	Pudovkin
1928	October (Ten Days That Shook The World)	Eisenstein
1928	Storm Over Asia	Pudovkin
1929	The General Line	Eisenstein
1938	Alexander Nevsky	Eisenstein
1939	Time in the Sun	Eisenstein
1944	Ivan the Terrible, Part I	Eisenstein
1946	Ivan the Terrible, Part II	Eisenstein
1953	The Return of Vasily Bortnikov	Pudovkin
1957	The Cranes Are Flying	Mikhail Kalatozov (b. 1903)
1958	The Overcoat	Alexis Batalov (b. 1928)
1960	Ballad of a Soldier	Grigori Chukhrai (b. 1921)

*All the films in Programs 36 through 47 are available on 16mm.

SUGGESTED SHORT FILMS

| 1960 | The Colt | Vladimir Fetin |
| 1962 | The Showman | |

SUGGESTED READING

Eisenstein, *The Film Form and The Film Sense.*
Leyda, *Kino.*
Nizhnii, *Lessons With Eisenstein.*
Pudovkin, *Film Techniques and Film Acting.*

PROGRAM THIRTY-SEVEN: Italian Directors and Their Films

1942	Ossessione	Luchino Visconti (b. 1906)
1942	The Children are Watching	Vittorio de Sica (b. 1902)
1945	**Rome: An Open City**	Roberto Rossellini (b. 1906)
1946	Shoeshine	de Sica
1948	N.U. (documentary)	Michelangelo Antonioni (b. 1912)
1949	The Bicycle Thief	de Sica
1950	Flowers of Saint Francis	Rossellini
1950	Stromboli	Rossellini
1951	The Miracle of Milan	de Sica
1952	Umberto D	de Sica
1952	The White Sheik	Federico Fellini (b. 1920)
1953	I Vitelloni	Fellini
1953	"Tentato Suicido" (from Love in the City)	Antonioni
1953	"Love Cheerfully Arranged" (from Love in the City)	Fellini
1954	La Strada	Fellini
1955	Il Bidone	Fellini
1955	Gold of Naples	de Sica
1956	The Roof	de Sica
1957	Nights of Cabiria	Fellini

1957	Il Grido	Antonioni
1959	General Della Rovere	Rossellini
1960	Night in Rome	Rossellini
1960	La Dolce Vita	Fellini
1960	L'Avventura	Antonioni
1960	La Notte	Antonioni
1961	"The Dream of Dr. Antonio" (from Boccaccio 70)	Fellini
1961	Eclipse (l'Eclipse)	Antonioni
1961	Two Women	de Sica
1963	The Condemned of Altona	de Sica
1964	The Red Desert	Antonioni
1964	Marriage Italian Style	de Sica
1964	The Gospel According to St. Matthew	Pier Paolo Pasolini (b. 1922)
1965	Juliet of the Spirits	Fellini

SUGGESTED SHORT FILM

| 1946 | Shoestring | de Sica |

SUGGESTED READINGS

Antonioni, *Screenplays.*
Budgen, *Fellini.*
Cowie, *Antonioni, Bergman, Resnais.*
Fellini, *La Dolce Vita.*
Fellini, *Juliet of the Spirits.*
Leprohon, *Michelangelo Antonioni.*
Nowell-Smith, *Luchino Visconti.*
Rondi, *Italian Cinema Today.*

PROGRAM THIRTY-EIGHT: British Directors and Their Films

1925	The Pleasure Garden	Alfred Hitchcock (b. 1899) (pre-Hollywood films listed)
1926	The Lodger	Hitchcock
1929	Blackmail	Hitchcock

1936	Night Mail	Harry Watt (b. 1906)
1945	Brief Encounter	David Lean (b. 1908)
1945	Henry V	Sir Laurence Olivier (b. 1907)
1946	Great Expectations	Lean
1958	Hamlet	Olivier
1952	Breaking the Sound Barrier	Lean
1957	The Bridge on the River Kwai	Lean
1961	The Innocents	Jack Clayton
1962	Lord of the Flies	Peter Brook (b. 1925)
1962	A Taste of Honey	Tony Richardson (b. 1928)
1962	The Loneliness of the Long Distance Runner	Richardson
1963	Tom Jones	Richardson
1963	Billy Liar	John Schlesinger (b. 1926)
1965	Darling	Schlesinger

SUGGESTED SHORT FILMS

1934	Granton Trawler	Edgar Anstey (b. 1907)
1954	Animal Farm	John Halas and Joy Batchelor
1962	The Plain Man's Guide to Advertising	Bob Godfrey
1964	Automania 2000	Halas-Batchelor

SUGGESTED READING

Bluem, *A Pictorial History of the Talkies*. (a British view)
Bogdanovich, *Cinema of Alfred Hitchcock*. (from England to U.S.A.)
Losey, *Losey on Losey*. (from U.S.A. to England)
Perry, *The Films of Alfred Hitchcock*.
Wood, *Hitchcock's Films*.

PROGRAM THIRTY-NINE: French Directors and Their Films

1924	Entr' Acte	Rene Clair (b. 1898) (pseudonym for Rene Chomette)
1927	The Italian Straw Hat	Clair

1930	Under the Roofs of Paris	Clair
1931	Le Million	Clair
1932	A Nous La Liberté	Clair
1932	Boudu Saved from Drowning	Jean Renoir (b. 1894)
1935	The Crime of Monsieur Lange	Renoir
1936	The Lower Depths	Renoir
1936-46	A Day in the Country	Renoir
1938	The Ghost Goes West	Clair
1938	Rules of the Game	Renoir
1942	I Married a Witch	Clair
1943	This Land is Mine	Renoir
1944	Les Dames du Bois de Boulogne	Robert Bresson (b. 1907)
1946	Beauty and the Beast	Jean Cocteau (b. 1892-1963)
1949	The Walls	Rene Clement (b. 1913)
1950	The River	Renoir
1950	Beauty and the Devil	Clair
1951	Diary of a Country Priest	Bresson
1952	Forbidden Games	Clement
1956	A Man Escaped	Bresson
1957	Gates of Paris	Clair
1959	Hiroshima, Mon Amour	Alain Resnais (b. 1922)
1959	The 400 Blows	François Truffaut (b. 1932)
1959	Lunch on the Grass	Renoir
1960	"The Marriage" (in Three Fables of Love)	Clair
1960	Pickpocket	Bresson
1961	Last Year at Marienbad	Resnais
1961	Jules and Jim	Truffaut
1963	Le Jour et l'Heure	Clement
1963	The Umbrellas of Cherbourg	Jacques Demy (b. 1931)
1965	La Guerre est Finie	Resnais

1966	Fahrenheit 451	Truffaut
1966	Is Paris Burning?	Clement
1966	A Man and A Woman	Claude Lelouch
1967	To Be a Crook	Lelouch

SUGGESTED SHORT FILMS

1948	Van Gogh	Resnais
1955	Night and Fog	Resnais
1956	The Red Balloon	Albert Lamorrisse
1958	Children Adrift	Edouard Luntz
1959	Vivre!	Carlos Vilardebo
1959	The Golden Fish	Edmond Sechan
1962	An Occurrence at Owl Creek Bridge	Robert Enrico
1963	The Chicken	Claude Berri
1964	The String Bean	Sechan and Marie Marc

SUGGESTED READINGS

Armes, *French Cinema Since 1946.*
Cowie, *Antonioni, Bergman, Resnais.*

PROGRAM FORTY: Swedish Directors and Their Films

1943	A Summer's Tale	Arne Sucksdorff (b. 1917)
1948	Port of Call	Ingmar Bergman (b. 1918)
1949	The Devil's Wanton	Bergman
1950	Summer Interlude	Bergman
1951	The Wind and the Rain	Sucksdorff
1952	Secrets of Women	Bergman
1952	Monika	Bergman
1953	The Great Adventure	Sucksdorff
1953	The Naked Night	Bergman
1954	A Lesson in Love	Bergman
1955	Dreams	Bergman
1955	Smiles of a Summer Night	Bergman

1956	The Seventh Seal	Bergman
1957	Wild Strawberries	Bergman
1957	Brink of Life	Bergman
1958	The Magician	Bergman
1959	The Virgin Spring	Bergman
1960	The Devil's Eye	Bergman
1961	Through a Glass Darkly	Bergman
1962	Winter Light	Bergman
1963	The Silence	Bergman
1964	All These Women	Bergman
1965	Persona	Bergman
1966	Night Games	Mai Zetterling (b. 1925)
1967	The Hour of the Wolf	Bergman
1967	Elvira Madigan	Bo Widerberg (b. 1930)
1968	The Shame	Bergman

SUGGESTED SHORT FILMS

1961	The Boy and the Kite	Widerberg

SUGGESTED READINGS

Bergman, *Four Screenplays.*
Cowie, *Antonioni, Bergman, Resnais.*
Cowie, *Swedish Cinema.*
Lauritzen, *Swedish Films.*

PROGRAM FORTY-ONE: Spanish Directors and Their Films

1928	Un Chien Andalou (co-directed with Salvador Dali)	Luis Buñuel (b. 1900)
1950	The Young and the Damned	Buñuel (in Mexico)
1951	Una Mujer sin Amor	Buñuel
1951	Subida al Cielo	Buñuel
1951	Esa Pareja Feliz (Co-directed with Bardem)	Luis Berlanga (b. 1921)

1952	Adventures of Robinson Crusoe	Buñuel
1952	El	Buñuel
1955	Death of a Cyclist	Juan Antonio Bardem (b. 1922)
1958	Nazarin	Buñuel
1961	Viridiana	Buñuel
1962	The Destroying Angel	Buñuel
1963	Diary of a Chambermaid	Buñuel (in France)
1967	Belle de Jour	Buñuel

SUGGESTED READINGS

Kyrou, *Luis Buñuel.*

PROGRAM FORTY-TWO: Japanese Directors and Their Films

1924	Sunday	Yasujoro Shimazu (b. 1897)
1939	Tomorrow's Dancers	Kimisaburo Yoshimura (b. 1911)
1945	Men Who Tread on the Tiger's Tail	Akira Kurosawa (b. 1910)
1948	Drunken Angel	Kurosawa
1950	Rashomon	Kurosawa
1952	Ikiru	Kurosawa
1952	Children of Hiroshima	Kaneto Shindo (b. 1912)
1953	Gate of Hell	Teinosuke Kinugasa (b. 1898)
1954	The Seven Samurai	Kurosawa
1955	I Live in Fear	Kurosawa
1957	The Burmese Harp	Kon Ichikawa (b. 1915)
1957	Throne of Blood	Kurosawa
1958	The Lower Depths	Kurosawa
1961	The Inheritance	Masaki Kobayashi (b. 1916)
1962	The Bad Sleep Well	Kurosawa
1963	High and Low	Kurosawa
1963	Woman in the Dunes	Hiroshi Teshigahara (b. 1927)

SUGGESTED SHORT FILMS

| 1960 | Animations by Yoji Kuri (b. 1928) |

SUGGESTED READINGS

Richie, *The Films of Akira Kurosawa.*
Richie, *The Japanese Movie.*

PROGRAM FORTY-THREE: American Pioneers of Film

1914	(35 short comedies, Keystone Films)	Charles S. Chaplin (b. 1889)
1915	(12 short films, Essanay Films)	Chaplin
1915	Birth of a Nation	David Wark Griffith (1875-1948)
1916	Intolerance	Griffith
	(Fun Factory: History of Film Series)	Mack Sennett (1880-1960)
1920	Nanook of the North	Robert J. Flaherty (1884-1951)
1923-25	Moana	Flaherty
1924	Greed	Erich Von Stroheim (1885-1957)
1924	Iron Horse	John Ford (b. 1895)
1925	The Gold Rush	Chaplin
1927	Long Pants	Frank Capra (b. 1897)
1932	Industrial Britain	Flaherty
1932-34	Man of Aran	Flaherty
1933	Duck Soup	Leo McCarey (b. 1898)
1938	Bringing Up Baby	Howard Hawks (b. 1896)

SUGGESTED READING

Barry-Bowser, *D. W. Griffith, American Film Master.*
Bowman, *Charlie Chaplin, His Life and Art.*
Chaplin, *My Autobiography.*
Chaplin (Jr.), *My Father, Charlie Chaplin.*
Griffith, *The Movies.*
Griffith, *The World of Robert Flaherty.*
Griffith (Mrs.) *When the Movies Were Young.*
Lahue, *World of Laughter.*
McDonald, *The Films of Charlie Chaplin.*
O'Leary, *The Silent Cinema.*
Ramsaye, *A Million and One Nights.*

Sennett, *King of Comedy.*
Wood, *The Fabulous Films of the Twenties.*

PROGRAM FORTY-FOUR: Films of the 30's and 40's
Directors Capra and Ford

1936	Mr. Deeds Goes to Town	Frank Capra (b. 1897)
1937	Lost Horizon	Capra
1938	You Can't Take it With You	Capra
1939	Mr. Smith Goes to Washington	Capra
1939	Stagecoach	John Ford (b. 1895)
1940	Drums Along the Mohawk	Ford
1940	The Grapes of Wrath	Ford
1940	The Long Voyage Home	Ford
1941	Tobacco Road	Ford
1941	Meet John Doe	Capra
1941	How Green Was My Valley	Ford
1944	Arsenic and Old Lace	Capra

PROGRAM FORTY-FIVE: Films of the 40's and 50's
Directors Mann and Wyler

1942	Mrs. Miniver	William Wyler (b. 1902)
1946	The Best Years of Our Lives	Wyler
1949	The Reign of Terror	Delbert Mann (b. 1902)
1949	Border Incident	Mann
1950	Devil's Doorway	Mann
1951	Detective Story	Wyler
1953	Roman Holiday	Wyler

PROGRAM FORTY-SIX: Films of the 40's and 50's
Directors Huston, Kazan and Zinnemann

1946	Boomerang	Elia Kazan (b. 1909)
1947	The Treasure of the Sierra Madre	John Huston (b. 1906)
1947	My Brother Talks to Horses	Fred Zinnemann (b. 1907)
1948	The Search	Zinnemann
1948	Key Largo	Huston
1949	Pinky	Kazan
1950	The Asphalt Jungle	Huston
1950	The Men	Zinnemann
1950	Teresa	Zinnemann
1950	A Streetcar Named Desire	Kazan
1951	The Red Badge of Courage	Huston
1952	The African Queen	Huston
1952	High Noon	Zinnemann
1952	The Member of the Wedding	Zinnemann
1952	From Here to Eternity	Zinnemann
1954	On the Waterfront	Kazan
1954	East of Eden	Kazan

PROGRAM FORTY-SEVEN: Films of the 50's
Directors Hitchcock and Sturges

1949	The Beautiful Blond from Bashful Bend	John Sturges (b. 1914)
1954	Bad Day at Black Rock	Sturges
1955	To Catch a Thief	Alfred Hitchcock
1955	The Trouble with Harry	Hitchcock
1956	The Man Who Knew Too Much	Hitchcock
1956	The Wrong Man	Hitchcock

Alfred Hitchcock with Sylvia Sidney on the set of SABOTAGE, *1936*

1958	The Old Man and the Sea	Sturges
1958	Vertigo	Hitchcock
1959	North by Northwest	Hitchcock
1960	The Magnificent Seven	Sturges
1960	Psycho	Hitchcock

Part Six

Practical Information

CITIZEN KANE, *1940*

Thirteen

Film Grammar and Properties

The annotated index to films in Appendix I of this book will help the lover of cinema know the *where, when* and *who* of film. The serious student knows that it is also important to know the *how* and *why* of film. However, he is not like the movie "buffs" who can give dates and name "stars" for nearly every film ever made. These fans too often miss the full importance and impact, the "message" and rich experience which a well-made film can excite. Rather, the true film lover makes an effort to become more aware of *what* the film maker is doing, and *how* he is doing it. While not allowing himself to place technique over content, the student of film is sensitive to the language and the various properties of film.

A few very fundamental terms are to be defined first. The most basic terms proper to film language are those of editing patterns. These were described at more length in Chapter Ten.

SHOT: the basic element of motion pictures, the single record of some action by the camera. OUT-IN and OUT-AWAY shots result from the camera moving into or out of and away from the screen or the action.

SCENE: successive shots in the same locale or time. To ESTABLISH or RE-ESTABLISH is to reveal the scene in which the action is to take place.

SEQUENCE: part of the film which is complete in itself, similar to that part of a drama called an "act." A sequence is normally bridged to another through establish or re-establish or re-establish shots.

With these basic terms we can describe some of the cinematic properties which a well-made film possesses. Additional film grammar is integrated with the following list of cinematic properties. Notable examples from the best films are given with each property. Films indexed in Appendix I will refer to these properties by indicating the **numbers** (of the properties) which a particular film illustrates:

1. MONTAGE: An impressionistic juxtaposition of brief shots, sometimes denoting a time change, often employed for the sake of general effect of quickly changing visual impressions. Notable examples include:

> (The Battleship) Potemkin (U.S.S.R. 25)
> Citizen Kane (41)
> Hiroshima, Mon Amour (France 59)
> Very Nice, Very Nice (Canada 61) Short
> 8½ (Italy 62)

2. CAMERA ANGLE: The view of a shot from above, or below, or head-on, often giving an unique interpretation to a scene. A HIGH SHOT is taken from above eye level with a downward tilt. A LOW SHOT is taken from below eye level with an upward tilt. A FLAT SHOT is at eye level on a horizontal plane. Each of these angles gives an interpretation to the shot and may have psychological significance.

> Detective Story (51)
> N.Y., N.Y. (57) Short
> The 400 Blows (France 59)
> Hud (63)
> Arabesque (U.K. 66)

3. CAMERA POSITION: Long, medium or close-up positions giving direction to a scene, signifying specific desired effects. A LONG SHOT is taken from a distance of the entire scene or subject. A MEDIUM SHOT is near enough for detailed view of most of the subject. A CLOSE-UP SHOT is only of a small portion of the subject.

> The Birth of a Nation (15)
> Vertigo (58)
> Psycho (60)
> Phoebe (64) Short
> In the Heat of the Night (67)

4. CAMERA MOVEMENT: Panning, tracking or circling indicating effect not possible from a stationary viewpoint. PAN movement of the camera is from side to side on the same horizontal plane. TILT movement is up or down on the axis of the camera. TRUCK or travel movement results from the camera following the action over a distance by being mounted in a truck or on a trolley. DOLLY movement is taken from a wheeled platform, or dolly. BOOM movement results from the camera and crew being lifted by crane to a position above the subject. A ZOOM movement is a rapid close-up resulting from an adjustment of camera lens which brings the subject quickly to a close-up position.

    Lonely Are the Brave (62)
    Stowaway in the Sky (France 62)
    The Birds (63)
    Blow-Up (Italy 66)

5. COLOR: While black and white is more appropriate for certain scenes or atmospheres, color can do more than reproduce natural lighting.

    Animal Farm (U.K. 44)
    An American in Paris (51)
    Gate of Hell (Japan 54)
    Lust for Life (56)
    The String Bean (France 64) Short
    2001: A Space Odyssey (68)

6. SOUND:

    a. NATURAL SOUND—the sounds from the environment of the action, without addition or major alteration.

    The Magnificent Ambersons (42)
    The Great Adventure (Sweden 53)
    Assembly Line (Canada 61) Short
    The Haunting (63)
    The Train (65)

    b. MUSIC—music added to or flowing from the scene, unobtrusively *letting* the viewer feel the effect, not *making* him or *telling* him what to feel. Besides the obvious examples from musicals (Singin' In The Rain, Sound of Music) and opera/operettas (Mikado, The Umbrellas of Cherbourg), the following films employ music as an integrated element.

    The Third Man (49)
    Anastasia (56)
    A Man Escaped (France 57)
    The Tender Game (62) Short

7. FILM DEVICES: These are properties peculiar to motion pictures. Besides fast motion, slow motion and stop motion, a shot may also be a:

FADE—gradually disappearing (fade-out) until the screen is dark, gradually lightening again on a new scene (fade-in);

DISSOLVE—a superimposition of a fade-out on a fade-in with no darkness between shots;

SUPERIMPOSITION—a shot is held and a succeeding shot(s) is superimposed so that both shots can be seen simultaneously;

WIPE—a shot forces a preceding one off the screen with an actual line between them;

CUT—splicing two different shots so that they follow one another;

BUILD-UP—increasing the tempo of cutting and editing a film in order to create a heightened sense of drama or movement.

BLUR or SWISH PAN—rapid movement of the camera to create a blur effect in making transitions from shot to shot or situation to situation.

Intolerance (16)
Berlin: The Symphony of a Great City (Germany 28)
Citizen Kane (40)
High Noon (52)
An Occurrence at Owl Creek Bridge (France 62) Short
Tom Jones (U.K. 63)
The Knack . . . And How to Get It (U.K. 65)

8. CATEGORIES: Chapter Twelve employs a *practical* list of film categories: foreign films, adaptations, documentaries, Westerns, mysteries, romances, musicals, comedies and short films. The following is a more *academic* listing which better indicates properties of film.

a. DOCUMENTARY—recording and/or interpreting actual subjects, generally non-fiction. (See Chapter Eight.)

Greed (24)
Rome: An Open City (Italy 46)
Night and Fog (France 55) Short
(See Program Four in Chapter Twelve.)

b. ADAPTATION from stage, television or another film. (See Chapter Four.)

Henry V (U.K. 45)
Hamlet (U.K. 48)
Stalag 17 (52)
Mister Roberts (53)

Twelve Angry Men (54)
Marty (55)
Dr. Strangelove (64)
(See Program Three in Chapter Twelve.)

c. ADAPTATION from novels, short stories, poems, etc. (See Chapter Three.)
The Grapes of Wrath (40)
Night of the Hunter (55)
The Bridge on the River Kwai (U.K. 57)
The Old Man and the Sea (58)
An Occurrence at Owl Creek Bridge (France 62) Short
Hangman (64) Short.
(See Program Three in Chapter Twelve.)

d. ANIMATION—the filming of drawings or objects in sequence so that they appear to be moving.
The Adventures of * (57) Short
The Violinist (59) Short
(See the many films by Walt Disney and his staff, in particular excerpts from Fantasia [41]. Also see the animated credit titles of Saul Bass. Two of his best are those for It's a Mad, Mad, Mad, Mad, World [63] and 2001: A Space Odyssey [68].)

e. SOCIAL or MORAL or SYMBOLIC COMMENTARY—
Umberto D (Italy 52)
My Uncle (France 58)
La Dolce Vita (Italy 61)
Lord of the Flies (U.K. 63)
Parable (64) Short
Darling (U.K. 65)

f. PURE FILM—a non-story use of objects or a simple combination of movement, color, sound, etc.
Fantasia (41)
Dream of the Wild Horses (60) Short
Lines Vertical, and Lines Horizontal (60) Short
Clay (64) Short

9. CINÉMA VÉRITÉ: The camera goes to reality, making use of non-professional actors and/or real locations, hand-held camera and the elements of naturalism or unposed life as it is. Not necessarily a documentary.
The Bicycle Thief (Italy 49)

He Who Must Die (Greece 57)
A View from the Bridge (61)
Good Night, Socrates (62) Short
Nobody Waved Goodbye (Canada 64)
That Man From Rio (France 64)

10. INTROCEPTIVE CAMERA: The use of camera capabilities to reveal subjective mental or psychological states of persons.

Thursday's Children (U.K. 52) Short
Helen Keller in Her Story (53) Short
Nights of Cabiria (Italy 57)
Judgment at Nuremberg (61)
Billy Budd (U.K. 62)
The Miracle Worker (62)

11. CHARACTER DEVELOPMENT: The writing, acting and camera coordinate to present a picture of a character's personality and traits.

The African Queen (U.K. 51)
Death of a Salesman (51)
Shane (53)
Caine Mutiny (54)
La Strada (Italy 54)
Ballad of a Soldier (U.S.S.R. 59)
A Thousand Clowns (65)
You're No Good (Canada 65) Short

12. TRANSITIONAL PHASES: Foreshadowings, bridges and similar anticipations or follow-ups can bring a film from isolated times and places to a woven integrity. As in music, a motif can intensify the emotional response by repetition of visual or audio devices.

Last Year at Marienbad (France 61)
The Loneliness of the Long Distance Runner (U.K. 62)
Phoebe (64) Short
Two for the Road (66)

13. VISUAL SYMBOLS: The use of sight, objects, movements, gestures which express an idea or have ideological content.

Ikiru (Japan 52)
The Golden Fish (France 59) Short
The Mouse that Roared (59)
La Dolce Vita (Italy 61)

Lord of the Flies (U.K. 63)
Fahrenheit 451 (U.K. 66)
Closely Watched Trains (Czech 68)

14. LIGHTING: Unusual use of light and shadows. Most of Bergman's films not only employ masterful lighting but also give light and darkness symbolic meaning.

The Best Years of Our Life (46)
A Time Out of War (54) Short
The Seventh Seal (Sweden 56)
The Hustler (61)
David and Lisa (62)
Days of Wine and Roses (62)
Requiem for a Heavyweight (62)

15. BEAUTY OF PHOTOGRAPHIC IMAGES AND COMPOSITION: While pure films (8f above) tend to be more concerned with the beauty of a scene, many movies with a definite storyline have illustrated awareness of a beautiful environment or the beauty of the persons and objects being filmed.

Morning on the Lievre (44) Short
Louisiana Story (48)
The Great Adventure (Sweden 53)
Sundays and Cybele (France 62)
A Man and a Woman (France 66)
Elvira Madigan (Sweden 68)

16. HIGHLY VISUAL SUBJECTS: Action, comedy, settings which are very photographic.

A Night at the Opera (35)
The Lady from Shanghai (47)
Singin' in the Rain (52)
On the Waterfront (54)
North by Northwest (59)
Lawrence of Arabia (U.K. 62)
Christmas In Appalachia (65) Short

SUGGESTED READINGS

Beck, *Light Show Manual.*
Fielding, *A Technological History of Motion Pictures and Television.*
Graham, *A Dictionary of the Cinema.* (See Glossary)

Halas, *Film and TV Graphics.*
Halliwell, *The Filmgoer's Companion.* (Terms occasionally defined)
Jacobson, *A Mass Communications Dictionary.*
Manoogian, *The Film-Maker's Art.*
Reisz, *The Technique of Film Editing.*
Spottiswoode, *Film and Its Techniques.*
Spottiswoode, *A Grammar Of Film.*
Stephenson, *The Cinema as Art.*

Like the other materials throughout this book, this list intends to be practical. Therefore it is based on 16mm films *only* which are, or soon should be, available for rental and/or purchase. Many of these films are also frequently booked by movie houses and television.

Although many other titles could be added to the listing, the titles here are among the best possible for serious film study.

Available information is arranged in this format:

FILM TITLE, country (other than USA, Canada), date of release/ length in minutes, color (all films are black and white unless indicated)/ director, animator, or producer/ **numbers** which key to the film properties as mentioned in Chapter Thirteen.* Following most entries are remarks prepared by teachers who have experienced the film and have experimented in various ways with it in the classroom or discussion groups. For foreign films, the last remark of the annotation indicates whether the film has English subtitles or is dubbed. Distributors are listed at the end of each annotation; their addresses are in Appendix II.

A film of less than 61 minutes in length, usually called a "short film," is indicated by the letter **s** in boldface preceding the titles.

The older films on this list have stood the test of time and audience endurance. Following the annotation on some of the more recent films are references to critical reviews which are easily available:

---

*The properties of film described in Chapter Thirteen will be found on every other page of Appendix I for ready reference.

PK — *I Lost It At The Movies* by **Pauline Kael**
PKK — *Kiss Kiss Bang Bang* by **Pauline Kael**
F — *Film 67/68* edited by **Richard Schickel** and **John Simon**

Short films are *described* in several books; these too are referenced after the film annotation. A key to some of these follows:

K — *Themes: Short Films for Discussion* by William **Kuhns**
M — *A Guide To Short Films In Religious Education* by Patrick **McCaffrey**
M2 — *A Guide To Short Films In Religious Education II* by Patrick **McCaffrey**

(The number following these references indicates the **page** on which the description/critical review may be found.)

s **A**, Poland, 1964/10 min., b/w animation/Jan Lenica/**4, 7, 8d, 8e, 13.** A comic cartoon, this film presents the topic of man's almost subservience to language. The letter A appears one day in a man's room and remains tauntingly, hauntingly, despite the man's efforts. He finally gives up, goes to sleep, and the next day is pleasantly surprised to note that A is gone. But in its place there is another intruder: B. **Distributed by Contemporary/Mass Media.   K 13**

s **THE ADVENTURES OF** *, 1957/10 min., color/John Hubley/**5, 6, 8d, 8e, 13, 15, 16.** Animated drawings depict the maturing process of man, symbolized by the figure * from early childhood through adulthood. The young * enjoys the fun of seeing, testing, doing, and getting to know his environment. A delightful study of animation, combinations of light, sight and sound, the film discusses, without words, the emotions and ideas of the characters. **Distributed by Brandon/Contemporary/Mass Media.   K 15**

THE AFRICAN QUEEN, United Kingdom, 1951/104 min./John Huston/ **2, 3, 6a, 9, 11, 15, 16.** The story of an offbeat and delightful romance between an inhibited missionary (Katherine Hepburn) and a roughneck skipper (Humphrey Bogart), this film is considered by many the finest in the careers of the actors, the director (Huston), and the writer (James Agee). The shy couple, at first incompatible, grow in tender affection as they pilot a battered old riverboat downstream to escape German troops during World War I hostilities in British East Africa. The journey down an African river is arduous and the sacrifices required to prove their very non-Hollywood variety of love grow with each new obstacle. The locale is splendidly used and the characterizations are both touching and real, with many touches of warmth and humor as well as drama. Based on the novel by C. S. Forester. **Distributed by Swank.   PKK 130, 180, 229**

s **ALEXANDER AND THE CAR WITH A MISSING HEADLIGHT,**
1966/12 min., color/Peter Fleischmann/**5, 8d-e, 13.** While intended for
children's programs, this excellent animation uses the drawing and voices of
children in a masterful way. Will appeal to adults and illustrate mixed-
animation at its best. Children's concept of space and time well presented
and a good reminder for adults who have forgotten the simple vision of
childhood. Compares to the similar approach used in **Moonbird. Distributed
by Weston Woods Studios.**

ALEXANDER NEVSKY, U.S.S.R., 1938/107 min./Sergie Eisenstein/**2,
6b, 16.** A large-scale historical drama. A classic of innovations in camera
technique. Music by Prokofiev (1891-1953) replaces the natural sounds
expected in the action sequences. English subtitles. **Distributed by Brandon.**

ALL ABOUT EVE, 1950/130 min./Joseph Mankiewicz/**7, 10, 11.** Winner
of five Academy Awards for best production, supporting actor, direction,
screenplay, black-and-white costume design, and sound recording, this sharp
characterization of an actress in the theater world is supported by a good
plot, lively dialog and witty satire. It stars Bette Davis at her best, along with
Anne Baxter, George Sanders and Celeste Holme. Marilyn Monroe has a
brief showing. **Distributed by Brandon/Films, Inc.   PKK 230**

ALL THE KING'S MEN, 1949/109 min./Robert Rossen /**8c, 10, 11, 14, 7.**
This drama of the rise and fall of a political demagog, adapted from Robert
Penn Warren's Pulitzer Prize novel of the same name, is said to be based
on the dubious career of the late Huey Long of Louisiana. It won three
Academy Awards in 1949, as well as the New York Film Critics' Award
for the Best Picture of the Year. Broderick Crawford is seen at his best.
Distributed by Audio/Brandon/Trans-World/etc.

AN AMERICAN IN PARIS, 1951/113 min., color/Vincente Minnelli/**2,
3, 4, 5, 6b, 7, 15.** A truly cinematic musical, **AMERICAN IN PARIS** is a
product of the era of the big MGM musicals. Written originally for the
screen and produced with a fantastic use of color, the film won nine Oscars.
Though unashamedly stagey in spots, it makes plentiful use of effects which
could never be achieved on the stage—from its three opening narratives to
the final exhilarating stairway scene. Its simple storyline is in keeping with
its musical purpose, and dancing of Gene Kelly is highlighted to its full

---

PROPERTIES OF FILM

1. Montage	b) Adaptation from Stage, TV	9. Cinema Verite
2. Camera Angle		10. Introceptive Camera
3. Camera Position	c) Adaptation of Novels, Short Stories, Poems	11. Character Development
4. Camera Movement		12. Transitional Phases
5. Color		13. Visual Symbols
6. Sound:	d) Animation	14. Lighting
a) Natural	e) Social/Moral/ Symbolic Commentary	15. Beauty of Photographic Images
b) Music		16. Highly Visual Subject
7. Film Devices	f) Pure Film	
8. Categories		
a) Documentary		

potential for film. Gershwin's music is especially well treated by his friend Oscar Levant. **Distributed by Brandon/Films, Inc.**

THE AMERICANIZATION OF EMILY, 1964/115 min./A. Hiller/**8a-e, 11.** Paddy Chayefsky adapts the novel of William Bradford Huie, and Hiller does the film version. Little is lost in the process. It is still a good satire about war, men and love. Julie Andrews and James Garner are the major personalities in the Americanization. Another fine opportunity to see adaptation at its best. **Distributed by Brandon.**

ANASTASIA, 1956/105 min., color/cinemascope/Anatole Litvak/**8b, 11, 12.** The question of identity provides the plot, a haunting musical score provides the background, and the brutal story of the princess who is in doubt herself as to her past and future provides the impact for this stageplay broadened to film life. The scope of action improves the basic plot line; the character portrayals are vivid, especially that of Dowager Empress Helen Hayes as she examines the "Imposter." **Distributed by Films, Inc.**

ANIMAL FARM, United Kingdom, 1954/75 min., color/John Halas and Joy Batchelor/**5, 8d-e.** A full-length animation based on George Orwell's fable. The satire on political and other human aspects of life is still timely. Interesting use of color. **Distributed by Contemporary.**

ARABESQUE, United Kingdom, 1966/105 min., color/Stanley Donen/**2, 3, 4, 5, 7, 8c, 10, 15, 16.** A very stylish spy satire, this film has little beyond the routine to offer in the way of content: an innocent outsider (Gregory Peck) becomes involved in the intrigues of Arab politics in London and eventually saves the good guy from various revolutionaries and imposters. Sophia Loren is the mystery woman who might be on his side, and then, might not. What makes the film remarkable is the photography, which has to be seen to be believed. Virtually everything is seen in reflection, and as a tool almost no shiny surface known to man is overlooked. Of many memorable sequences, two stand out: Peck staggering about a freeway under the influence of a truth drug; and a fabulous chase through an aquarium-zoo. **Distributed by Cultural.**

s   ASSEMBLY LINE, 1961/35 min./Morton Heilig/**6a, 9, 11, 14, 16.** Life is an assembly line, a parade of the same old thing day after day. Eddie Ryan, Mr. Typical, exists to work on an assembly line, live with an unemployed roommate, and face boredom. The film says that this is the plight of more people than the viewer would like to admit. **Distributed by Brandon/Mass Media.   K 19**

s   AUTOMANIA 2000, United Kingdom, 1964/10 min., color/John Halas and Joy Batchelor/**8d, 5, 6c, 3, 13, 1.** A highly imaginative animated film, it plays cinematically with the wonders of automation today, and the possible results by the end of the century. Cartooning and camera work reveal a humor and a satire which merited it an Academy Award nomination. It also won first prize for the best animated film at the International Film

Festival in Moscow, Locarno, and Barcelona. **Distributed by Contemporary/ Mass Media. K 21**

s **A VALPARAISO,** Chile, 1963/30 Min., partly color/Joris Ivens/**8e, 9, 15, 8a, 6.** A slow-moving and at times labored film, **A VALPARAISO** is a cinematic study of the contrasts and tensions which exist between the two worlds of Valparaiso: the world of the very rich and that of the poor. The camera takes a searching look at the hovels of the poor and the homes of their unaware neighbors. A poetic commentary, by Chris Marker, asks the existential question of "why live" and "how find happiness?" **Distributed by Contemporary. K 23**

L'AVVENTURA, Italy, 1959/145 min./Michelangelo Antonioni/**7, 8e, 10, 11.** An adult looks at the morals of high society. Easily one of the great films. Expert direction and acting. English subtitles. **Distributed by Janus. PK esp. 134-135**

BAD DAY AT BLACK ROCK, 1954/81 min., color/John Sturges/**2, 3, 5, 11.** In this mid-50's adult Western, John Sturges low-keys the action and the actors to sustain a controlling tone of violence. This audience anxiety stems from the too-carefully-measured exposition of Spencer Tracy's reasons for visiting Black Rock, Arizona. As the plot slowly unfolds, Tracy's intent is exposed. He is to clear up a long-suspected murder. The close-mouthed townspeople attempt to foil the investigation. Tracy, Sturges, & Co., win of course. The film definitely comes off as melodrama, but if the audience were prepared, it could be profitably compared with **High Noon, Lonely Are the Brave, Shane, Ox-Bow Incident,** and **Occurrence at Owl Creek Bridge.** In 1955 this film was a visual power-pack; today its emotional torque seems self-conscious. **Distributed by Films, Inc. PKK 233**

THE BAD SLEEP WELL, Japan, 1959/135 min./Akira Kurosawa/**8e, 11, 15, 16.** The director of **Ikiru** again comments on corruption in society. Similarities with modern America will be obvious. Japanese actor Toshiro Mifune will be remembered from Kurosawa's **Rashomon** and **Seven Samurai.** English subtitles. **Distributed by Brandon.**

BALLAD OF A SOLDIER, U.S.S.R., 1959/89 min./Gregori Chukhrai/**2, 3, 4, 6b, 9, 11, 15, 16.** After disabling enemy tanks, a young Russian soldier

PROPERTIES OF FILM		
1. Montage	b) Adaptation from Stage, TV	9. Cinema Verite
2. Camera Angle		10. Introceptive Camera
3. Camera Position	c) Adaptation of Novels, Short Stories, Poems	11. Character Development
4. Camera Movement		12. Transitional Phases
5. Color		13. Visual Symbols
6. Sound:	d) Animation	14. Lighting
a) Natural	e) Social/Moral/ Symbolic Commentary	15. Beauty of Photographic Images
b) Music		16. Highly Visual Subject
7. Film Devices	f) Pure Film	
8. Categories		
a) Documentary		

goes home to visit his mother. On the way, he meets a young girl and gradually falls in love with her amid the horror and brutality of war. The sentimentality of this film is potentially dangerous. Yet, the action of the camera focusing on the Russian landscape, for example, absorbs the intense emotion. The final scene of the soldier with his mother demonstrates, especially for an American audience exhausted by a Cary Grant-Doris Day relationship, that familial love is a precious experience. The shot of the mother running through the wheat fields is the climax to a beautiful story. A good discussion might center around the notion of a graphic ballad. In the light of this, it would be necessary to analyze the powerful musical score. **Distributed by Audio.**

BECKET, United Kingdom, 1964/148 min./Peter Glenville/**8b, 10, 11. Distributed by Films, Inc.**

s   **BEGONE DULL CARE,** 1949/7 min./Norman McLaren/**8d, 8e. Distributed by Contemporary/International Film Bureau.**

BEHOLD A PALE HORSE, 1964/112 min./Fred Zinnemann/**6b, 8c, 15.** From the novel by Pressburger. Gregory Peck and Anthony Quinn dominate the scenes. Spanish Civil War guerrilla fighter refuses to stop his raiding, though the war was over two years ago. Excellent music score by Maurice Jarre, who also did the music for **Lawrence of Arabia** and **Dr. Zhivago. Distributed by Audio.**

BERLIN: THE SYMPHONY OF A GREAT CITY, Germany, 1928/90 min./Walter Ruttmann/**3, 4, 7, 8f, 15.** The director created a city symphony which emphasizes visual rhythms in the cutting and makes the everyday life of this great city very like the parts of an organized symphony. Notable in the film are the contrasting presentations of objects of different bulk and shape, and the use of motif and symbol. **Distributed by Brandon/Museum of Modern Art.**

THE BEST YEARS OF OUR LIVES, 1946/175 min./William Wyler/**8c, 2, 3, 7, 10.** This Samuel Goldwyn production portrays the return of World War II veterans to their special problems of personal and social readjustment. Striking in the film is the illusion of the absence of "direction" due to the effortless realism created by Gregg Toland's extraordinary deep-focus photography and natural lighting. It won seven Academy Awards and also the New York Film Critics Award, One of the Best Ten Films of the Year Award, and Best Director Award for 1946. From a novel by MacKinlay Kantor. **Distributed by Brandon/Museum of Modern Art.**

s   **BETWEEN THE TIDES,** United Kingdom/22 min./**5, 8a, 9, 15.** A successful attempt to convey the drama of natural life enacted on the narrow strand over which land and sea contend, all within a few hours, between the flowing and the ebb of the tides. **Distributed by Contemporary.**

THE BICYCLE THIEF, Italy, 1949/87 min./Vittorio deSica/**9, 11, 8a, 6a,**

2, 3, 13. This is one of deSica's most important films in the Italian neo-realist school. A man and his son search for a lost bicycle at a time when the man most needs a bicycle to earn a living. It presents the post-war world where one needs to rethink a hierarchy of values in life. Such a value structure will be arrived at only after a good deal of human suffering. A notable feature of this film is the face of the child as he wanders about with his father; the child needs someone to help form and mold his life. Like **The 400 Blows,** the conclusion of this film sets the problems into sharp focus and leaves the audience with an impact. English subtitles. **Distributed by Brandon.**

THE BIG SLEEP, 1946/114 min./Howard Hawks/**8c, 11, 2, 3.** This is probably the most popular of the hard-boiled detective thrillers of the forties. It is fast moving, brutal, and often as confusing as it is enjoyable. Humphrey Bogart and Lauren Bacall star in this adaptation of the novel by Raymond Chandler. **Distributed by Audio/Brandon/Contemporary/Films, Inc.**

BILLY BUDD, United Kingdom, 1962/123 min./Peter Ustinov/**3, 4, 10, 11, 16.** Herman Melville's story presented without "unnecessary" elements, revealing the basic action line and tension of Billy's tragic life. Terence Stamp as Billy is excellent casting, but he is to achieve even more in **The Collector.** A worthwhile film but not the Billy Budd of Melville's genius. Discussion will center on the tragedy of unfortunate circumstances and the control of justice over compassion. **Distributed by Audio/Cultural.   PK 211-215, 285**

s   **BILLY LIAR,** 1963/96 min./John Schlesinger/**1, 2, 3, 4, 7, 8e, 10, 11, 12, 13, 14, 15, 16.** Billy Fisher (Tom Courtenay) is a young clerk in the office of a funeral director. He has a vivid imagination and has dreams of being a writer. Imaginary episodes well edited and excellent acting. Could be a source film for contemporary cinematic properties. **Distributed by Continental 16.**

s   **BIOGRAPHY OF JACKIE ROBINSON,** 1965/26 min./David L. Wolper/**8a, 8e, 16. Distributed by Sterling.   M2 46**

s   **THE BIRD HUNT,** 1951/11min./**6a, 6b, 8e, 9, 13, 14, 15, 16. Distributed by University of California.   M 25**

PROPERTIES OF FILM		
1. Montage	b) Adaptation from Stage, TV	9. Cinema Verite
2. Camera Angle		10. Introceptive Camera
3. Camera Position	c) Adaptation of Novels, Short Stories, Poems	11. Character Development
4. Camera Movement		12. Transitional Phases
5. Color		13. Visual Symbols
6. Sound:	d) Animation	14. Lighting
a) Natural	e) Social/Moral/ Symbolic Commentary	15. Beauty of Photographic Images
b) Music		16. Highly Visual Subject
7. Film Devices		
8. Categories	f) Pure Film	
a) Documentary		

BIRDMAN OF ALCATRAZ, 1962/143 min./John Frankenheimer/**2, 3, 4, 6a, 8c, 11, 14.** This is the incredible story of a two-time murderer, forced by a series of brutal injustices to spend nearly a half-century in solitary confinement, who devotes his life to the study and care of birds. Despite the physical limitations of the setting, the film is constantly fascinating in describing the prisoner's relations with his birds and other humans (convicts, guards, outsiders, his mother). The result is a powerful indictment of the penal system, as well as a moving tribute to the beauty of the human spirit. As the convict-hero, Burt Lancaster gives perhaps the finest performance of his career. There are several scenes of violence, but Frankenheimer chiefly demonstrates that the medium can successfully handle subtle character relationships without abundant action or a multiplicity of exterior locations. **Distributed by United Artists.**

THE BIRDS, 1963/119 min., color/Alfred Hitchcock/**2, 3, 4, 10, 13, 14, 16. Distributed by Contemporary/Twyman/United World.**

THE BIRTH OF A NATION, 1915/175 min./D. W. Griffith/**1, 2, 3, 7, 16. BIRTH** is famous, not because of subject matter, length, or complexity alone, although Griffith employs all to best advantage. It established once and for all the basic nature of the motion picture, and its unique capacities as an art medium. Viewers will note the artistic use of emotionally effective succession of long shots, medium shots and extreme close-ups, as well as rapidly alternation cross-cutting of scenes. The film has been called a classic of camera placement, editing, and restrained acting, and, as such, influenced movie makers throughout the world. Based on **The Clausman** by Thomas Dixon. Sound has been synchronized with the original silent film. **Distributed by Museum of Modern Art.**

s   BLIND GARY DAVIS, 1962/11 min./Harold Becker/**4, 6a, 6b, 8a, 9, 10, 11, 14, 15, 16.** The film is an impressionistic profile of a Negro street singer. The Reverend Gary Davis, blind since youth, combines in his style and guitar virtuosity great musical talent and genuine depth of feeling. Visual images have been played against the soundtrack of Davis' songs as a counterpoint to comment upon this man and his world. The final scenes are especially relentless and effective. **Distributed by Contemporary.   M 26**

s   BLINDNESS, 1964/28 min./**3, 4, 8a, 13, 14. Distributed by Contemporary.   M2 47**

s   BLINKITY BLANK, 1955/5 min./Norman McLaren/**8d. Distributed by Contemporary/International Film Bureau.**

BLOW-UP, Italy, 1966/111 min., color/Michelangelo Antonioni/**1, 2, 3, 4, 5, 13, 14, 15, 16.** Something is sad and something is said in this film about "illusion and reality." Not all agree on the meaning or intention. Antonioni is making a comment on the contemporary scene and, it seems, is revealing himself to us as he does. Is it autobiographical? Vanessa Redgrave dominates the beautiful aspects of the film, sometimes saving it from being very drab, in spite of all the purple paper. Excellent editing, especially in the sequence in which the young hero blows up a series of photographs and discovers that he has photographed a murder. But the film is much more than a murder mystery. Discussion may reveal that it is accomplishing much even in those who will not like or understand the film. For adults.   **F esp 274-281; PKK 31-37**

BOOMERANG, 1946/88 min./Elia Kazan/**8e, 11.** A semi-documentary murder mystery based on the murder of a priest in a small town. An excellent opportunity to see Kazan's early style, even before **On The Waterfront. Distributed by Films, Inc.**

s **BOSWELLE'S BON VOYAGE,** 1966/9 min., color/**2, 3, 4, 5, 14, 15, 16. Distributed by Sterling.   M2 102**

BOUDU SAVED FROM DROWNING, France, 1932/87 min./Jean Renoir/**2, 13, 15.** Renoir's more famous **The River** was shot in India. Twenty years earlier, he showed similar sensitivity to environments by shooting **Boudu** mainly along the left bank of the Seine. The two films would make an interesting program. **Distributed by Contemporary.**

s **BOUNDARY LINES,** 1947/9 min., color/Philip Stapp/**1, 2, 3, 4, 5, 6, 7, 8d, 8e, 8f, 13, 15.** This forceful message tells the viewer to learn to live in harmony with the rest of the world if the horrors of war are to be avoided. New techniques are employed in the film to get the point across. Conceived of as an intelligent and highly artistic piece, it is both a social commentary and a novel experiment in film making. **Distributed by Contemporary/International Film Foundation/Trans-World Films.   K 27; M 27**

THE BRIDGE, Germany, 1960/102 min./Bernhard Wicki/**2, 3, 6a, 8c, 11.** The idealism of German youth meets the disillusionment of the Nazi army during the last days of World War II as a group of high school boys is conscripted into the army and assigned to defend a bridge in their own town. An ironical turn of events twists the attempt to save the youths from the horrors of war into a savage waste of budding life. A courageous con-

---

PROPERTIES OF FILM

1. Montage	b) Adaptation from Stage, TV	9. Cinema Verite
2. Camera Angle		10. Introceptive Camera
3. Camera Position	c) Adaptation of Novels, Short Stories, Poems	11. Character Development
4. Camera Movement		12. Transitional Phases
5. Color		
6. Sound:	d) Animation	13. Visual Symbols
a) Natural	e) Social/Moral/ Symbolic Commentary	14. Lighting
b) Music		15. Beauty of Photographic Images
7. Film Devices		
8. Categories	f) Pure Film	16. Highly Visual Subject
a) Documentary		

frontation of the realities of war, this film is also a powerful cinematic accomplishment. (English dubbed.) **Distributed by Audio.**

THE BRIDGE ON THE RIVER KWAI, United Kingdom, 1957/161 min., color/David Lean/**2, 3, 4, 5, 6a, 8c, 9, 11, 16.** David Lean's directing and Alec Guinness' acting highlight a gripping and highly entertaining film. Winner of Academy Awards for Best Picture, actor, director, cinematography, screenplay, musical score, and editing. A good example of a film adaptation, since it is based on a novel by Pierre Boulle, who also did the screenplay for the film. It is an extremely ironic, yet exciting and suspenseful comment on war. **Distributed by Audio/Brandon/Contemporary/Trans-World/Twyman.**

s **BUSTER KEATON RIDES AGAIN,** Canada, 1965/55 min./Spotton/ **2, 3, 4, 7, 8c, 16.** Keaton is shown on location during the filming of Potterton's **The Railrodder** (65). A fine companion to one of Keaton's earlier films, it would go especially well with **Sherlock, Jr.,** which he directed as well as acted. **Distributed by Contemporary.**

CABINET OF DR. CALIGARI, Germany, 1919/70 min./R. Wiene/**3, 4, 7, 13.** Expressionistic sets, even surrealistic, surrounded this classic thriller. To discuss the role of technical tricks in film, compare this masterpiece to the 1962 remake available from Films, Inc. or Continental 16 (104 minutes). A synchronized soundtrack has been added to the original silent film. **Distributed by Continental 16.   PKK esp. 242-243**

CAINE MUTINY, 1954/125 min., color/Edward Dmytryk/**3, 8c, 10, 13.** Expertly directed, this film uses effective camera positions and movements to capture the events leading up to the mutiny on the U.S.S. Caine, climaxed by the trial. Character development, the element of suspense and taut dramatic action combine to raise fascinating questions of authoritarianism (indictment vs. vindication of it) and the role of the individual (become involved or play things safely). **Distributed by Audio/Brandon/Contemporary/Institutional Cinema/Modern Sound/Pictura/Trans-World/Twyman.**

CALL NORTHSIDE 777, 1947, 111 min./Henry Hathaway/**4, 10, 14. Distributed by Films, Inc.**

s **A CHAIRY TALE,** 1957/10 min./Norman McLaren/**6, 8e, 13, 14, 16.** A humorous and provocative film which explores one aspect of the world which we take for granted. McLaren's habit of stop photography and fast and slow camera work actually put a playful and impish kind of life into an ordinary kitchen chair, to the delight of the viewer. And by catching the chuckling viewer off guard, the film says a good deal about human relationships. **Distributed by Contemporary/International Film Bureau/Mass Media/Trans-World Films.   K 29**

s **THE CHICKEN,** France, 1963/15 min./Penn Productions/**13, 8e, 9, 3, 4, 6, 10, 16.** The story of the pet chicken destined for the stewpot is treated with comedy, excellent photography, whimsy in both cinema and musical aspects. The film is unique in its simplicity of subject and skillful method of presenting this same subject. **Distributed by Contemporary.** M2 103

s **CHILDREN ADRIFT,** France, 1958/26 min./Edouard Luntz/**8e, 9, 10, 11, 14, 15, 16.** In documentary and touching interpretive filmwork, this is the study of the children of a Paris slum. It looks at their relationships, their play, and the tragedies that fill their young lives, and it does so through a one-day concentration on a simply loveable little boy. Luntz explained, "We wanted to do nothing within the film except to reveal by cinematic means, and to create empathy for our little characters without offering any explanation." **Distributed by Contemporary/Mass Media.** K 31; M2 49

s **CHILDREN OF THE DUST,** 1965/27 min., color/**5, 8a, 8e, 9, 15.** Distributed by World Horizon.   M2 50

s **CHRISTMAS CRACKER,** 1964/9 min., color/Norman McLaren/**1, 2, 3, 5, 6c, 8d, 8e, 8f, 13.** A Christmas film in three parts: boy and girl paper cutouts dance to "Jingle Bells"; a ballet troupe of ten toys perform in animation; a man attempts to trim a tree with a star stolen from the sky. The fantasy here is enhanced even further by the judicious use of sound, music, and the bizarre effects that can be produced with well-chosen lighting and costuming. **Distributed by Contemporary.**   M 30

s **CHRISTMAS IN APPALACHIA,** 1965/29 min./CBS-TV/**2, 8a, 8e, 15, 16. Distributed by Carousel.**   M2 53

CHRONICLE OF A SUMMER, France, 1961/90 min./Jean Rouch & E. Morin/**8a, 9, 15, 16.** English subtitles. **Distributed by Contemporary.**

CITIZEN KANE, 1941/119 min./Orson Welles/**1, 2, 3, 4, 6a, 7, 10, 11, 12, 13, 14.** One of the great films of all time. Based on the life of William Randolph Hearst, this classic has intrinsic interest for students of journalism. The creative cinematography explores the potentials of the camera in a manner unparalleled in 1941. The story does not follow a chronological order, but rather tries to dramatically interpret the last words of a dying

PROPERTIES OF FILM		

1. Montage
2. Camera Angle
3. Camera Position
4. Camera Movement
5. Color
6. Sound:
  a) Natural
  b) Music
7. Film Devices
8. Categories
  a) Documentary
	b) Adaptation from
	  Stage, TV
	c) Adaptation of
	  Novels, Short Stories,
	  Poems
	d) Animation
	e) Social/Moral/
	  Symbolic
	  Commentary
	f) Pure Film
		9. Cinema Verite
		10. Introceptive Camera
		11. Character Development
		12. Transitional Phases
		13. Visual Symbols
		14. Lighting
		15. Beauty of Photographic
		  Images
		16. Highly Visual Subject

magnate. As in **The 400 Blows, The Loneliness of the Long Distance Runner,** and **Ikiru,** the last shot crystalizes the entire structure of the story. In addition, the deep focus shooting, the coated lens, the wide angle shots, and the use of echoes and sounds make this film an American classic. The size of Kane's estate reflects his ambitions, but the haunting, masterful final shot reveals the value of his achievements. Welles plays Kane, expertly supported by Joseph Cotton, Everett Sloane, Agnes Moorehead, George Coulouris, Ray Collins and Paul Stewart. **Distributed by Brandon/Contemporary/Films, Inc.**   **PKK esp. 247-248**

s   **THE CITY,** 1939/30 min./Willard Van Dyke & Ralph Steiner/**1, 2, 6b, 7, 8a, 9, 13, 15.** This film, contrasting the simplicity of planned community life with the inhuman and chaotic state of urban living, was the hit of the 1939 New York World's Fair. The film is especially good in portraying the hectic pace of big-city living. Indeed, the vitality of the lunch-hour scene and the weekend outing in contrast to the somewhat anemic portrayal of rustic life reveals the film-makers as confirmed urbanites and subtly belies the intended purpose of the film. **Distributed by Contemporary.**

s   **CLAY,** 1964/8 min./Eliot Noyes, Jr./**7, 8f, 13, 16.** One of the most intriguing of the many animation films which use clever molding and re-molding of materials. Too much could be read into the evolutionary symbols of man eating animal, animal eating animal, animal eating man, etc. However, even these symbols provoke alarming varieties of discussion. One of those shorts which should not be followed immediately by a "feature" without time for reaction. Best considered for its media, not its message—if it does have a message. **Distributed by Contemporary/Mass Media.**

CLOSELY   WATCHED   TRAINS, Czechoslovakia, 1967/92 min./Jiri Menzel/**3, 4, 8a, 8c, 8e, 10, 13.** Adapted from a novel by Bohumil Hrabal, this effective presentation of adolescence takes place during World War II. At times funny, often disturbing, sometimes bizarre, but always a presentation of a personal philosophy of life. Highly aware of symbols, especially the most visual ones, Menzel has presented a memorable day in the young life of an apprentice railwayman. Presently not available for distribution.   **F esp. 18-21; 119-121**

THE COLLECTOR, 1965/119 min./William Wyler/**4, 8e, 10, 11.** Based on John Fowles' novel about a young man (played by Terence "Billy Budd" Stamp) who lays aside his butterfly collection and kidnaps a girl (Samantha Eggar). His spiritual possession of her interests him more than her obvious sex appeal or her ransom value. The tension and suspense are even more convincing than in Wyler's earlier **Wuthering Heights.** It is better drama than his **Detective Story** and certainly has more substance than **Funny Girl.** It ranks with **The Best Years of Our Lives** as one of Wyler's triumphs. The film may have been more suitable in sombre black-and-white. While considering the mental balance of the collector, discussions will most likely reconsider the mental state of "normal" people and society. **Distributed by Columbia Cinematheque.**

THE COLLECTOR, *1965, Terence Stamp and Samantha Eggar*

s **THE COLT,** Russia, 1960/42 min./Vladimir Fetin/**2, 4, 6a, 7, 8c, 8e, 11, 13, 16.** This moving parable, based on the story by Mikhail Sholotov, tells of the effect of a young colt upon soldiers on both sides, in the midst of war. Acting, direction, and photography tell the story, with a minimum of words. The viewer is made readily aware that human concerns can overcome, at least for a brief moment, the human differences which exist across the lines of fire. Russian dialogue with English subtitles. **Distributed by Brandon.   K 33**

s **CONFORMITY,** 1963/49 min./David Wilson/**8e. Distributed by Carousel/Mass Media.   K 35**

s **CORNET AT NIGHT,** 1964/15 min./**2, 6b, 8e, 9, 10, 11, 14. Distributed by Contemporary.   M2 57**

s **CORRAL,** 1954/12 min./Colin Low/**1, 2, 3, 4, 6b, 7, 8f, 9, 10, 12, 13, 15.** The roping and riding of a high-spirited, half-broken horse is the subject of this film which makes visual poetry. Movement and music (by Pete Seeger) combine with unusual camera angles and very strong symoblism to tell a story completely without words, as the viewer watches the cowboy perform the traditional bronco-breaking ritual. **Distributed by Contemporary/International Film Bureau.   K 37**

THE COWBOY, 1954/69 min./**6a, 8a, 9.** One of the few and one of the best documentary films on past and present man of the West. **Distributed by Modern Sound/Swank.**

THE CRANES ARE FLYING, U.S.S.R., 1957/94 min./Mikhail Kalatozov/**7, 11, 4, 13.** A notable post-Stalin romantic drama of lovers caught in the tragic events of 1941-45. It has fine acting and "all the camera tricks that the Soviet cinema had schooled itself to disregard," and these are used effectively in revealing the World War II Russian mood, of individuals marked by war, and their hopes for peace and life. English subtitles. **Distributed by Brandon/Films, Inc.**

CRIME AND PUNISHMENT, France, 1935/103 min./Josef Sternberg/**8b, 11.** Compare to the 1958 French version, or the 1956 British version. Both available from Brandon with subtitles. An American version was done in 1959, available from Twyman and Ideal Pictures. A classic with several worthwhile points for comparative study. Subtitles. **Distributed by Brandon. PKK esp. 252**

CRISIS, 1950/96 min./Richard Brooks/**2, 3, 4. Distributed by Films, Inc.**

s **THE CRITIC,** 1963/4 min., color/Ernest Pintoff/**5, 6, 7, 8d, 8e, 11.** A hilarious cartoon, the film spoofs art shows and the people who go to them. This humorously new look at modern art is seen through the eyes of comedian Mel Brooks. **Distributed by Brandon/Contemporary/Mass Media/Twyman.   K 39**

s   **CROSS-COUNTRY RUNNER,** 1961/13 min./UCLA Students/**8e, 9, 13. Distributed by University of California.   M2 58**

CYRANO DE BERGERAC, 1950/112 min./Stanley Kramer/**4, 11, 8b, 14.** Jose Ferrer won an Academy Award for his performance of the tragic hero in the film presentation of Edmond Rostand's popular romantic stage play. Especially noteworthy are the duel scenes, the careful use of light and shadow in the romance scenes, and the artistic arrangements of groupings. **Distributed by Audio/Brandon/Contemporary/Institutional Cinema/Modern Sound/Pictura/Trans-World/Twyman.**

s   **THE DAISY,** Bulgaria, 1965/6 min., color/Todor Dinov/**5, 6, 7, 8d, 8e, 13.** The ironical story of a daisy which could not be destroyed by a person insensitive to beauty, this film combines musical score and cinematic properties to study both the intensity of human feelings and the interesting effect of sights and sounds upon the viewer. **Distributed by Brandon/Mass Media.   K 41**

s   **A DANCER'S WORLD,** 1957/30 min./Nathan Kroll/**2, 3, 4, 8a, 16, 9, 14.** The delightful interpretation of the tensions between freedom and discipline is presented in a narration which accompanies a kind of documentary on the training and exercises of the ballet dancer. Martha Graham discusses the dancer as a creative artist, and she explains the craft simply and clearly while members of the dance company execute a dance to illustrate her theories. **Distributed by Rembrandt Films.   M2 59**

DARLING, United Kingdom, 1965/127 min./John Schlesinger/**1, 2, 3, 4, 7, 8e, 9, 10, 11, 13.** Happiness requires more than a warm puppy for Julie Christie. Through a series of flashbacks and well-edited montages, we see a beautiful girl's rise to the heights of success and wealth. She has the world at her well-manicured feet, but her heart is imprisoned by her tragic quest for self-fulfillment. She cannot give herself to another person. A youthful fling with an aspiring writer lingers in her star-struck mind, but a return to him is impossible. "The Happiness Girl" has reached the top of the ladder, but without the love she seeks. Discussion will gravitate toward the contemporary theme of alienation: as such, the discussion leader will have to hold the group's focus to the person ("Darling") and not allow it to concede to generalities. It will then be an effective critique of modern society

---

PROPERTIES OF FILM

1. Montage	b) Adaptation from Stage, TV	9. Cinema Verite
2. Camera Angle		10. Introceptive Camera
3. Camera Position	c) Adaptation of Novels, Short Stories, Poems	11. Character Development
4. Camera Movement		12. Transitional Phases
5. Color		13. Visual Symbols
6. Sound:	d) Animation	14. Lighting
a) Natural	e) Social/Moral/ Symbolic Commentary	15. Beauty of Photographic Images
b) Music		
7. Film Devices		16. Highly Visual Subject
8. Categories	f) Pure Film	
a) Documentary		

and values, as well as a valuable cinema study. **Distributed by Audio.**
PKK 158-159

DAVID AND LISA, 1962/94 min./Frank Perry/**1, 2, 3, 10, 11, 13.** This
movie could be seen as a companion to **Sundays and Cybele** because of
the nature of the boy-girl relationship in each. It could well demonstrate the
difference between the French outlook on life and the American outlook.
The symbolic gestures in this film, the fear of touch, the speech pattern in
rhyme, the clock, and the statue in the museum all contribute to make this
a valuable American film. David and Lisa learn to appreciate one another
only by forgetting themselves and looking into the other interests in a way
which David's mother and father could not understand. The story is carefully set in a larger framework of other young adults, who, like David and
Lisa, must come to help and love one another. **Distributed by Contempo-**
rary/Continental 16.

DAVID COPPERFIELD, 1934/133 min./George Cukor/**8b, 11.** A "Hollywood classic." The period and style of Dickens is captured in convincing
settings and costumes. This great "what's-his-name" film stars W. C. Fields,
Edna May Oliver, Basil Rathbone, Roland Young, Lionel Barrymore, etc.,
etc. As literary adaptation, the film may be criticized; as a fine example of
early Hollywood, the film is invaluable. **Distributed by Brandon/Films, Inc.**

s **DAY AFTER DAY,** 1962/27 min./Clement Perron/**6a, 3, 4, 8a, 8e, 9,**
10, 12, 13, 16. An experience of what factory workers go through, and how
they are at times destroyed by the existence, are created for the viewer by a
careful and powerful combination of sight and sound. Views throughout
the day of the machines and men whom they mold and distort are presented against the music and sound of the mighty machine. **Distributed by**
Contemporary/Mass Media.   **K 43**

DAYS OF WINE AND ROSES, 1962/117 min./Blake Edwards/**4, 10, 11,**
12, 13. Music by Henry Mancini underscores the brutally corrosive effects
of alcoholism shown here. The film's writing, direction and performances
are convincing as well as painfully absorbing as we see breezy public relations man Jack Lemmon and his wife take the road from social to anti-
social drinking. **Presently not available for distribution.**

DEAD BIRDS, 1963/83 min./**2, 3, 4, 8f, 14, 15. Distributed by Con-**
temporary/Mass Media.

DEATH OF A SALESMAN, 1951/115 min./Laslo Benedek/**8b, 8e, 10, 11,**
12. Distributed by Audio/Brandon/Contemporary/Institutional Cinema/
Modern Sound/Pictura/Trans-World/Twyman.

DESERT VICTORY, United Kingdom, 1942/62 min./David MacDonald/
6a, 8a, 9. There is nothing sensational about this war documentary of the
North African campaign. Yet, the skill and restraint of the camera and
editing. use of natural sounds and commentary, blend together to create
one of the finest of war fact-films. **Distributed by Museum of Modern Art.**

s **THE DETACHED AMERICANS,** 1965/27 min./Don Matticks/**1, 6, 7, 8a, 12. THE DETACHED AMERICANS** was originally produced by CBS News as a special documentary. Non-involvement is the too-oft-repeated theme of this offering. There are a few clever bits of editing in a history-of-U.S.-apathy sequence and the construction of a prefabricated "Ticky-tacky" housing development. The opening sequence, concerning the Genoese murder, represents a good example of TV reporting and editorializing. Despite the redundance of the kinescope, it could serve well as a contrast with **Very Nice, Very Nice** or as a comparison with **Harvest of Shame.** If utilized in this fashion, this film could be helpful in demonstrating visually the difference between TV and film as art. **Distributed by Carousel/Mass Media/Roa.   K 45; M2 60**

DETECTIVE STORY, 1951/103 min./William Wyler/**2, 3, 7, 8b, 11.** The **DETECTIVE STORY** displays extensive use of good camera angles and artistic cutting, though its theatrical origins are apparent throughout. Wyler's version of Sydney Kingsley's play centers around a police detective (Kirk Douglas) who thinks he is a "rock." The setting, rather sharply limited to the confines of a New York precinct police station, allows for good character development and some subjective camera work. **Distributed by Films, Inc.**

s **DIALOGUE WITH MALCOLM BOYD,** 1967/60 min./Georgia Educational TV Network and Protestant Radio & TV Center/**8a, 8e, 9.** Included here as a fine example of interview-camera. A discussion between college students and the liberal priest. Too long, but need not be seen at one sitting. A solo performance, not a dialogue. **Distributed by Emory University.**

DIARY OF A COUNTRY PRIEST, France, 1950/95 min./Robert Bresson/**3, 6a, 8c, 9, 10, 11, 13.** A French curè realizes that his own spiritual and physical limitations will not transform his congregation as he would wish. The photography reveals a desolate countryside which reflects the loneliness of this priest. Bresson stressed the visual repetition to highlight the plight of this small village. The chateau park, the priest making his rounds, the parishioners, all contribute to reveal the social and spiritual problems which the man must face. Sanctity is not a gift, but a task one must desire and seek. English subtitles. **Distributed by Brandon.   PKK 259**

PROPERTIES OF FILM		
1. Montage	b) Adaptation from Stage, TV	9. Cinema Verite
2. Camera Angle		10. Introceptive Camera
3. Camera Position	c) Adaptation of Novels, Short Stories, Poems	11. Character Development
4. Camera Movement		12. Transitional Phases
5. Color		13. Visual Symbols
6. Sound:	d) Animation	14. Lighting
a) Natural	e) Social/Moral/ Symbolic Commentary	15. Beauty of Photographic Images
b) Music		16. Highly Visual Subject
7. Film Devices	f) Pure Film	
8. Categories		
a) Documentary		

THE DIARY OF ANNE FRANK, 1959/170 min., cinemascope/George Stevens/**2, 3, 6a, 8c, 11, 12.** This familiar story, based on a diary attributed to a young Jewish girl during the Nazi persecutions of World War II, is extraordinary in the sense that this young girl could articulate her deepest experiences in such a mature manner. The routine quarrels, anxieties, acts of kindness, and fears take on a new significance because of the conditions outside the attic. Anne's sensitivity to the needs of others as she tries to understand herself is clearly revealed. For students of journalism, a discussion might center around the problems the author has in achieving unity, coherence and artistic development when he takes a document not meant for the film and tries to make this document graphically significant. **Distributed by Films, Inc.**

DR. STRANGELOVE, OR: HOW I LEARNED TO STOP WORRYING AND LOVE THE BOMB, 1964/93 min./Stanley Kubrick/**1, 3, 2, 6b, 8e, 11, 13, 16.** Critic Stanley Kauffman called Stanley Kubrick's wry and poignant comedy of nuclear catastrophe the best American film made since 1947. The film is high comedy and merits serious attention. The performances of George C. Scott, Sterling Hayden, and Peter Sellers (who plays three roles) highlight this illumination of the corner into which mankind has painted itself. Major points for cinema study are ironic use of music, Ken Adam's imaginative sets, and the terrific cutting which builds suspense. Based on Peter George's novel **Red Alert. Distributed by Columbia Cinematheque/ Royal 16.**

LA DOLCE VITA, Italy, 1961/180 min./Federico Fellini/**2, 3, 6b, 8e, 9, 11, 13, 14.** Fellini said that this movie "puts a thermometer" to a sick world. The patient is analyzed and observed by a young journalist as he moves among the decaying Roman society. The film exposes the cruel and wierd instincts and preoccupations of people who have no sense of the spiritual beauty of men. In a most graphic manner, the scandals of Roman society are enumerated and dramatized. For all the sordid reality, however, there emerges a potential relationship between the journalist and an innocent young girl he meets. At the conclusion, the sound of the waves, the water that separates them, and the mental preoccupation of those capturing the sea monster turn the journalist away from the one person in life who could give some meaning to a brilliantly vulgar existence. English subtitles. **Distributed by Audio.   PK esp. 161-166; 237-239**

s **THE DRAG,** 1966/9 min., color/**8e. Distributed by Contemporary. M2 61**

s **DREAM OF THE WILD HORSES,** 1962/9 min., color/**3, 4, 5, 7, 8f, 15, 9, 16.** Color and slow-motion photography combine to form a beautiful poem of the movements of the wild horses of Camargue, an island in the delta of the Rhone. **Distributed by Contemporary.**

DUCK SOUP, 1933/72 min./Leo McCarey/**2, 3, 16.** This is probably the most consistently funny of the vintage Marx Brothers' comedies. Set in the tiny warring nation of Fredonia, it features Groucho as prime minister and Harpo and Chico as professional spies working with and for both sides. Compare to **Night at the Opera. Distributed by Contemporary.**

EAST OF EDEN, 1955/115 min./Elia Kazan/**2, 8c, 11, 13.** In this modern Cain and Abel story, high drama and high cinema capture the audience. The film covers one-half of the Steinbeck novel. The portrayals of James Dean and Julie Harris are intense as is the delivery of dialogue from all concerned, and might be profitably compared to the portrayals by Dean and Natalie Wood in **Rebel Without a Cause,** Dean's earlier attempt. **Check area distributors, public libraries, and college audio-visual libraries.**

ECLIPSE (L'ÉCLIPSE), France-Italy, 1962/123 min./Michelangelo Antonioni/**10, 14, 15.** English subtitles. **Distributed by Audio Film Classics.**

8-1/2, Italy, 1962/138 min./Federico Fellini/**1, 2, 3, 4, 6b, 10, 11, 12, 13, 15.** Few films in the last decade have tried to deal with such a difficult theme: the inquisitive and disenchanted artist who seeks to explore and create a masterpiece. The film rhythmically reveals the dreams, pressures, impressions and aspirations of a movie director as he comes to grips with his talent and limitations. Ironically, the director participates in a circular dance at the end of the film which is reminiscent of Dante's dance of heavenly unity and human perfection. English dubbed. **Distributed by Embassy.   PK 235-239**

s **END OF SUMMER,** 1964/27min./Michel Brault/**3, 4, 6a, 6b, 9, 10, 7, 13, 16.** A kind of cinema verite presentation of the end of a summer and what it means to the charmed world of the adolescent. The film has French dialogue with English subtitles, and this in itself seems to strengthen the somewhat intimate, listening-to-their-secret-thoughts impression. Especially effective with girls, since girls form the heart of the story and do the bulk of the talking. **Distributed by Contemporary/Mass Media.   K49; M2 63**

EVA, 1962/111 min./Joseph Losey/**3, 4, 8e, 9, 10, 11.** The symbols are not as subtle here as in Losey's much earlier **The Boy with the Green Hair.** A gambler loses his heart to a prostitute who bets her life that all men are bad. The twists are not the usual ones. Losey's direction is expert and the

---

PROPERTIES OF FILM

1. Montage	b) Adaptation from Stage, TV	9. Cinema Verite
2. Camera Angle		10. Introceptive Camera
3. Camera Position	c) Adaptation of Novels, Short Stories, Poems	11. Character Development
4. Camera Movement		12. Transitional Phases
5. Color		13. Visual Symbols
6. Sound:	d) Animation	14. Lighting
a) Natural	e) Social/Moral/ Symbolic Commentary	15. Beauty of Photographic Images
b) Music		16. Highly Visual Subject
7. Film Devices	f) Pure Film	
8. Categories		
a) Documentary		

visual effects are fittingly dramatic. We see hints of his **Modesty Blaise** ready to be dealt out next. **Distributed by Audio.**

FAHRENHEIT 451, United Kingdom, 1966/112 min./Francois Truffaut/ **1, 5, 6, 8c, 11, 12, 13.** Oskar Werner and Julie Christie (plays dual role) team up in Brave-New-World-type tale adapted by Truffaut from Ray Bradbury's short story. The story is strong. The film is a bit strained in its stylized attempt to involve the viewer in the future. Nonetheless, the film would lend itself well to a discussion of color, photography, visual symbol, and characterization—an interesting comparison with **Fail Safe** or **Dr. Strangelove. Distributed by United World.**   **PKK 146-150**

FAIL SAFE, 1964/111 min./Sidney Lumet/**1, 2, 3, 4, 6a, 7, 10, 11, 12, 14, 16.** A gripping story of the point of no return in nuclear war is made even more tense through effective camera action, convincing character portrayal, and editing which cuts from the planning room of the Strategic Air Command to the individual lives of the men who must make the ultimate decisions. Lighting is employed artfully, and the last minutes of the film can be called impact at its greatest. Could be compared with **Dr. Strangelove. Distributed by Ideal/Trans-World.**

s   **FELICIA,** 1965/13 min./**8a, 8e, 9, 16. Distributed by University of California.**   **M 35**

s   **FIDDLE-DE-DEE,** 1947/3 min./Norman McLaren/**6b, 8d. Distributed by Contemporary/International Film Bureau.**

FILM AND REALITY, United Kingdom, 1941/105 min./Ernest Lindgren/ **8a, 8f.** Contains a highly controversial account of the sources and history of the documentary film in terms of excerpts from important films of all periods and many countries. It by no means agrees with the views of eminent documentarists such as Paul Rotha, John Grierson and others, but does include scenes from key films not now available in complete form. **Distributed by Museum of Modern Art.**

s   **FLAVIO,** 1964/12 min., color/Gordon Parks/**8a, 8e, 11, 16.** This film tells the un-romanticized story of the real life of an impoverished family in Rio de Janiero, through the eyes of the 12-year-old Flavio. He carries out his responsibilities, as eldest of the family's ten children; and the film, in concentrating on him, conveys the real story of poverty with a compassion undiluted by either sentimentality or condescension. **Distributed by Contemporary/Mass Media.**   **K 51; M 36**

s   **FLOWERS ON A ONE-WAY STREET,** 1968/58 min./Robin Spry/ **8e, 9, 13.** Music by the Beatles and Ravi Shankar. Unlike many "documentaries" on the hippie scene, this on-location-type film gives the viewer a walk-through visit. Could be an interesting partner to the too-infrequently screened **The Anatomy of Cindy Fink. Distributed by Films, Inc.**

THE 400 BLOWS, France, 1959/98 min./Francois Truffaut/**2, 3, 4, 6a, 9, 11.** A 12-year-old boy grows up quickly when he finds that his mother has few moral values and that his father cannot handle the marital problems in a mature way. The boy is put into an institution which he finds intolerable. He escapes and runs to the sea. The last shot forces a response from the audience. The boy's world is small and centers mostly around a few friends. It is in this milieu that he must find meaning. His brilliant reply to the teacher, "Ma mere est morte," shows the childlike, yet perceptive, reaction that he is forced into. Many of the scenes are shot from above to show the immaturity of the boy. Gradually, however, the camera assumes a more natural position as the boy faces his problems. There are no slick answers to the ambivalent questions. English subtitles. **Distributed by Audio.**

s   **THE GAME,** 1966/27 min./George Kaczender/**2, 3, 4, 8e, 9, 16, 10, 11.** A young high school student is taunted by the rest of his gang to live up to his claimed ability as a seducer. He tried to win over one of the school's most attractive and impressive girls. Eventually he drops her because of his guilty feelings over his dishonesty and the really selfish ways in which he is exploiting someone he is coming to be fond of. The simple plot introduces, with a sensitivity and a propriety, the problems of relationships of people to people, in particular of boys to boys and boys to girls. **Distributed by Contemporary/McGraw-Hill/Roa.   K 55**

GATE OF HELL, Japan, 1954/89 min., color/Teinosuke Kinugasa/**2, 3, 5, 6b, 8b, 13, 14, 15.** Based on a twelfth-century chronicle and set in ancient Japan, the film is the story of a feudal warrior who saves the life of a beautiful married noblewoman but who ultimately destroys her when his frenzied passion drives him to forsake his code of personal honor. The extraordinary visual beauty of this first Japanese film to use color depends on the static design of light and shade in beautifully composed individual frames as well as on the carefully controlled use of color. The unusual choice of color for a tragedy succeeds because it is used with a psychological awareness of its effects, which reinforces the emotions excited by the action and the spectacle. **Distributed by Audio.**

PROPERTIES OF FILM

1. Montage	b) Adaptation from Stage, TV	9. Cinema Verite
2. Camera Angle		10. Introceptive Camera
3. Camera Position	c) Adaptation of Novels, Short Stories, Poems	11. Character Development
4. Camera Movement		12. Transitional Phases
5. Color		13. Visual Symbols
6. Sound:	d) Animation	14. Lighting
a) Natural	e) Social/Moral/ Symbolic Commentary	15. Beauty of Photographic Images
b) Music		16. Highly Visual Subject
7. Film Devices		
8. Categories	f) Pure Film	
a) Documentary		

s **GENERATION WITHOUT A CAUSE** (Part One: **Self-Portrait**), 1959/ 26 min./Henwar Roackiewicz/**8a, 8e, 9, 14, 16. Distributed by Carousel. K 57**

GEORGY GIRL, 1966/100 min./S. Narizzano/**3, 4, 6b, 8e, 11.** Lynn Redgrave, Alan Bates and James Mason present plausible characters in an unplausible story. Expert directing, interesting settings and fine camera work could distract from the fundamental lack of integrity in the film as well as in the main characters. Nevertheless, it is a film worth comparing with others which present a character seeking to find his place in a mix-up world, or a world which he has mixed up. Pauline Kael considers **Georgy** alongside **Alfie, Marty** and **Morgan! Distributed by Columbia Cinematheque.   PKK esp. 20-25**

s **GIUSEPPINA,** Italy, 1961/33 min., color/James Hill/**2, 3, 4, 8e, 9, 11, 14, 16.** English subtitles. **Distributed by Radiant.   M 37**

s **GLASS,** Holland, 1959/8 min./Bert Haanstra/**1, 2, 5, 6b, 8f, 9, 15.** A beautiful Dutch film by Bert Haanstra, harmonizing editing with a jazz composition, this work stresses the value of human labor in contrast to the automated machine. **Distributed by Contemporary.**

THE GOLD RUSH, 1925/81 min./Charlie Chaplin/**2, 3, 11.** As "the lone prospector," Charlie silently pans out a living. One of the Chaplin classics. Rhythm and timing are perfect and each gesture a graceful masterpiece of humor. The first publication of the "screenplay" compiled from the film by Timothy J. Lyons appears in CINEMA, Vol. 4, No. 2 (Summer 1968). This would be a unique opportunity to study screenplay construction as well as the Chaplin style. **Distributed by Brandon.   PKK 248, 273**

s **THE GOLDEN FISH,** France, 1959/20 min., color/Edmond Séchan/ **2, 4, 5, 6c, 8e, 9, 10, 12, 13, 14, 15, 16.** A rare experience created by the photographer of **The Red Balloon,** this film tells in cinema and extremely effective music the story of one little boy and the most beautiful goldfish in the world. The viewer is held breathless as the story progresses and a cat seems ready to catch the goldfish. The film creates its effects without dialog through careful and judicious use of sight, sound effects, and musical background. TIME called it, "Altogether the most charming short subject in live action since **The Red Balloon." Distributed by Brandon/Columbia Cinematheque/Contemporary/Mass Media/Twyman.   K 59; M 91**

GOLDEN MOMENTS WITH CHAPLIN, 1915/120 min./Charlie Chaplin/**2, 3, 4, 8a.** A well-edited collection of Chaplin shorts: **The Champion, Between Showers,** and **The Police** date around 1915. Also included is **The Rounders,** which is one of the few films in which he starred but did not direct. **Distributed by Trans-World.**

s **GOOD NIGHT, SOCRATES,** 1962/34 min./Stuart Hagmann/**2, 3, 4, 6a, 7, 8a, 9, 10, 12, 16.** A neighborhood dies before the eyes of its inhabitants and before the eyes of the viewer. Seen through the vision of one ten-year-old boy, this film discusses the often forgotten suffering brought about by urban renewal. Careful and creative camera work makes incisive statements regarding the almost soulless way in which the old is destroyed. **Distributed by Contemporary/Mass Media.   K 61; M 38**

THE GOSPEL ACCORDING TO ST. MATTHEW, Italy, 1967/136 min./ Pier Paolo Pasolini/**2, 3, 4, 6b, 7, 9, 13, 15.** This is the story of Christ told in the simple, stark, direct cinema verite style of the TV news cameraman. The film confines itself to St. Matthew's text, omitting the embellishments that have marred most "biblical" films and bringing the viewer face to face with an intense and angry Christ who clearly came "to bring not peace, but a sword." While Pasolini's portrait of the human Christ is moving and powerful, the divine and supernatural elements are also described with childlike frankness. As never before in movies, Jesus is seen as a preacher of religious revolution and reform, and the divine context is uncompromised. Most striking are the use of non-professional Italian peasants in the key roles and the desolate areas of Southern Italy to represent the Holy Land. The background music, ranging from the African **Missa Luba** to Bach and American Negro spirituals, is highly experimental. **GOSPEL** will go down in cinema history as one of the most unusual and provocative of films. **Distributed by Brandon.**

s **GRANTON TRAWLER,** United Kingdom, 1934/11 min./John Grierson/**1, 2, 8a.** John Grierson intended this simple but strikingly photographed and edited account of life aboard a fishing trawler off the coast of Scotland as a textbook for his fellow documentarists. **Distributed by Contemporary/ Museum of Modern Art.**

THE GRAPES OF WRATH, 1940/115 min./John Ford/**1, 3, 4, 6b, 8c, 9, 11, 12, 13, 14, 15.** This is a dark film, yet brilliant in its portrayal of the Joads as they leave their home and move westward to California. The land and the family unit are the basic ingredients for survival: when either is disturbed, there is hardship. The documentary realism of this film is seen in the tractors leaving the ravaged land, the car caravans, the migrant camps, and the first glimpse of California. It might be interesting to discuss how Ford changes the story since Steinbeck gave Ford complete control

PROPERTIES OF FILM		
1. Montage	b) Adaptation from Stage, TV	9. Cinema Verite
2. Camera Angle		10. Introceptive Camera
3. Camera Position	c) Adaptation of Novels, Short Stories, Poems	11. Character Development
4. Camera Movement		12. Transitional Phases
5. Color		13. Visual Symbols
6. Sound:	d) Animation	14. Lighting
a) Natural	e) Social/Moral/ Symbolic Commentary	15. Beauty of Photographic Images
b) Music		
7. Film Devices		16. Highly Visual Subject
8. Categories	f) Pure Film	
a) Documentary		

over the film and did not interfere with its production. **Distributed by Brandon/Contemporary/Films, Inc.**   **PKK 275-276, 350-351**

THE GREAT ESCAPE, 1963/169 min./John Sturges/**8c, 16. Distributed by United Artists 16.**

GREAT EXPECTATIONS. United Kingdom, 1947/115 min./David Lean/ **3, 8c, 11, 12, 14.** The story of young Pip and his relationship with the escaped convict Magwitch and the rich Miss Havisham are well known to many students of Charles Dickens. When Pip sets off to London and meets different people, he gradually changes his mode of living. By helping his old friend to escape arrest, and by assisting the beautiful Estella, he learns to grow up quickly in a difficult world. One must accept the film on its own grounds and not criticize the exaggerated sounds, the gloomy grave-yard, or the dark room of Miss Havisham's residence. One memorable scene occurs when Pip and Magwitch confront each other for the first time. A discussion might center on the methods used by Lean to create and sustain an atmosphere. **Distributed by Contemporary/Twyman/United World. PKK 276-277**

s **THE GREAT HOLIDAY MASSACRE,** 1957/54 min./CBS-TV/**8a, 8e, 16. Distributed by Association/Carousel.**   **M2 65**

GREED, 1924/109 min./Erich von Stroheim/**3, 4, 7, 8c, 10, 11.** Written and directed by Erich von Stroheim, the film is acknowledged as his greatest, and one of the classics of the motion picture. Adapted from the novel **McTeague** by Frank Norris, it is outstanding in its direction, acting, and screen visualization as it portrays the distortions of human nature when confronted by a passion for money. A close look at a powerful silent film will reveal much to students of the uniquely visual possibilities of film. **Distributed by Brandon.**

LA GUERRE EST FINIE, France, 1965/Alain Resnais/**10, 12, 13.** Like the untranslatable title, which means much more than "the war is over," the film has tones of irony throughout. As in Resnais' **Hiroshima, Mon Amour,** this film says more indirectly about war than hard-core pacifist comments. The setting is the Spanish underground that continues to fight the Falange from exile in France, even thirty years after Franco. The hero (played well by Yves Montand) presents the tense situation of being committed to a cause which has no future. His mistress (played by Ingrid Thulin) is a fine study in the greatness of secondary characters who allow the "star" to dominate—or is it the director who balances such touchy situations? Excellent for adult viewers who have had some experience with the Resnais style. **Distributed by Brandon.**   **PKK 162-166; F esp. 126-131**

THE GUNS OF NAVARONE, United Kingdom, 1961/155 min., color/ J. Lee Thompson/**2, 3, 4, 16. Distributed by Brandon/Twyman.**

GUYS AND DOLLS, 1955/150 min., color/Joseph Mankiewicz/**6b, 8c,**

11. This is a highly exciting modern musical presenting the best of Damon Runyon, Broadway lingo and settings perfect in tintype, neon-lighted Broadway sophistication. Hilarious choreography brightens an already versatile plot in which an invertebrate gambler courts a mission lass. **Distributed by Brandon/Films, Inc.**

HALLELUJAH THE HILLS, 1963/82 min./Jonas & Adolfas Mekas/**2, 3, 4, 7.** The Mekas brothers made this feature-length comedy at a moment when Europe was closely watching the New American Cinema. It received rave reviews as an export presumed to be the best of the American underground. American critics, however, were far from unanimous in their praise. Superb camera work and interesting spoofs of and allusions to the Keaton-Chaplin films keep this movie on the standard lists of independent film. Appreciation of the film depends a great deal on the viewer's experience of the Mack Sennett schools of comedy. See "Objections to the New American Cinema" by Dwight Macdonald in Gregory Battcock's **The New American Cinema. Distributed by Films, Inc./Janus.**

HAMLET, United Kingdom, 1948/152 min./Laurence Olivier/**2, 3, 4, 8b, 10, 11, 12, 14.** The reduction of four and one-half hours of drama to a two and one-half hour film often means a loss of characters and incident. But Sir Laurence Olivier's austere and thrifty presentation of Shakespeare's play shows a thorough understanding of both stage and film medium. Discussion might center on why it is sometimes considered to be one of the best films made from a Shakespearean text. Compare to the 1964 Russian version directed by Grigori Kozintsev. **Distributed by Contemporary/United World.**

s   **THE HAND,** Czechslovakia, 1967/19 min. color/Jiri Trnka/**8d, 8e.** Award winning puppet animation photographed by Jiri Safar. Symbolic suggestions vague and provocative. **Distributed by Contemporary.**

s   **HANGMAN,** 1964/12 min., color/Les Goldman/**1, 6b, 8b, 8d, 8e, 10, 12, 13, 8c.** Visual images and an effective final montage of symbolic pictures suggest the thought that social evil untended and ignored can destroy mankind. This film, set to the background of a poetry reading, can be effectively used back to back with others such as **The Detached Americans, Night and Fog,** and **Harvest of Shame.** In synopsis, a hangman comes to town and

PROPERTIES OF FILM		
1. Montage	b) Adaptation from Stage, TV	9. Cinema Verite
2. Camera Angle		10. Introceptive Camera
3. Camera Position	c) Adaptation of Novels, Short Stories, Poems	11. Character Development
4. Camera Movement		12. Transitional Phases
5. Color		13. Visual Symbols
6. Sound:	d) Animation	14. Lighting
a) Natural	e) Social/Moral/ Symbolic Commentary	15. Beauty of Photographic Images
b) Music		16. Highly Visual Subject
7. Film Devices	f) Pure Film	
8. Categories		
a) Documentary		

eventually kills everyone there, including the narrator of the poem. **Distributed by Contemporary/Mass Media.**   K 63; M2 66

A HARD DAY'S NIGHT, United Kingdom, 1964/85 min./The Beatles/**1, 3, 4, 6b, 14, 16.** An interesting effort to let the Beatles play themselves and yet not force their viewpoint on the viewer. The camera is far from passive as it flashes montage over montage. Even so, the impression is that humor is discovered for the first time by the viewer and was not structured by the players. A good companion to consider with **Don't Look Back** with Bob Dylan doing his thing as the Beatles do here. (Not yet on 16 mm.)   F **esp. 251-252**

s   **HARVEST OF SHAME,** 1961/58 min./Palmer Williams/**3, 4, 8a, 9, 10, 11, 16.** One of the strongest and most piercingly beautiful documentaries presented on American television, this study of the plight of the migrant worker is discussed in Chapter Eight of this book. **Distributed by Contemporary/McGraw-Hill/Mass Media.**   K 65

s   **THE HAT: IS THIS WAR NECESSARY?** 1964/18 min., color/John Hubley/**5, 6b, 6c, 8d, 8e, 13.** This cartoon depicts two soldiers patrolling a border, keeping a suspicious and hostile eye on each other. The hat of one of the soldiers falls off and into enemy territory. Whose hat is it now? Who is to decide, since this dilemma now becomes a national problem. **THE HAT** has shades of **Boundary Lines,** but is more effective because it is more subtle and more full of suggested meanings. **Distributed by American Friends/Brandon/Mass Media/University of Southern Illinois.**   K 67; M 39

THE HAUNTING, 1963/112 min., cinemascope/Robert Wise/**2, 3, 4, 6a, 6b, 7, 8c, 10, 12, 14.** This adult ghost story, adapted from a Shirley Jackson novel, is one of the most frightening films ever made. Besides being hair-raising, it also has abundant moral and psychological depth. Julie Harris is the oddly inhibited young woman who finds herself morbidly attracted by an evil old New England mansion. Script and acting are first-rate, but the remarkable thing is the way Wise creates a mood of absolute terror through setting and camera alone, without once showing a ghost. The film is particularly a good example of the use of sound and camera angle. This gloomy cinema masterpiece is not for the faint of heart. **Distributed by Brandon/Films, Inc.**   PK 9-11

s   **HAVE I TOLD YOU LATELY THAT I LOVE YOU?,** 1958/16 min./ U. of Southern California Students/**3, 4, 6a, 7, 8a, 8e, 8f, 9, 10, 11, 13.** This film spoofs the breakdown of human interpersonal communication. It focuses on the technological giants that control the present age: the electric shaver, the radio-deafened freeway driver, the television set that is a god in itself and makes human conversation unnecessary. The film zeroes in on one family, and concludes with the frightening feeling that this is our world: a vacuum without human communication, and the only time individuals touch one another with words or signs is when the machines and mechanical gadgets break down. The film has weak points in technique, since it is the work of students with a very small budget. But it is valid and powerful, and a good jumping off point for discussion and further experimentation with film expression. **Distributed by Mass Media/U. of Southern California. K 69; M 40**

HE WHO MUST DIE, Greece, 1957/116 min./Jules Dassin/**2, 3, 4, 6a, 8c, 9, 11, 13.** The setting is a poor village in Turkish-occupied Greece in 1920, and the point is that if Christ were reincarnated in that or perhaps any context, he would again be crucified. This is what happens when a shepherd, appointed to act Christ in a passion play, begins to take his part seriously and speaks up about the superficialities of the Church and the exploitation of the poor. The saint, the film suggests, is inevitably in conflict with the Establishment of his time, and there is a powerful plea not only for social and moral reform but for violence, if necessary, to overthrow the evil system. Since the other passion play "actors," heroes and villains, also begin to play out their roles in real life, another point is that a man is as good or bad as we expect him to be. The film, adapted from a Nikos Kazantzakis novel, is angry and often heavy-handed, but it remains one of the most forceful and disturbing religious films in movie history. Dassin uses the desolate locations to create an effect of both universality and utter realism. **Distributed by United Artists 16.**

s **HELEN KELLER IN HER STORY,** 1953/45 min./William Carver Wood/**8a, 9, 10, 11, 14, 16.** The inspirational meeting of a woman whose openness to the world and passion to communicate with it make this film worthwhile, although it is not outstanding cinema. **Distributed by Contemporary/Mass Media.** **K 71; M2 68**

HELP!, United Kingdom, 1965/92 min./Richard Lester/**1, 2, 3, 4, 5, 6a, 6b, 7, 9, 16.** Every possible camera angle, motion, device, and color effect is explored by Richard Lester in this visual probe of the Liverpool Wonders. Everything's fun in this satire of and on Beatlemania. The token plot serves as a vehicle to transport the stars from one shooting sight to the next. The plot shows the Beatles being chased all over the world by a group of Keystonish toughs who want to recover a ring mistakenly given to Ringo. Because he cannot remove the ring, which is to be worn only by the one selected to be a fit human sacrifice, Ringo must be exterminated. Of course,

PROPERTIES OF FILM		
1. Montage	b) Adaptation from	9. Cinema Verite
2. Camera Angle	Stage, TV	10. Introceptive Camera
3. Camera Position	c) Adaptation of	11. Character Development
4. Camera Movement	Novels, Short Stories,	12. Transitional Phases
5. Color	Poems	13. Visual Symbols
6. Sound:	d) Animation	14. Lighting
a) Natural	e) Social/Moral/	15. Beauty of Photographic
b) Music	Symbolic	Images
7. Film Devices	Commentary	16. Highly Visual Subject
8. Categories	f) Pure Film	
a) Documentary		

he eventually rids himself of the ornament of death, but not before Lester's camera has shown us everything there is to see about the Beatles, including a delightful visual interpretation of a whole album of song hits. **Distributed by Ideal.   PKK esp. 116-117**

s **HELP! MY SNOWMAN'S BURNING DOWN,** 1964/10 min., color/ Carson Davidson/**1, 5, 6a, 6b, 7, 8e, 8f, 13.** A total lack of story and/or clear meaning, this film plays and pokes fun at American society and its sex standards. It appears at times a free-form and undisciplined look-through-cinema at pretenses, U.S.A. **Distributed by Contemporary/Mass Media.   K 73**

HENRY V, United Kingdom, 1945/137 min., color or b/w/Laurence Olivier/**2, 3, 4, 5, 6b, 8b, 11, 12.** Many consider **HENRY V** the most successful attempt to translate Shakespeare onto film. Despite the drawback of artificial sets, Olivier uses the camera and the medium to increase the impact of the text. The Battle of Agincourt is superbly staged, aided by brilliant editing and mobile camera, and the use of a performance of the play at the Globe Theater as a framework for the film presentation is ingenious. **HENRY V** has many elements in it that appeal to young people, and the form of Olivier's film makes an ideal tool for discussing Shakespeare and his time, the differences between stage and film, etc. **Distributed by Contemporary/ United World.**

s **HEY, STOP THAT!,** 1965/6 min./Robert Faldman/**1, 4, 7, 8e.** One of the most successful anti-war comments. Very clever start and credits. Contrasts audio and visual as it pans the childish aspects of adult patriotism. **Presently not available for U. S. distribution.**

HIGH NOON, 1952/85 min./Fred Zinnemann/**1, 2, 3, 6b, 8c, 7, 11.** This is the prototype of the socially conscious Western, which has always had heroes and badmen, but not so often a conflict between the marshal and the people he represents. The story reaches a climax when the marshal has a gunfight at noon with a convict and some of the convict's friends. Ultimately, the marshal's bride remains by his side and when the battle is over, they go on their honeymoon. What makes this unique is the fact that the real time and the time in the film seem to coincide but do not. Dimitri Tiomkin's music ("Do Not Forsake Me, O My Darling"), the frequent absence of dialogue, and the rapid rate of cutting, heighten the emotional mood of the film. (See also Chapter Six.) **Distributed by Brandon/ Cinema Guild/Cinema, Inc./Contemporary.   PKK esp. 151-152, 280-281**

HIROSHIMA, MON AMOUR, France, 1959/88 min./Alain Resnais/**1, 8a, 10, 12, 13.** A timely commentary on war, love and life. A French actress falls in love with a Japanese man of Hiroshima. She tells her own past, including a tragic affair with a German soldier in an occupied France. The nuclear destruction of Hiroshima is also recalled as personal and global tragedy become integrated. Resnais flashes back and forth in time with amazing clarity, a contrast to many pseudo-impressionistic films. A key film of the French New Wave. His expert direction is best seen in the montage and special effects which Resnais masterfully keeps from dominating the story. English subtitles. **Distributed by Audio Film Classics.**

s   **THE HOLE,** 1962/15 min., color/John Hubley/**5, 6a, 8d.** In his Nobel Prize speech, William Faulkner said that the basest of all things is to be afraid. We should experience the threat of the atomic bomb and then forget this experience and live creative lives. Faulkner would have enjoyed **The Hole,** which is a cartoon about the anxieties of nuclear warfare. Two construction workers discuss the meaning of warheads and missiles as they work at their jobs beneath the city streets. The dialogue and art work are excellent. **Distributed by Brandon/Mass Media/Roa.   K 77; M 41**

THE HOME OF THE BRAVE, 1949/88 min./Mark Robson/**6a, 8b, 10, 12, 14, 16.** A screen adaptation of the Broadway hit by Arthur Laurents, is brilliantly acted against a background of racial intolerance. Five men, four white and one black, are sent on a top secret, suspense-filled adventure behind enemy lines in the South Pacific. The melodrama induced by the subject matter is carefully handled, and camera techniques and artistic editing create a strong effect. **Distributed by Contemporary/Ideal.**

s   **HOOKED,** 1965/20 min./**8a, 8e, 9. Distributed by Churchill.   M2 69**

s   **THE HOUSE,** Holland, 1961/32 min./Louis van Gasteren/**1, 7, 10, 12.** An interesting montage of all that made up the reality of an old house: the loves and hates, the lives and deaths that took place in it. Few films have attempted (and succeeded) to move back and forth rapidly in time to give fragmentary glimpses of the lives that filled the house: the waltz, the shooting of a man, the happy entrance by bride and groom. **Distributed by Contemporary.   K 79**

HOUSE ON 92ND STREET, 1945/88 min./Henry Hathaway/**8e, 10, 16.** Louis de Rochemont, producer of this masterpiece of Hathaway's direction, reveals his March of Time technique in this quasi-documentary. One of the journalistic films which undoubtedly influenced television's many detective and spy shows. Excellent camera work and editing. **Distributed by Films, Inc.**

PROPERTIES OF FILM		
1. Montage	b) Adaptation from Stage, TV	9. Cinema Verite
2. Camera Angle		10. Introceptive Camera
3. Camera Position	c) Adaptation of Novels, Short Stories, Poems	11. Character Development
4. Camera Movement		12. Transitional Phases
5. Color		13. Visual Symbols
6. Sound:	d) Animation	14. Lighting
a) Natural	e) Social/Moral/ Symbolic Commentary	15. Beauty of Photographic Images
b) Music		16. Highly Visual Subject
7. Film Devices	f) Pure Film	
8. Categories		
a) Documentary		

THE HUNTERS, 1958/73 min., color, cinemascope/Dick Powell/**3, 11.** Robert Mitchum, Robert Wagner, Richard Egan and May Britt are some of the stars in this Korean War film. Excellent action and fair romance. **Distributed by Contemporary.**

HUSH . . . HUSH, SWEET CHARLOTTE, 1964/133 min./Robert Aldrich/ **3, 4, 10, 13, 14, 16. Distributed by Films, Inc.**

THE HUSTLER, 1961/135 min., cinemascope/Robert Rossen/**2, 3, 8e, 11, 13, 16.** Pool is not usually considered as a legitimate game by which to make a living. Rossen's world of gamblers and pool-sharks has a built-in tension unknown to most people. The action between "Fast Eddie" and the champ "Minnesota Fats" (Jackie Gleason) shows how the tense and grueling conflict of a pool match can be expressed by using different camera shots and angles. In this film, Fats has the feel and cunning of an old professional. Eddie, however, has to fight his own interior battle, which makes the combat with Fats and the gambler (George Scott) even more intense. The stakes are worth more than money. **Distributed by Brandon/Films, Inc.**

s   **I WAS A NINETY-POUND WEAKLING,** 1960/24 min./John Kaminy/**1, 4, 6a, 7, 8a.** Documentary, edited portions of interviews, and the juxtaposition of surprising elements raise questions which the film does not attempt to answer. As in other productions by the National Film Board of Canada, **I WAS A NINETY-POUND WEAKLING** never states bluntly what the film maker is saying, nor what its conviction is with regard to the subject matter. This particular film takes a sharp poke at the physical unfitness of American society and leaves to the viewer the task of deciding "just where this puts us". **Distributed by Contemporary.**   **K 81; M2 70**

s   **I WONDER WHY,** 1965/5-½ min./Frederic Abeles & Stephan Segal/ **2, 3, 4, 8c, 8e, 10, 11, 14, 16. Distributed by Contemporary/Mass Media. K 83; M 43**

IKIRU, Japan, 1952/140 min./Akira Kurosawa/**3, 9, 10, 11.** Japanese films such as this one have their own tempo which is difficult for Americans to appreciate because of our affection for speed and efficiency. This film is an extraordinary document of one man who feels that he must do something significant with his life because he has little time to live. It is not a pretty thing because interior and exterior suffering are difficult to watch. Yet, the film is a visual masterpiece: the focus on the stacks of paper in the office, the night of drunkenness, the finale in the park, the silence as he leaves the doctor, the loneliness of the old man at the bottom of the stairs, all reveal an atmosphere which points to the spiritual value of the individual. English subtitles. **Distributed by Brandon.**

THE INFORMER, 1935/100 min./John Ford/**1, 3, 6b, 8c, 8e, 10, 11, 12, 13, 14.** This artful psychological study of guilt, which won Academy Awards for Ford, writer Dudley Nichols and star Victor McLaglen, is a genuine all-time film classic and a superb example of a novel adaptation. The story takes place in Dublin during the Irish uprising of 1922; the hero betrays his friend to the British and, pursued both by the vengeful Irish and his own conscience, eventually finds forgiveness in death. The film is especially skillful in revealing the hero's inner moods through visual symbols, choice of locale and outer incidents and action. Certainly revolutionary for its time, the movie is tragic in tone, with an imperfect though human hero who sins, suffers and finally dies (in a superbly staged death scene in a church). The cutting during the early killings of the hero's friend by police is also memorable. But the triumph of the movie is its creation of a complex and sympathetic human being, largely by visual means. **Distributed by Brandon/Contemporary/Films, Inc./Ideal.**

s **THE INHERITANCE,** 1964/60 min./Harold Mayer/**6b, 8a, 16.** Using the history of the Amalgamated Clothing Workers of America as a skeleton, Millard Lampell's script attempts to trace the story of Americans struggling for human rights. An example of effective use of skills in motion pictures, proper balance in visual and narrated impact, and well-wedded musical score. An extraordinary documentary. **Distributed by Contemporary/Mass Media. K 85**

THE INNOCENTS, United Kingdom, 1961/99 min., cinemascope/Jack Clayton/**2, 3, 4, 6a, 7, 8c, 9, 10, 11, 13.** "What an enchanting child," says the governess (Deborah Kerr) of one of the haunted children early in the film; and thus begins the horror, irony, and ambiguity of the film version of James' **Turn of the Screw.** Who are the "innocents," the children or the governess and other adults? Are the children possessed, or is the governess herself psychotic? The director has clearly left an ambiguous statement as a challenge to comfortable audiences, and he does so with full art, as does the writer of screenplay, Truman Capote. This excellent example of an intellectual horror film could be compared to **The Bad Seed** or **Rosemary's Baby. Distributed by Brandon/Films, Inc. PK 147-155**

s **THE INTERVIEW,** 1960/5 min., color/Ernest Pintoff/**6b, 8d.** An animated commentary on the problems of communication which contrast the jazz vocabulary (slightly dated) of a musician and the conventional language of a newsman. A characterization of both is extreme. Excellent discussion starter on the failure to listen and the difficulty of expressing what we think and feel. **Distributed by Brandon/Mass Media.**

PROPERTIES OF FILM

1. Montage
2. Camera Angle
3. Camera Position
4. Camera Movement
5. Color
6. Sound:
   a) Natural
   b) Music
7. Film Devices
8. Categories
   a) Documentary

b) Adaptation from Stage, TV
c) Adaptation of Novels, Short Stories, Poems
d) Animation
e) Social/Moral/ Symbolic Commentary
f) Pure Film

9. Cinema Verite
10. Introceptive Camera
11. Character Development
12. Transitional Phases
13. Visual Symbols
14. Lighting
15. Beauty of Photographic Images
16. Highly Visual Subject

INTOLERANCE, 1916/170 min./D. W. Griffith/**1, 3, 7, 10, 12.** Griffith's **Birth of a Nation** aroused a considerable amount of opposition, and this film, following a year later, was in part an answer to this censure. Today it is generally considered the masterpiece of the movies, and has had a world-wide influence. Very short shots, a quadruple story, enormous sets, and rapid crosscutting combine with close-ups of hands, faces, and objects, unseen before the appearance of this film. This is another example of the power of the film medium unsupported by sound. The **Fall of Babylon** consists of the most impressive parts of **INTOLERANCE,** recut in 1919. **Distributed by Audio/Museum of Modern Art.**

s INTRODUCTION TO FEEDBACK, 1960/12 min., color/Charles & Ray Eames/**8d, 8e.** The film is a subtle presentation of the fact that our communication depends on feedback. It explains this phenomenon in history and follows it into present society. Several principles are suggested as essential for successful feedback: information, response, the ability to guide and control the communication situation. **Distributed by IBM.   K 87**

INTRUDER IN THE DUST, 1949/87 min./Clarence Brown/**2, 3, 8c, 9, 11.** Faulkner's novels challenge visual portrayal because of their subtle linguistic style. Faulkner rarely tells a story in linear fashion; he prefers to weave his account with the thread of the story going back and forth over the same matter until its fabric is complete and unified. This film concerns a young white boy, Chick, who helps a proud Negro, Lucas, escape a lynching. Incidents and insights presented could be compared with those in **To Kill A Mockingbird. Distributed by Brandon/Films, Inc.   PKK 283-286**

s IT'S ABOUT THIS CARPENTER, 1963/10 min./**2, 3, 4, 7, 8e, 9, 11, 13, 14, 16. Distributed by New York University.   M2 71**

THE JAZZ SINGER, 1927/89 min./Alan Crosland/**6.** Often called the first talking film, this classic is admittedly sentimental. Al Jolson's songs and personality dominate. Compare to the 1953 remake starring Danny Thomas. Sound remade and synchronized with the original film. **Distributed by Brandon.**

LE JOLI MAI, France, 1962/124 min./Andre Heinrich/**9, 13, 15, 16.** Part One: "A Prayer from the Eiffel Tower," shows Paris in cinema verite. Part Two: "The Return of Fantomas" scans the socio-political life of the city. **Distributed by Contemporary.**

JUDGMENT AT NUREMBERG, 1961/178 min./Stanley Kramer/**3, 7.** Ostensibly, four Nazi judges are on trial; actually, the German nation is on trial. There are film clip inserts of Buchenwald and dialogue patterns that deliver actual courtroom lines. A balance of close-ups and long shots contrast individual character reactions effectively. The narrative of atrocities is rough in spots—but truth may be clear sometimes only with such rough exterior. Spencer Tracy provides a humane yet just characterization in his role. **Distributed by United Artists 16.**

JULES AND JIM, France, 1962/104 min./Francois Truffaut/**1, 2, 3, 4, 7, 8a, 10, 12, 15, 16.** In this film, François Truffaut's brilliant imagery brings into focus a nostalgic portrait of living joyously, yet tragically, on the brink of sorrow. Although the director does not ignore the sorrowful consequences of love with its ambiguities and irresolutions, yet he also lifts a toast to the joys of loving. The film may be called Truffaut's tribute to the visionary romanticism of Renoir. Contrast, especially the ending, to **Georgy Girl,** English subtitles. **Distributed by Janus.   PK esp. 195-200**

JULIET OF THE SPIRITS, Italy, 1965/135 min., color/Federico Fellini/ **1, 5, 12, 13.** Like Gelsomina, Cabiria, and the other heroines of Fellini's cinema, Juliet is simple and lovable. Her fantasies, however, are complex. (Compare to **Rachel, Rachel.**) Her search for identity and stability brings on dread of childhood fears (as in the themes of **8-½**). Fellini's ninth feature is the first in color and he uses it expertly. English subtitles. **Distributed by Audio Film Classics.**

KANCHENJUNGHA, 1962/102 min./S. Ray/**9, 11, 14, 15, 16.** The story takes place within a few hours. Much does and does not happen to a family on the last day of their vacation. Bengali with English subtitles. Adult. **Distributed by Audio.**

KING AND COUNTRY, 1964/86 min./Joseph Losey/**3, 4, 5, 13, 16.** A timely comment on institutionalism and the patterned-man. Losey zooms in on tense moments when a young soldier is to be executed for desertion. **Distributed by Audio.**

THE KING AND I, 1956/113 min./Walter Lang/**2, 5, 6b, 8b, 11, 16.** When an English widow becomes a teacher in an Eastern potentate's household, a colorful story unfolds. The music of Rodgers and Hammerstein and staging of this film is valuable insofar as it emphasizes Yul Brynner's magnetic personality as he struts and exclaims his way through the film. The most imaginative part is the Uncle Tom's Cabin scene, beautifully executed with an oriental charm. The story of segregation takes on new implications when seen through the romantic eyes of a foreign culture. This scene alone justifies the entire film. Also, a parade of Siamese children has a freshness and spirit unusual for a musical production. Compare to the earlier "straight" version **Anna and the King of Siam** (1946). Both based on the book by Margaret Landon. **Distributed by Films, Inc.**

PROPERTIES OF FILM

1. Montage	b) Adaptation from Stage, TV	9. Cinema Verite
2. Camera Angle		10. Introceptive Camera
3. Camera Position	c) Adaptation of Novels, Short Stories, Poems	11. Character Development
4. Camera Movement		12. Transitional Phases
5. Color		13. Visual Symbols
6. Sound:	d) Animation	14. Lighting
a) Natural	e) Social/Moral/ Symbolic Commentary	15. Beauty of Photographic Images
b) Music		
7. Film Devices		16. Highly Visual Subject
8. Categories	f) Pure Film	
a) Documentary		

s **THE KING AND THE LION,** 1953/13 min., color/Stevens-Wallace Puppet Films/**8e, 13. Distributed by Athena/Contemporary.** **M 44**

s **KINO-PRAVDA,** 1922/series of 12 newsreels/Dziga Vertov/**1, 8a, 8f.** A Soviet newsreel edited by Dziga Vertov who attempted a you-are-there style. An important contribution to the theory of documentary film. The excerpts in the Museum of Modern Art reel include the trial of the Social Democrat "conspirators" and shots of youthful victims of famine. (Museum of Modern Art's reel is eighteen minutes.) **Distributed by Museum of Modern Art.**

THE KNACK, United Kingdom, 1965/84 min./Richard Lester/**1, 2, 3, 4, 6a, 6b, 7, 8b, 9, 11.** This wild, very cinematic adaptation of Ann Jellicoe's stage comedy is a remarkably beautiful and funny job by the film-makers responsible for the first two Beatles films. It is about a painfully eager young schoolteacher (Michael Crawford) who wants to emulate a successful Don Juan neighbor by learning his "knack" with the ladies. But he cannot be a rogue: he falls in love with the first girl he meets (Rita Tushingham) and then struggles to keep her from falling into the Don Juan's harem. Basically, this is a comic picture of the sexual predicament among "emancipated" British youth, but it also serves as an excellent satire on the sex obsession of the age, opting for a middle ground between eroticism and puritanism. The humor is virtually all visual and spontaneous, with marvelous use of sight gags, visuals, sound and cutting to produce magical comic effects. **Distributed by United Artists 16.** **PKK esp. 116-117**

KNIFE IN THE WATER, Poland, 1962/95 min./Roman Polanski/**14, 15.** A journalist and his wife pick up a young boy on the road. They spend a week-end on a yacht. The husband tries to use the youth's presence as a spur to his own ambition and virility. The results are rather unexpected and disturbing. A brilliant first feature film by Polanski. English subtitles. **Distributed by Brandon.**

s **KU KLUX KLAN,** 1965/47 min./CBS-TV/**8a, 8e, 14. Distributed by Carousel.** **M2 75**

THE LADY FROM SHANGHAI, 1948/87 min./Orson Welles/**1, 2, 3, 16.** A sailor (Welles) steps out of the night into the strangest and most sinister adventures of his life. At the cinematically brilliant conclusion in a multi-mirrored fun palace, Welles walks out, leaving Rita Hayworth and Everett Sloan dead among the shattered mirrors. This scene, and the wonderfully sneaky, mean, and villainous acting of Sloan and Glenn Anders, are what makes this movie worth seeing. Note also the lovers' meeting in front of a tank of octopuses, and the courtroom scene. **Distributed by Brandon.**

s **THE LAKE MAN,** 1964/27 min./**8e, 9, 11, 16. Distributed by Contemporary.** **M2 76**

LAST YEAR AT MARIENBAD, 1961/93 min./Alain Resnais/**1, 4, 7, 12, 14.** Joining Antonioni and Fellini in their more introverted moments, Resnais presented a confusingly beautiful impression of time's influence on man, man's reaction to time and, in general, abstract scenes which mean different things to as many different people. There may be a commentary on society and morals, but most of all there is a display of cinematic possibilities which should be experienced. English subtitles. **Distributed by Audio Film Classics.** PK esp. 161-176

LAUREL AND HARDY'S LAUGHING 20'S, 1965/90 min./Robert Youngson (compiler)/**2, 3, 4, 11.** Some of Mr. L.'s and Mr. H.'s best moments compiled from their silent two-reelers. **Distributed by Brandon.**

LAWRENCE OF ARABIA, United Kingdom, 1962/221 min., color, Cinemascope/David Lean/**2, 3, 4, 5, 6a, 6b, 9, 10, 11, 12, 15, 16.** Like **West Side Story,** this film makes splendid use of color, angles, shapes, textures, motions and sounds—all united to a powerful story. From the death sequence on an English road in 1935 to Lawrence's meeting with Prince Feisal and the consequent entrance into Damascus, the hero displays great dynamism. He has been accused of all sorts of weaknesses; without detracting from his power, the film shows the interior limitations of this sensitive, yet heroic individual. It is rare that a "spectacular" such as this can also be a successful and moving motion picture. **Presently not available for distribution.**

s **LET MY PEOPLE GO,** 1965/54 min./Marshall Flaum/**8a, 8e, 9, 10, 4, 7, 12.** This film, originally prepared as a CBS documentary, has shades of **Exodus** and reminds one in parts of Resnais' **Night and Fog.** It tells the story of the return of the Jews to Israel with outstanding commentary, impressive photography, and a sustained inspiration. **Distributed by University of Michigan/Xerox.**   K 89

LILITH, 1964/110 min./Robert Rossen/**2, 3, 4, 6a, 6e, 9, 10, 11, 13, 14, 16.** A very successful presentation of persons in need of psychiatric help, persons in love, persons in general. A second screening could be held for awareness of symbols (water is especially used). Warren Beatty and Jean Seberg star. **Distributed by Audio/Brandon.**

s **LINES (HORIZONTAL),** 1960/6 min./Norman McLaren/**8d.** **Distributed by Contemporary/International Film Bureau.**

PROPERTIES OF FILM		
1. Montage	b) Adaptation from	9. Cinema Verite
2. Camera Angle	Stage, TV	10. Introceptive Camera
3. Camera Position	c) Adaptation of	11. Character Development
4. Camera Movement	Novels, Short Stories,	12. Transitional Phases
5. Color	Poems	13. Visual Symbols
6. Sound:	d) Animation	14. Lighting
a) Natural	e) Social/Moral/	15. Beauty of Photographic
b) Music	Symbolic	Images
7. Film Devices	Commentary	16. Highly Visual Subject
8. Categories	f) Pure Film	
a) Documentary		

s **LINES (VERTICAL),** 1960/6 min./Norman McLaren/**8d. Distributed by International Film Bureau.**

THE LITTLE FOXES, 1941/116 min./William Wyler/**11, 16. Distributed by Brandon/Films, Inc.**

THE LONELINESS OF THE LONG DISTANCE RUNNER, United Kingdom, 1962/103 min./Tony Richardson/**1, 4, 7, 8e, 10, 11, 16.** The theme of a young man challenging his environment and seeking his place in the world has been common for the Western world. Huck Finn, Holden Caulfield, and Gene Forrester have always been popular heroes. This film explores the problems of a young man placed in a borstal (reform school) who can win a race against a neighboring school and receive the favors of the warden, or he can lose the race and be acceptable to his peers. The decision whether to win or not is made all the more difficult by the fact that the boy likes to run very much; in fact, the magnificent scenes where he is practicing his running reveal the freedom and ecstasy possible for someone who has committed himself to a project. In various subtle ways, the sound track and the different sequences overlap to create a new form of graphic continuity. The use of William Blake's song, "Jerusalem," with its mystical-socialistic overtones, the constant build-up of flashback shots, the final freeze shot, and humorous TV episode make this film well worth seeing several times. **Distributed by Contemporary/Continental 16.**

LONELY ARE THE BRAVE, 1962/107 min., Cinemascope/David Miller/**8e, 9, 11, 13, 16.** The Western myth catches up with itself as Kirk Douglas, the lonely individualist cowboy, is defeated in a modern, mechanized America, which no longer needs him. The film, once described as an "existential Western," provides an excellent starting point for a study of the classic American myth. A fine blend of humor is provided by Walter Matthau's portrayal of the sheriff, the cowboy's reluctant pursuer. A battle between the cowboy and a hostile helicopter is the film's highpoint. **Distributed by Contemporary/United World.**

s **LONELY BOY,** 1962/27 min./Wolf Koenig & Roman Kroiter/**1, 2, 4, 6b, 7, 8a, 9, 10, 11, 12.** A cinema biography of the young singing sensation, Paul Anka, this film presents, through camera and background music and sound effects, the extreme loneliness of the idol revered, but never really touched, by millions. A photographer lived with Anka and his troupe for several months and took miles of film. Careful editing reveals the deep futility of the young star. **Distributed by Contemporary.   K 91; M2 77**

LORD OF THE FLIES, United Kingdom, 1963/90 min., Peter Brook/**2, 3, 6a, 8c, 8e, 9, 11, 13, 15.** This film captures, with only a few exceptions, all the elements of Golding's novel. The dramatic build-up, witnessed in the music changing from "Kyrie Eleison" to "Kill the Pig", and from the orderly marching at the beginning of the film to the frantic chase at the end, shows cinematic technique and insight. Personalities are carefully established with the symbolic elements of glasses, the conch, fire, the mask, and the boar's head. Simon's prophetic utterances are juxtaposed with Piggy's humor in much the same way as Jack is balanced with Ralph. The visual treatment of Simon's death is superb, although none of the children are professional actors. The structure and progression of this film are important, especially in a discussion of it as an allegory. **Distributed by Contemporary/Continental 16.**

LOUISIANA STORY, 1948/77 min./Robert Flaherty/**3, 4, 8a, 9, 10, 14, 15, 16. LOUISIANA STORY** is the last of the significant films made by Robert Flaherty. The viewer sees the beauty and majesty of the bayous of Louisiana through the eye of a wondering camera, and also through the eyes of a 12-year-old Cajun boy as he plays, hunts, fishes in the swamplands, and fights an alligator. The discovery of oil gives a new and exciting direction to the film and to the boy's view of life. Compare to **The Great Adventure. Distributed by Contemporary.**

LOVE WITH THE PROPER STRANGER, 1963/100 min./Robert Mulligan/**2, 3, 4, 6a, 6b, 9, 11.** A modern love story in a romantic-realistic setting. A likeable musician (Steve McQueen) finds that he is responsible for the pregnancy of a casual girlfriend (Natalie Wood). The story of how he reacts to this news is at first starkly tragic, then romantically humorous, and finally touching. This moral tale about ordinary people is told with cinematic imagination with especially good use of New York city locations. On this point, compare to **The Odd Couple** and **Barefoot in the Park.** The abortion sequence, from its beginnings in the Manhattan fish market district to its finale in an almost Dante-esque slum apartment, is exceedingly powerful and could be contrasted to the much briefer abortion sequence in **Alfie. Distributed by Films, Inc.**

THE LOWER DEPTHS, Japan, 1957/125 min./Akira Kurosawa/**7, 8b, 8e.** Adaptation of Maxim Gorky's play. An interesting program would be to compare Kurosawa's direction to that of Jean Renoir, who also did **The Lower Depths** in 1936 (available from Contemporary, 91 minutes). **Distributed by Brandon.**   **PKK 302**

LUST FOR LIFE, 1956/122 min., color, cinemascope/Vincente Minnelli/**1, 5, 10, 11, 15.** The fields of the Borinage region of Belgium and Auvers sur-l'Oise knew the secret of Van Gogh's art. He painted with masterful

PROPERTIES OF FILM		
1. Montage	b) Adaptation from Stage, TV	9. Cinema Verite
2. Camera Angle		10. Introceptive Camera
3. Camera Position	c) Adaptation of Novels, Short Stories, Poems	11. Character Development
4. Camera Movement		12. Transitional Phases
5. Color		13. Visual Symbols
6. Sound:	d) Animation	14. Lighting
a) Natural	e) Social/Moral/ Symbolic Commentary	15. Beauty of Photographic Images
b) Music		
7. Film Devices		16. Highly Visual Subject
8. Categories	f) Pure Film	
a) Documentary		

strokes and at times with vengeance. The beauty of this film is in the fusion of the real scenes with Van Gogh's graphic portrayal of them. The dividing line between genius and madness is often a thin one: this film shows the unusual perspective suffering gives to life, and is famous for its extraordinary beauty of color as well as for Anthony Quinn's Oscar-winning performance as Gaugin. **Distributed by Brandon/Films, Inc.**

s **THE MAGICIAN,** Poland, 1964/13 min./Tad Markarcynski/**6, 8e, 9, 11, 13.** The story of the Pied Piper was a popular one, and this modern Pied Piper tale explores the fact of man's being attracted to what he originally finds evil. Little children are the chief characters, lured by the tricks and games of the magician. The film is similar to **The Parable,** but not as intricate or sophisticated. **Distributed by American Friends Service Committee/Mass Media.   K 93; M 47**

THE MAGNIFICENT AMBERSONS, 1942/88 min./Orson Welles/**2, 3, 4, 7, 8c, 11, 12, 14.** In this film adaptation of Booth Tarkington's Pulitzer Prize novel, experimental use of camera and sound demonstrates the expandable boundaries of the film form. **AMBERSONS** ranks with Welles' **Citizen Kane** as a virtuoso performance of real film-history importance. It portrays an aristocratic American industrial family around the turn of the century, who fears the challenge of the growing power of the automobile and the nouveaux riches, and does so with a strength and an impact rarely equaled. **Distributed by Brandon/Contemporary/Modern Sound/Trans-World.   PKK 304**

THE MAGNIFICENT SEVEN, 1960/John Sturges/**6b, 8c.** An American Western take-off or remake of the Japanese classic **Seven Samurai** directed by Kurosawa six years earlier. Yul Brynner leads the mercenaries in defense of a village against bandits, led by Eli Wallach. Elmer Bernstein's musical score compliments very active camera art. Excellent character studies of the seven, often primarily visual. **Distributed by United Artists 16.**

A MAN ESCAPED, France, 1957/94 min./Robert Bresson/**2, 3, 6a, 8a, 9, 10, 14, 6b.** This is a remarkably economical reconstruction of an actual event, the escape of a Frenchman from a Nazi prison, and it can be taken purely as a suspense drama or as an existential moral drama in which all fate conspires to allow the hero to fulfill his destiny, i.e., to escape. The film is notable chiefly for its restriction to a single point of view, achieved partly by subjective camera, elimination of all sights and sounds that would not be seen or heard by the prisoner himself, and partly by matter-of-fact first-person commentary. No detail is included in the film that does not relate directly to the problem of escape. The music (Mozart's Mass in C Minor) and exterior sounds also make thematic contributions. As usual with Bresson, the actors are all (amazingly) non-professionals, and the sets are either the actual locations or meticulously detailed reconstructions. English subtitles. **Distributed by Contemporary.   PKK esp. 305-306**

A MAN FOR ALL SEASONS, 1966/120 min./Fred Zinnemann/**8b, 11.**

One of those rare films which somehow allows its original stage style to remain intact without forgetting the ability of the camera. The play of Robert Bolt remains evident; Zinnemann masterfully remains the director, not the author. Bending history for the sake of good drama, and rightly so, the Thomas More (Paul Scofield) of tne script is immaculate—the kind of super man we may not want around our all too human self. He is a **type** we can admire if not imitate. So, too, the film should not be a model for **real** motion picture art, but can be referred to as existing and friendly. **Distributed by Columbia Cinematheque.   PKK esp. 154-155**

MAN OF ARAN, United Kingdom, 1934/77 min./Robert Flaherty/**9, 8a, 15, 16.** Flaherty produced this masterpiece of photography artistry on the Aran Islands off the west coast of Ireland. The film, which depicts man struggling against the elements for his existence, is typical of Flaherty's approach to all subjects he films. He does not preconceive, he explores. And the exploration and freedom to let the material tell its own story are strikingly evident throughout **MAN OF ARAN.** Compare to the classic **Nanook of the North** (1922). **Distributed by Contemporary.   PKK esp. 306-307**

THE MANCHURIAN CANDIDATE, 1962/126 min./John Frankenheimer /**8c, 10, 11.** An excellent exercise in combining science fiction, political satire, and grim irony, this is a thrilling melodrama. It stars Frank Sinatra, Laurence Harvey, Angela Lansbury, and Janet Leigh. Excellent casting and acting are evident in the story of a silent, efficient assassin who has been captured and brainwashed by the communists, and who functions as the unwitting tool of his mother who plans to take over the U.S. **Distributed by United Artists.**

MARTY, 1955/91 min./Delbert Mann/**4, 11, 16.** Shortly after a comparatively minor role in **Bad Day at Black Rock,** Ernest Borgnine plays one of those rare triumphs in which the actor is perfectly cast. In the title role, Borgnine plays a male version of the less successful **Georgy Girl,** but the role is cleaner and more convincing. Marty is a direct contrast to **Alfie;** he is sensitive to real love and develops a capacity to respond to the risk which love brings. Excellent for singles, informative for the married and disturbing for the playboy. If **MARTY** is on the late show tonight and the television is working, there should be no doubt about "what 'cha wanna do tonight".

PROPERTIES OF FILM		
1. Montage	b) Adaptation from	9. Cinema Verite
2. Camera Angle	Stage, TV	10. Introceptive Camera
3. Camera Position	c) Adaptation of	11. Character Development
4. Camera Movement	Novels, Short Stories,	12. Transitional Phases
5. Color	Poems	13. Visual Symbols
6. Sound:	d) Animation	14. Lighting
a) Natural	e) Social/Moral/	15. Beauty of Photographic
b) Music	Symbolic	Images
7. Film Devices	Commentary	16. Highly Visual Subject
8. Categories	f) Pure Film	
a) Documentary		

If the TV is out of order, you may have to resort to reading something by Mickey Spillane. "Boy, that Mickey Spillane—he sure can write." (**MARTY** has lines which are now famous and often attributed to later sources.) **Distributed by United Artists 16.**

s   **MARVELS OF THE HIVE,** 1964/20 min., color/John J. Carey/**5, 8a, 15. Distributed by Contemporary.   M 92**

s   **MEMORANDUM,** 1966/58 min./Donald Brittain & John Spotton/**8a, 9, 10, 6, 16.** A discussion in cinema verite style, this film asks again the questions about mankind's responsibility for the atrocities of the concentration camps. Interviews, documentary film clips, combine to raise the questions in a subtle and absorbing manner. Reminiscent of Resnais' **Night and Fog, MEMORANDUM** appeals to the heart and to the mind and makes its impact in a reality-centered presentation of man's inhumanity to man, and willingness to pass off this inhumanity as merely the result of following the orders of the top command. **Distributed by Contemporary. K 95; M2 81**

s   **THE MEMPHIS BELLE,** 1944/40 min./William Wyler/**1, 8a, 9.** William Wyler's account of the twenty-fifth mission of a B-17 on a bombing raid over Germany stands out as one of the best of the war documentaries. The negatives of the film have been lost, but even the somewhat distorted color of the print of a print of a print does not take away from the share of danger, expectancy and uncertainty which the skillful composition evokes. **Distributed by Museum of Modern Art.**

s   **THE MERRY-GO-ROUND,** 1966/23 min./Tanya Ballantyne/**1, 2, 3, 4, 7, 8a, 9, 10, 11, 12, 14.** This film presents the development of relationships between a boy and a girl from the viewpoints of three divergently thinking authorities on sex. It also points out vividly the gap that yawns between the understandings of these three adult experts and the questions that plague young people. Clever editing and camera work make it clear to the viewer that the film takes the side of the boy and girl, in condemning the pat answers of the adults. And so it becomes more than a discussion of sex, a commentary on the communications which do not exist between the two age groups. **Distributed by Contemporary/McGraw-Hill/Mass Media/Roa.   K 99**

s   **MINT TEA,** France, 1962/20 min./Pierre Kafian/**2, 3, 4, 6a, 6b, 7, 8e, 9, 14.** In **MINT TEA,** a group of perceptive film makers have captured the depth of loneliness and the futility of man's attempts to conquer it. A young man sits, like a canary in a cage, in a glass-enclosed Parisian sidewalk cafe, alone despite the cars and people, the noise and movement going on around him. Camera work, skillful use of sound, and careful editing combine to create a touching and honest picture of individual man's isolation from the rest of mankind. **Distributed by Contemporary.   M 49**

THE MIRACLE WORKER, 1962/106 min./Arthur Penn/**2, 3, 4, 7, 8b, 10, 11.** The greatness of this film is that it doesn't merely tell a story, but rather involves the audience in the story itself. The nightmarish action of the camera as it swivels about during Helen's struggle at the dinner table is a masterpiece of involvement and subjective camera, and is beautifully contrasted with the peace and quiet of the small house wherein Helen and Annie (Anne Bancroft) learn to tolerate and love one another. The final scene at the pump, in which Helen (Patty Duke) associates w-a-t-e-r with the liquid flowing over her hands, is an almost palpable experience for the audience. Another example of cinematic concentration on simple but profound realizations is the grainy texture of the flashback scenes of Annie's childhood, which allows us to more realistically enter the hazy world of the blind. Compare Penn's direction in this film to that in his recent **Bonnie and Clyde** (1967). **Distributed by Cultural.**

s **THE MISCHIEF MAKERS,** 1957/27 min./François Truffaut/**2, 3, 4, 7, 8e, 10, 11, 13, 14, 15, 16. Distributed by Brandon.   M2 82**

THE MISFITS, 1961/124 min./John Huston/**2, 3, 4, 8e, 11, 13, 16.** Usually billed merely as the last film of both Clark Gable and Marilyn Monroe, **THE MISFITS** has cinematic merit as drama and good camera work. Arthur Miller did the screenplay about modern cowboys and very modern cowgirls. **Distributed by United Artists.**

MOANA, 1925-1926/90 min./Robert Flaherty/**14, 9.** Paramount sent Flaherty to the South Seas to film Samoan life. He not only made an excellent film, he found his way into the closed social life of a people entirely foreign to him. Traditional Samoan culture is recorded through everyday events as hunting, feasting, dancing, and the ritual of the Tattoo. The film should be seen more than once in order to discover the method behind the apparent disorder. It was John Grierson's review of this film which first introduced the term "documentary" to the language. **Distributed by Contemporary/Museum of Modern Art.**

MONIKA, Sweden/1952/83 min./Ingmar Bergman/**3, 4, 14. Distributed by Janus.** English subtitles.

s **MOONBIRD,** 1959/10 min., color/John Hubley/**6a, 5, 8d, 8e, 13, 15.** This Academy Award winning animated film is one of the most beautiful and captivating ever made. It tells the story of how two little boys go out

PROPERTIES OF FILM		
1. Montage	b) Adaptation from Stage, TV	9. Cinema Verite
2. Camera Angle		10. Introceptive Camera
3. Camera Position	c) Adaptation of Novels, Short Stories, Poems	11. Character Development
4. Camera Movement		12. Transitional Phases
5. Color		13. Visual Symbols
6. Sound:	d) Animation	14. Lighting
a) Natural	e) Social/Moral/ Symbolic Commentary	15. Beauty of Photographic Images
b) Music		
7. Film Devices		16. Highly Visual Subject
8. Categories	f) Pure Film	
a) Documentary		

one night to catch the moonbird. The drawings, the color, and the soundtrack combine to entrance the viewer back into the magical time and mentality of childhood. **Distributed by Brandon/Contemporary/Mass Media. K 101**

THE MORALIST, Italy, 1959/120 min./Alberto Sordi & Vittorio de Sica/ **8e, 13, 16.** A not-too-funny satire on self-appointed censors and their self-appointed art. Good for adult discussion. Compare to the first episode in **Boccaccio 70.** English subtitles. **Distributed by Brandon.**

MY DARLING CLEMENTINE, 1946/97 min./John Ford/**2, 3, 4, 6b, 7, 9, 11, 13, 14, 15, 16.** Wyatt Earp's pacification of Tombstone, as visualized with extreme pictorial beauty and typical human warmth by the recognized dean of Western movie directors. Henry Fonda gently underplays the hero who agrees to become marshal after an arrogant gang murders his kid brother, then leaves for new frontiers after the famous gunfight at the O.K. Corral. While the shoot-out is the highlight of the movie, a lingering Sunday morning sequence ending in a church dance is equally memorable. The film is loaded with virtuoso visual technique, but the emphasis on character and the depth of relationships involving women is exceptional for the Western genre. Walter Brennan makes a salty villain and Victor Mature appears as Doc Halliday. **Distributed by Brandon/Films, Inc.**

s   **MY OWN YARD TO PLAY IN,** 1959/7 min./Phil Lerner/**3, 6a, 8e, 9, 16. Distributed by Harrison.   M2 83**

MY UNCLE (MON ONCLE), France, 1958/114 min., color/Jacques Tati/ **3, 6b, 10, 16.** The indestructible enchantment of slapstick comedy as it was performed by the classic screen comedians Chaplin, Keaton and Lloyd comes through strongly in this hilarious satire on the contemporary addiction to mechanical gadgetry. Tati wrote, directed, and starred in the production which was a Special Award winner at the Cannes Film Festival. Compare to the serious treatment of technology in the James Bond films or the TV series **Mission: Impossible.** English subtitles. **Distributed by Contemporary.**

s   **NAHANNI,** 1962/19 min., color/William Weintraub/**2, 3, 4, 5, 6, 7, 8a, 8e, 9, 10, 11, 15, 16.** Reminiscent of **Old Man and the Sea,** this film tells the story of one old man's desire to conquer the mighty Nahanni River. Like the old man in Hemingway's novelette, Albert Faille is persistent through many hardships. His goal is to discover the cache of gold which he believes is at the river's end. Cinema, sound, and the bewitchingly beautiful background of Northwestern Canadian wilderness make this a striking film, and one well worthwhile including in film study programs. **Distributed by Contemporary.   K 103**

THE NAKED EYE, 1957/70 min./Louis Clyde Stoumen/**2, 3, 4, 5, 6, 8a, 14, 15, 16.** A documentary about the camera and still photography, its history, art and the dedication of photographers. An entertaining adult introduction to a consideration of cinematic properties. **Distributed by Contemporary.**

s **NANOOK OF THE NORTH,** 1922/55 min./Robert Flaherty/**3, 8a, 9.** Robert Flaherty's record of Eskimo life based upon his own long and careful observations as an explorer in Northern Canada has long been hailed as a classic in film. The Rousseauistic view of the so-called "primitive" makes the film an interesting discussion piece. **Distributed by Audio/Brandon/ Contemporary/Museum of Modern Art.   K 105**

s **NEIGHBORS,** 1952/10 min., color/Norman McLaren/**3, 5, 7, 8d, 8e, 11, 13. NEIGHBORS** is an allegory in film, the story of man's inability to be neighbor to his fellowman. It is more effective, and more subtle, than **Boundary Lines,** a film on the same subject and also animated. **NEIGHBORS** employs the stop-action technique and other special effects. In brief, it shows two men fighting over possession of a single flower that has sprouted exactly on the boundary line between their property. The ensuing violence and eventual final ending make the film's point without any need for dialogue explanation. **Distributed by Contemporary/Trans-World.   K 107; M 51**

s **NEW BORN AGAIN,** 1966/30 min./Clarence Rivers/**6b, 8e, 14.** Distributed by The Grail.   **M 52**

s **N.Y., N.Y.,** 1957/15 min./Francis Thompson/**1, 2, 3, 5, 6, 7, 8f, 13, 15, 16.** Using previously unknown camera distortions, Francis Thompson's film moves swiftly through a day in New York, transforming the city's familiar scenes into a new world of fantasy. The camera transforms and manipulates the actual scene so that buildings float, limp automobiles swallow themselves, trumpet horns distend, and each sequence is organized into a visual structure of movement and mood. **Distributed by Museum of Modern Art.**

s **NIGHT AND FOG,** France, 1955/31 min./Alain Resnais/**1, 4, 5, 6b, 7, 8a.** Alain Resnais' film of the Nazi concentration camps is at once beautiful, gruesome and forceful. It is more than a historical record of something which took place "at a certain time and in a certain place." Resnais' film and Jean Cayrol's narration are an exploration into man's

---

PROPERTIES OF FILM

1. Montage	b) Adaptation from Stage, TV	9. Cinema Verite
2. Camera Angle		10. Introceptive Camera
3. Camera Position	c) Adaptation of Novels, Short Stories, Poems	11. Character Development
4. Camera Movement		12. Transitional Phases
5. Color		13. Visual Symbols
6. Sound:	d) Animation	14. Lighting
a) Natural	e) Social/Moral/ Symbolic Commentary	15. Beauty of Photographic Images
b) Music		16. Highly Visual Subject
7. Film Devices		
8. Categories	f) Pure Film	
a) Documentary		

paradoxical need both to forget and recall. **Distributed by Chicago Public Library/Contemporary/Mass Media.   K 109, M 54**

A NIGHT AT THE OPERA, 1935/90 min./Sam Wood/**6b, 11, 16.** The Marx Brothers provide filmic comedy at its best after the advent of sound. This film has importance because of its historic value of showing sound film in its early stages when the camera begins to come out of its box. The Marx Brothers created a kind of humor which was ideally suited for the sound camera, since it depended on both action and dialogue. Each Brother had some unique quality of voice or movement which set them apart from one another. Harpo was especially suited to the film because of his total use of pantomime (he never spoke a word). Particularly noticeable in their films is the dialogue which had a racy quality of its own and was itself highly picturesque. The classic scene is the hilarious (and highly cinematic) destruction of the opera **Il Trovatore** with its unreal settings and backdrops. **Distributed by Brandon/Films, Inc.   PKK 317**

s   **NIGHT MAIL,** United Kingdom, 1936/24 min./Harry Watt & Basil Wright/**1, 2, 3, 4, 6a, 6b, 7, 8a, 9.** Made by the G.P.O. Film Unit under the leadership of John Grierson, and directed by Harry Watt, the film follows the nightly run of the "Postal Special" from the south of England to Edinburgh. The work and dedication of the workers who serve the sleeping community is crystallized in the closing sequence of the film where the train hurries northward to the poetic commentary of W. H. Auden and the music of Benjamin Britten. **Distributed by Audio/Brandon/Museum of Modern Art.**

NIGHT OF THE HUNTER, 1955/93 min./Charles Laughton/**2, 3, 4, 6a, 6b, 8c, 10, 11, 12, 13, 14, 15.** This masterpiece of terror is about as off-beat as movies come. Robert Mitchum plays a half-crazed country preacher who woos and murders women for their money; the bulk of the film concerns his relentless pursuit of two small children who know his secret. The style is expressionistic, low-key and haunting, and the movie is one of the few American attempts to develop a plot more in terms of symbolism and atmosphere than realism. This was actor Laughton's only attempt at directing; although it was criticized at the time for being arty and pretentious, it was probably only ahead of its time. The script, by the noted film critic James Agee, is based on Davis Grubb's novel and has heavy psychological overtones, and works also as a moral allegory about the relations between good and evil, adults and children. But the movie, for all its oddity of style, will stand on fright value alone. The storyline could be compared to Flannery O'Connor's novel **The Violent Bear It Away. Distributed by United Artists 16.   PKK 317**

NIGHTS OF CABIRIA, Italy, 1957/110 min./Federico Fellini/**2, 3, 4, 6b, 8e, 9, 11, 12, 13.** Federico Fellini directs his wife, Guilietta Masina, who beautifully portrays a Roman prostitute who has every reason to give up on life but whose personality and indomitable spirit triumph in the most adverse of circumstances. This film asks questions about the true nature of good and evil, and is best considered in comparison with the Gelsomina figure first introduced in **La Strada**. English subtitles. **Distributed by Brandon. PKK esp. 318**

s **NO HIDING PLACE,** 1963/51 min./Herschel Daugherty/**8b, 8e, 9. Distributed by Carousel/Mass Media.   K 113**

s **NO REASON TO STAY,** 1965/28 min./John Kemeny (producer)/**1, 2, 4, 6a, 7, 8a, 9, 10.** "Why not stay in school?" is candidly answered by the young Christopher Wood, whose totally frustrating experiences in school have given him no reason whatever to stay. And his teachers and guidance counselor can add nothing that will convince him of the value of school. The film makes teachers viewing it cringe, because it says some very incisive and unsettling things about education today. Most impressive about the film is that it centers around a very intelligent young man who simply cannot prostitute his mind any longer in the face of what is daily more and more repellant to him. **Distributed by Contemporary.   K 115; M2 84**

NOBODY WAVED GOODBYE, 1964/80 min./Don Owen/**2, 3, 6a, 8a, 9, 11.** The first feature film by the National Film Board of Canada portrays, in the style of cinema verite, the conflicts of a teen-age boy who has rejected the middle-class values of his surroundings but who is unable to supplant those rejected values with any of his own. Real locations are used and sound is recorded on the spot. **Distributed by Brandon.**

NORTH BY NORTHWEST, 1959/136 min., color/Alfred Hitchcock/**2, 3, 4.** A chain of novel situations and fascinating escapades extends from the UN Building and Grand Central Station in New York to South Dakota's Mt. Rushmore. The film moves along rapidly within one surprise after another with that mixture of tension and sly humor which is the Hitchcock trademark. **Distributed by Brandon/Films, Inc.   PKK 318-319**

NORTHWEST PASSAGE, 1940/126 min., color/King Vidor/**8c, 11, 15.** A film adaptation of the first part of Kenneth Roberts' novel. The remainder was never filmed. Consequently, the northwest passage is hardly mentioned in the film. A classic Western in early Technicolor, starring Spencer Tracy. This film is interesting from several angles: as an adaptation, as an excellent Western, as an early film using color, as a well-directed and acted story, and

PROPERTIES OF FILM		
1. Montage	b) Adaptation from Stage, TV	9. Cinema Verite
2. Camera Angle		10. Introceptive Camera
3. Camera Position	c) Adaptation of Novels, Short Stories, Poems	11. Character Development
4. Camera Movement		12. Transitional Phases
5. Color		13. Visual Symbols
6. Sound:	d) Animation	14. Lighting
a) Natural	e) Social/Moral/ Symbolic Commentary	15. Beauty of Photographic Images
b) Music		
7. Film Devices		16. Highly Visual Subject
8. Categories	f) Pure Film	
a) Documentary		

as an excellent discussion starter on respect for persons and dedication to a cause. **Distributed by Films, Inc.**

s **THE NOSE,** France, 1963/11 min./Alexander Alexeieff & Claire Parker/**1, 8c, 8d, 8e.** This subtle cartoon is based on the short story by Nikoli Gogol and tells the story of a man whose nose escapes. It is captured in a dream, and a struggle ensues to make it stay on the man's face. Surprising elements throughout the short film need to be noted and perhaps prepared for by a pre-reading of Gogol's story. **Distributed by Contemporary. K 119**

NOTHING BUT A MAN, 1963/92 min./Michael Roemer/**9, 14, 11, 10, 4, 12.** Independent film-makers Michael Roemer and Robert Young have made a distinguished and moving drama of the personal struggle of a Southern Negro and his wife in a society hostile to them, especially since he refuses to play the role expected of a Negro in Alabama today. The very fact of its being produced independently may be responsible for the starkly simple and, therefore, poignantly effective presentation of Negroes who face problems in recognizable settings. The film earned two awards at the Venice International Film Festival, 1964, and the National Council of Churches Award in 1965. **Distributed by Brandon.**

THE NUN'S STORY, 1959/154 min./Fred Zinnemann/**2, 3, 4, 5, 8c, 9, 11, 13.** Excellent use of color, sound and subjective camera, as well as outstanding acting make the film a good example of novel adaptation. Much visual symbolism and careful and effective camera movement are complimented by music by Franz Waxman. Traditionalists may object to the obvious departures from the original novel by Kathryn Hulme. The early convent scenes are slow-moving but lovingly detailed, and help give the final half of the film a tremendous moral wallop. It is one of the few films primarily about an interior moral struggle. The nun is convincingly played by Audrey Hepburn. **Distributed by United Artists 16.**

s **AN OCCURRENCE AT OWL CREEK BRIDGE,** France, 1962/27 min./Robert Enrico/**1, 2, 3, 4, 6a, 6b, 7, 8c, 9, 10, 11, 13, 15.** Robert Enrico's rendering of Ambrose Bierce's story of a man about to be hung during the American Civil War makes a strong statement about death, concentrating as it does on man's strong will to live. More subtly, the film is a statement about war, that matrix where deaths take place merely as "occurrences." The film provides an excellent opportunity for cross-media analysis (short-story to film) and is a good example of the film's "subjective" view of time. **Distributed by Contemporary/Mass Media.**   **K 121; M55**

OCTOBER, U.S.S.R., 1928/68 min./Sergei Eisenstein & Grigari Alexandrov/**1, 2, 3, 8a.** A reconstruction of the events which culminated in the Russian Revolution of October 1917. Eisenstein used the actual locations and many actual participants in the event. The classic, however, is not strictly speaking a documentary as much as it is a powerful use of fact for emotional impact. Also called TEN DAYS THAT SHOOK THE WORLD. **Distributed by Brandon/Museum of Modern Art.**

s **OF STARS AND MEN,** 1961/53 min., color/John & Faith Hubley/**5, 8c, 8d, 8e, 12.** An interesting and appealing approach to the reality of the universe and its greatness, this animated cartoon also looks at man as the king of the universe. It poses, to man himself, the question: Where is it all leading, and just what is man's place, as king, in this whole complex? **Distributed by Brandon.   K 123**

s **OF TIME, WORK, AND LEISURE,** 1963/29 min./Ralph J. Tangney/ **1, 6a, 7, 8a, 8b, 13. Distributed by Indiana University/Mass Media. K 125**

OKLAHOMA!, 1955/140 min./Fred Zinnemann/**2, 6, 8b.** Love and rivalry of a generation ago is unfolded in a zestful Rodgers and Hammerstein musical. Its philosophy is now a part of Americana. The use of the new Todd-AO process with a soundtrack nearly unequalled in film history help to create spectacular effects. A good illustration of the film's versatility as opposed to stage presentation—dance routines, two horse runaway, and scene changes. Compare to Coppola's direction of **Finian's Rainbow** (1968). Contrast to the film version of **The Music Man** which, as some critics stress, could have been filmed on stage up to its final scene of the street parade. **Distributed by Audio/Trans-World.**

THE OLD MAN AND THE SEA, 1958/86 min./John Sturges/**8c, 8e, 9, 11, 15.** In Hemingway's novel, the old man forces himself to face the larger dimensions of life as symbolized in his quest for the fish. The book operates on many levels: that of spiritually achieving one's identity in the face of evil forces, that of psychologically fulfilling one's vocation in life even when others would excuse you, and that of creatively appreciating all the elements of life in order to find a unity and coherence in the world. Unfortunately, the film doesn't manifest all these dimensions. The spoken interior monologue of the film weakens the action which should have been expressed graphically rather than verbally. A discussion might center around seeing the book in itself, the movie in itself, and questioning whether it is really necessary to compare them. In what way is a film an autonomous work of art? **Presently not available for distribution.**

PROPERTIES OF FILM

1. Montage	b) Adaptation from Stage, TV	9. Cinema Verite
2. Camera Angle		10. Introceptive Camera
3. Camera Position	c) Adaptation of Novels, Short Stories, Poems	11. Character Development
4. Camera Movement		12. Transitional Phases
5. Color		13. Visual Symbols
6. Sound:	d) Animation	14. Lighting
a) Natural	e) Social/Moral/ Symbolic Commentary	15. Beauty of Photographic Images
b) Music		16. Highly Visual Subject
7. Film Devices		
8. Categories	f) Pure Film	
a) Documentary		

s **OLYMPIC GAMES 1936,** 1936/Leni Riefenstahl/**2, 3, 4, 8a, 14, 16. Distributed by Museum of Modern Art.**

ON THE WATERFRONT, 1954/108 min./Elia Kazan/**2, 3, 6a, 6b, 8c, 9, 11.** Heroism is not a popular topic for Hollywood when the hero must admit his limitations as a man. A priest represents more than his individual personality reveals and, therefore, unlike the Bing Crosby sweetness and light portrayal, the development of a priest in a film must be delicately handled because of the preconceived notions of the audience. In this film from Budd Schulberg's novel, theatrical techniques add to the natural surroundings of the waterfront to make this film rewarding. The portrayal of the priest, however, especially over Duggan's body in the hole, never quite comes off because a dogmatic caricature cannot replace a sincere spontaneous response. Nevertheless, the acting of Brando, Eva Marie Saint, Rod Steiger and Lee Cobb makes this movie worth seeing. Brando especially displays the better fruits of "method acting." (See the discussion following Chapter Four.) **Distributed by Audio/Brandon/Contemporary/Institutional Cinema/Modern Sound/Pictura/Swank/Trans-World/Twyman.   PK esp. 41-48**

s **ONE OF THEM IS BRETT,** 1964/30 min./Derrick Knight/**8a, 8e, 9, 16. Distributed by Contemporary.   M2 85**

OTHELLO, 1955/92 min./Orson Welles/**4, 8b, 10.** Welles produced, directed and acted in this adaptation from Shakespeare. Unsuccessful efforts were made to let the camera move and help the actors project their character. Somehow, it is still a film to be seen as a study of the art of adaptation. **Distributed by Contemporary.   PKK 173-175**

THE OVERCOAT, U.S.S.R., 1953/73 min./Alexi Batalov/**1, 3, 4, 7, 8c, 10, 11, 12, 14, 16.** This is the famous Nicolai Gogol story in a new screen version remarkably faithful to the author's vision, with the added dimension of a creative cinematic imagination. Acting and direction are superb, and camera work adds intensity to the portrayal of the pathetic little clerk in a grotesquely cruel world, whose new overcoat changes his destiny. English subtitles. **Distributed by Contemporary.**

THE OX-BOW INCIDENT, 1943/75 min./William Wellman/**2, 4, 8c, 11, 13, 15.** One of the victims in this film writes to his wife, "Law is a lot more than words you put in a book, or judges or lawyers or sheriffs you hire to carry it out. It is everything people have found out about justice and what's right and what's wrong. It's the very conscience of humanity." Every community needs such a conscience in order to evaluate the truth and not act hastily. This carefully constructed Western, in which even the weather is expressive, juxtaposes action with brooding still shots as Major Tetley, Jeff Farnley, and Marty Smith oppose Davies and Sparks. From the novel by Walter Van Tilburg Clark. A discussion might center on the notion of a Western parable. **Distributed by Brandon/Films, Inc.   PKK esp. 328**

s **PACIFIC 231,** France/10 min./**1, 2, 3, 4, 6a, 6b, 7, 8f, 9, 15, 16.** This winner of a Cannes editing award, called by its makers an "essay", is a kind of visual poem. A train ride, from the time the engine is taken from the roundhouse until the train arrives at its destination, is seen against a musical composition by Arthur Honegger. There is no narration. **Distributed by Audio/Contemporary.**

s **PADDLE TO THE SEA,** 1966/28 min., color/**2, 3, 4, 8e, 16. Distributed by Contemporary.   M2 104**

s **PARABLE,** 1964/22 min., color/Tom Rook & Rolf Forsberg/**2, 3, 4, 5, 6b, 8e, 11, 12, 13, 14, 15, 16.** A controversial film depicting in vivid symbolism the role of the true Christian today, the **PARABLE** is not at all subtle in presenting its message. A clown takes upon himself the suffering of minority personalities and is, in the end, murdered. But his murderer reacts by taking up the grease paint and becoming a clown himself. **Distributed by Protestant Council of Churches/Contemporary.   M 57**

s **PATTERNS OF THE MIND,** 1964/27 min./Board of Parish Education, Lutheran Church in America/**8a. Distributed by Mass Media Ministries. M2 88**

THE PAWNBROKER, 1964/119 min./Sidney Lumet/**10, 11, 14, 16.** The pawnbroker, brilliantly played by Rod Steiger, learns the necessity of involvement with mankind. Based on the novel by Edward Lewis Wallant. The Catholic Legion of Decency gave a "condemned" rating to a brief scene in which a prostitute exposes her breasts. The better reviews include TIME, April 23; SATURDAY REVIEW, April 3; NEW YORK TIMES, April 21, all in 1965. The early review was in VARIETY, July 8, 1964. **Distributed by Audio.   PKK esp. 160-161**

THE PEARL, Mexico, 1947/77 min./**11, 14, 16.** English subtitles. **Distributed by Brandon/Creative Film Society.**

PERSONA, Sweden, 1965/Ingmar Bergman/**1, 2, 3, 4, 7, 8e, 10, 11, 12, 13, 14, 15, 16.** English subtitles. **Distributed by Janus Films.   PKK 171-172; F 18-21; 194-200**

PHILADELPHIA STORY, 1940/112 min./George Cukor/**2, 4, 7, 11. Distributed by Films, Inc.**

PROPERTIES OF FILM		
1. Montage	b) Adaptation from Stage, TV	9. Cinema Verite
2. Camera Angle		10. Introceptive Camera
3. Camera Position	c) Adaptation of Novels, Short Stories, Poems	11. Character Development
4. Camera Movement		12. Transitional Phases
5. Color		13. Visual Symbols
6. Sound:	d) Animation	14. Lighting
a) Natural	e) Social/Moral/ Symbolic Commentary	15. Beauty of Photographic Images
b) Music		16. Highly Visual Subject
7. Film Devices		
8. Categories	f) Pure Film	
a) Documentary		

s **PHOEBE,** 1964/28 min./George Kaczender/**1, 8e, 9, 11, 4, 7, 10, 14.**
The story here attempts to explore the mind of a teen-age girl who realizes
she's pregnant. She is afraid and confused; how can she tell people about it.
Phoebe cannot tell Paul, her boy friend, nor can she face her parents with
the truth. She visualizes several possible reactions on the part of Paul, her
parents, the principal at her school. There is no opening for the human and
personal communication she so urgently needs in this painful moment of
truth. **Distributed by Contemporary/McGraw-Hill/Mass Media.**   **K 129;
M2 90**

s **PHYLLIS AND TERRY,** 1965/35 min./Eugene & Carol Marner/**2, 3,
4, 8a, 9, 16.** New York's Lower East Side viewed with two Negro teenage
girls. For adults, although a good teacher could probably try to bridge the
film's subtle touch and use it with high schoolers. Poor sound and some
technical errors do not keep this from being a fine on-the-spot and impro-
vised documentary. **Distributed by Center for Mass Communications.**

A PLACE IN THE SUN, 1951/120 min./George Stevens/**2, 3, 4, 6a, 6b,
8c, 10, 11, 12, 13, 15.** Based upon Theodore Dreiser's **An American Tragedy.**
Montgomery Clift plays the young man anxious to get ahead in the world;
Elizabeth Taylor plays the girl who embodies all that the young man
aspires to; Shelly Winters is the girl who gets in the way. A searing social
critique is turned into personal romantic tragedy, but some of Dreiser's bite
remains. The careful control and building of atmosphere is masterful. **Distributed by Films, Inc.**   **PKK 331-332**

THE POISONED AIR, 1966/50 min./CBS-TV/**2, 8a, 9, 16.** Well-documented and narrated treatment of the big-city problem. Satire and humor
comparable to that in **Sixteen In Webster Groves.** As with most documentaries on such challenges, the conclusion is that personal involvement is
needed. Cinematically excellent. **Distributed by Carousel Films.**

POTEMKIN (THE BATTLESHIP), U.S.S.R., 1925/67 min./Sergei Eisen-
stein/**1, 3, 7, 8a, 9, 10, 12, 14.** Directed by the master film artist, Sergei
Eisenstein, this is the complete version of the most famous of Russian films,
which recreates the spirit of the 1905 revolution through the depiction of
just one of its incidents. It introduced a new film technique, providing a
newly conscious conception of the manipulation of film materials to communicate physical sensation. Its influence on subsequent film-making has
been second to none. The "Odessa Steps" sequence is often screened as a
separate film and is available as a ten-minute film. Sound has been added
to the original silent film. **Distributed by Brandon/Museum of Modern Art.**
PKK esp. 333-334, 357-358

THE PRISONER OF ZENDA, 1937/101 min./John Cromwell/**2, 3.** Compare this Douglas Fairbanks and Ronald Coleman classic to the 1952
version, available from Films, Inc. **Distributed by Creative Film Society.**

PSYCHO, 1960/109 min./Alfred Hitchcock/**2, 3, 6a, 14.** Hitchcock is at
his bizarre best with this film of a psychological problem between a young

boy, his mother, and a pretty girl who happens off the main highway on a rainy night and checks in at an off-beat motel. From a novel by Robert Bloch, it is one of the first films to deal with a psychopathic problem in a horror film context. It is no doubt one of the most frightening films ever made. This film provides an excellent example of the Hitchcock style of camera direction. It also demonstrates first-rate use of sound and visual atmosphere. It is a strong film, and one for mature audiences. **Distributed by Brandon.**

s **THE PUSHER,** Yugoslavia, 1962/17 min./Ante Babaja/**8e, 10, 11, 13.** There's always got to be an underdog. People are born pushing, and they continue all their lives pushing the top dog away in a vain struggle to make it themselves. This film, stylized and allegorical, tells the simple story of two boys, born at the same time, growing up in competition, with the stronger of the two exercising the pushing technique so successfully that he wins his teacher's favor, his brother's girl, and finally his brother's position. The underdog at this point enrolls in a pushing class, and results take the natural course. **Distributed by Brandon/Mass Media.   K 133**

QUEEN ELIZABETH, United Kingdom, 1938/70 min. **Distributed by Film Classic Exchange.**

THE QUIET ONE, 1948/67 min./Sidney Meyers/**3, 4, 7, 8a, 8e, 9, 10, 11, 14, 16.** A fatherless boy, Donald, is the chief character in this story of the wreckage that results from the horror of ghetto living. Most of the film takes place in the Wiltwyck School for boys, and focuses on Donald and his inability to make meaningful contact with much of his environment. Donald's is a disturbing plight, but one which must be brought as forcefully as possible to the attention of today's society. **Distributed by Association/ Audio/Brandon/Contemporary.   M2 91**

A RAISIN IN THE SUN, 1961/100 min./Daniel Petrie/**2, 3, 8b, 11.** Lorraine Hansberry's poignant drama concerns a Negro family in the ghetto of Chicago trying to find itself in a world that is rapidly changing. Each person in the film has to find some type of love and self-fulfillment. Mama's basic values are the touchstone for finding happiness while moving into a white residential neighborhood. Ruby Dee, Claudia McNeil, and Sidney Poitier are outstanding. As in **The Diary of Anne Frank,** the camera limits

---

PROPERTIES OF FILM

1. Montage
2. Camera Angle
3. Camera Position
4. Camera Movement
5. Color
6. Sound:
   a) Natural
   b) Music
7. Film Devices
8. Categories
   a) Documentary

b) Adaptation from Stage, TV
c) Adaptation of Novels, Short Stories, Poems
d) Animation
e) Social/Moral/ Symbolic Commentary
f) Pure Film

9. Cinema Verite
10. Introceptive Camera
11. Character Development
12. Transitional Phases
13. Visual Symbols
14. Lighting
15. Beauty of Photographic Images
16. Highly Visual Subject

itself to the apartment; nevertheless, each character develops with dignity and honesty. The whole world of suffering and seeking maturity is focused on this one apartment. **Distributed by Brandon/Contemporary/Institutional Cinema/Twyman.**

REBEL WITHOUT A CAUSE, 1955/111min./Nicholas Ray/**2, 3, 4, 5, 6a, 8c, 11.** "What makes Jimmy Dean run?" The question is unresolved by this Academy Award nominee story of an alienated adolescent whose ever-loving girlfriend (Natalie Wood) tries to bring a glimmer of hope into his life. The story is open-ended, but the portrayal of the parents is rather saccharine. It is one of the first portrayals of delinquents coming from the rich man's environment. The film would provide an interesting discussion in comparison with **Loneliness of the Long Distance Runner, 400 Blows, Nobody Waved Goodbye,** or contrasted to **West Side Story.** Based on the book **Children of the Dark** by Irving Schulman. **Distributed by Swank/Trans-World.**

s **THE RED BALLOON,** France, 1956/34 min./Albert Lamorisse/**2, 3, 4, 5, 8e, 9, 12, 13, 15, 16.** One of the most beautiful of the modern short films, **RED BALLOON** tells its story with no dialogue, unobtrusive music, and one brilliant and sustained spot of color, the red of the balloon itself, which stands out sharply against the drab and dreary remainder of the little boy's day. A tender friendship grows between the little boy, played eloquently by Pascal Lamorisse, and a huge red balloon. But this idyllic life is immediately burst upon by a gang of street urchins, and is eventually destroyed when this same gang captures and kills the balloon. But the film's conclusion tells more about the boy and his balloon than the mere first-glance happy ending. **Distributed by Brandon/Roa.   K 137, M 93**

RED DESERT, Italy, 1964/116 min., color/M. Antonioni/**2, 3, 4, 5, 6a, 7, 8e, 9, 11, 13, 14, 15, 16.** Discussion could center on how Fellini's first use of color **(Juliet of the Spirits)** compares to this first color film of Antonioni. An appropriate short to accompany this if the approach is to be the storyline of the film would be **Assembly Line.** In both films, lonely people seek escape from the noise and depression of an industrial environment. English subtitles. **Distributed by Audio.   PKK esp. 23-25**

s **THE RED KITE,** 1966/17 min., color/**8c, 8e, 9, 10, 11, 13, 15.** This film tells of a man and his attempt to find meaning in this life. He observes different individuals and their apathetic or defeatist commentaries on the emptiness of life, and experiences the moment of truth in which he has to admit that his life has empty moments also. A trip to a windy hill for kite flying with his little daughter helped restore his faith and put a new perspective into his life. The film presents its message clearly, but not offensively. **Distributed by Contemporary/Mass Media/Roa.   M2 92**

REQUIEM FOR A HEAVYWEIGHT, 1962/85 min./Ralph Nelson/**1, 2, 3, 4, 7, 8b, 9, 11.** The problem of a man desperately seeking to retain his innate decency in an unfamiliar and hostile world becomes a trenchant indictment of the corrupt world of boxing. Based on the television play by Rod Serling, **REQUIEM** reflects the stark realism of the lower levels of the sporting world with its cheap hotels, dingy bars, and dirty streets, while graphically showing the plight of a decent man cut adrift from the only life he knows. The acting by Anthony Quinn, Jackie Gleason, Mickey Rooney, and Julie Harris is outstanding, and Ralph Nelson's direction makes effective use of camera techniques in the dressing room and ring sequences. **Distributed by Audio/Brandon/Contemporary/Institutional Cinema/Trans-World/Twyman.**

s   **RIEN QUE LES HEURES,** France, 1926/45 min./Alberto Cavalcanti/**9, 3, 4.** An impressionistic look at the commonplace man and life in Paris. Cavalcanti presents a social commentary of city life, even when setting up painting-like shots of the everyday scenes of Paris. Suitable for adult audiences. **Distributed by Museum of Modern Art.**

RIFIFI, France, 1956/116 min./Jules Dassin/**9, 1, 2, 3, 6a, 7, 8c, 10, 11, 16.** Success can kill you, a small-time crook learns in this Gallic version of Chicago gangster films. For the twenty-seven minutes it takes to cop the contents of a jeweler's safe, not a word is spoken. There is only the sound of men working—as skillfully and delicately as surgeons. The tension grows in the audience as it does in the actors during one of film history's most celebrated crimes. This is the grand-daddy of the modern caper films. From a novel by Auguste le Breton. Available subtitled or dubbed. **Distributed by Audio.**   **PKK esp. 338-339**

s   **THE RIVER,** 1937/30 min./Pare Lorentz/**1, 6, 8a, 9, 15.** This classic American documentary, written and directed by Pare Lorentz, with music by Virgil Thompson, gives a panoramic and historical view of the Mississippi River Valley. The film traces the relationship of the river to agricultural and industrial expansion, emphasizing man's exploitation of the river and nature's retribution. An epilog presents recent responsible approaches to the river: flood and erosion control, especially that effected by the TVA. **Distributed by Brandon.**

ROMAN HOLIDAY, 1953/119 min./William Wyler/**11, 12, 13.** A blend of high comedy with deeper emotional overtones in a modern fairytale about a princess who breaks through protocol for an unsupervised day on

PROPERTIES OF FILM		
1. Montage	b) Adaptation from Stage, TV	9. Cinema Verite
2. Camera Angle		10. Introceptive Camera
3. Camera Position	c) Adaptation of Novels, Short Stories, Poems	11. Character Development
4. Camera Movement		12. Transitional Phases
5. Color		13. Visual Symbols
6. Sound:	d) Animation	14. Lighting
a) Natural	e) Social/Moral/ Symbolic Commentary	15. Beauty of Photographic Images
b) Music		
7. Film Devices		
8. Categories		16. Highly Visual Subject
a) Documentary	f) Pure Film	

the town. The script draws fine contrasts between the stiff elaborate royal palace and the eternal city of Rome with its color and lights and humanness. **Distributed by Brandon/Films, Inc.**

ROME: AN OPEN CITY, Italy, 1946/103 min./Roberto Rossellini/**2, 3, 6a, 9.** Roberto Rossellini's story of underground resistance during the final phase of the German occupation of Rome, filmed on the streets of the city and utilizing many non-professional actors, marks the birth of Neo-realism, a new cinematic style which was to change the whole direction of Italian and, eventually, world cinema. **Distributed by Contemporary.   PKK esp. 324**

s **RUN!,** 1965/16 min./Jack Kuper/**1, 3, 4, 6b, 7, 8e, 9, 10, 12.** A symbolic interpretation of man's ability to bury himself in his haste to go and do, this film demands attention. It employs rapid cutting, judicious editing, and a raccous sound track which intensifies the effect. The running man tramples people, destroys things, and finally buries himself. **Distributed by Brandon/Mass Media.   K 139**

s **RUNNER,** 1962/12 min./Don Owen/**8c, 16, 2, 3, 4, 7, 15.** The film pictures and discusses Bruce Kidd, Toronto's long-distance runner. With excellent photography and the beautifully flowing lines of poetry by W. H. Auden, it, like **Dancer's World,** celebrates both the magnificent possibilities within the human body and the necessity for discipline and continual effort at perfection. **Distributed by Contemporary.   K 141**

s **SATAN'S CHOICE,** 1967/28 min./Donald Shebib/**4, 6a, 6b, 8a, 8e, 9, 16.** This is the documentary study of modern day rebellion on a motorcycle. "Satan's Choice" is the name of a Toronto motorcycle gang, and shows the reactions of the individual gang members to the staid and secure middle-class values and life patterns they see in their parents and neighbors. They do what they feel like doing, they move on their bikes without anyone "on my back", and they find their meaning in the motorcycles they ride. **Distributed by Contemporary.   K 143**

s **A SCRAP OF PAPER AND A PIECE OF STRING,** 1964/6 min., color/John Korty/**6c, 7, 8f, 13. Distributed by Contemporary.   M 67**

SEVEN BRIDES FOR SEVEN BROTHERS, 1954/103 min., color, cinemascope/Stanley Donen/**1, 2, 3, 4, 5, 6c, 12.** A charming, unpretentious original musical product of the golden age of MGM musicals, **SEVEN BRIDES** is a take-off on the ancient story of the Romans' abduction of the Sabine women, set in frontier Oregon in the 1850's. A family of female-hungry backwoodsmen kidnap seven refined young ladies from town, and in the end are civilized by them. The story is a bit silly and the outdoor backdrops are often painted, but the Johnny Mercer songs and the choreography by Michael Kidd are among the best examples on film. The barn-raising ballet is exhuberant and ingenious, and an expertly edited salute to the arrival of Spring foreshadows some of the best techniques in contemporary musicals. Jane Powell and Howard Keel are the stars; the supporting cast includes many who went on to later stardom, e.g., Jacques D'Amboise, America's leading male ballet dancer. **Distributed by Films, Inc.**

THE SEVEN SAMURAI, Japan, 1954/141 min./Akira Kurosawa/**3, 4, 6, 7, 10, 11, 14, 16.** This film is considered by many to be **the** Japanese film masterpiece. It is a raging, sensuous epic acclaimed as the perfect example of what a Hollywood Western should be. Vigorous editing, an almost devastating use of the camera, and careful use of the many possibilities of light and shadow tell the story of arms and men powerfully. The plot centers around the defense of a 16th century village by seven recruited, professional soldiers who organize the villagers and succeed in wiping out the attacking bandits. Into this basically simple plot, Kurosawa has introduced a profusion of events and subplots aimed at giving each of his characters an intensely distinctive personality. The work as a whole is one of overpowering immediacy. John Sturges' Western **The Magnificent Seven** (1961) was based on this Japanese classic. English subtitles. **Distributed by Audio.**   **PK esp. 107-111**

THE SEVENTH SEAL, Sweden, 1956/96 min./Ingmar Bergman/**3, 4, 6a, 10, 11, 12, 13, 14, 16, 8e.** In a heavily symbolic film, Bergman approaches many of the questions which have been considered by dramatists, novelists and artists for centuries. A crusader returns home during the plague-ridden Middle Ages. He confronts Death (Bengt Ekerot) and plays a chess game with him, a game which will seal not only his fate but the fates of several other people who are accompanying him. The film is accompanied by English subtitles which, depending upon the quality of the print, may or may not be difficult to read. The film demands very much by way of understanding and interpretation, and should not be planned for beginning film students. English subtitles. **Distributed by Janus.**   **PKK esp. 346**

SHANE, 1953/117 min., color/George Stevens/**2, 3, 4, 5, 6a, 6b, 8c, 9, 10, 11, 15, 16.** Jack Schaefer's novel is a compact, controlled portrayal of a mysterious stranger who tries to escape his past but whose past catches up with him as he chooses to defend a family of settlers besieged by a rancher and his ruthless henchmen. George Stevens' movie, a classic among Westerns, apotheosizes the usual insubstantial cliches of the typical Western and is remarkable for the depth of its visual characterizations of all the

---

PROPERTIES OF FILM

1. Montage	b) Adaptation from Stage, TV	9. Cinema Verite
2. Camera Angle		10. Introceptive Camera
3. Camera Position	c) Adaptation of Novels, Short Stories, Poems	11. Character Development
4. Camera Movement		12. Transitional Phases
5. Color		13. Visual Symbols
6. Sound:	d) Animation	14. Lighting
a) Natural	e) Social/Moral/ Symbolic Commentary	15. Beauty of Photographic Images
b) Music		16. Highly Visual Subject
7. Film Devices		
8. Categories	f) Pure Film	
a) Documentary		

figures of the Western myth. (See also Chapter Seven.) **Distributed by Films, Inc.   PKK 347**

s **SHOESTRING,** Italy, 1946/Vittorio De Sica/**9, 16. Distributed by Brandon.**

SHOOT THE PIANO PLAYER, 1961, France/François Truffaut/**1, 2, 3, 4, 6b.** Truffaut's protagonist in this excellent film is the pianist Charles Aznavor, acting out a creation of an unique imagination in whom we recognize something of ourselves as well as Truffaut himself. Life and Fate play on the lives of Charlie and his love (Marie Dubois). The story is sad but compelling. An **Elvira Madigan** type film which recalls other tragic Romeos and Juliets. There are beautiful sensitivities to the rhythm of bodies in love with music integrated so well the two seem one. Adult audiences will discuss the symbols but will experience the mystique of life in an indifferent and unchartered world. **Distributed by Brandon.   PK esp. 189-194**

THE SHOP ON MAIN STREET, Czechoslovakia, 1964/128 min./Jan Kader and Elmar Kes/**2, 6a, 8e, 10. Distributed by Audio.**

THE SILENCE, Sweden, 1963/94 min./Ingmar Bergman/**2, 3, 4, 8e.** Two sisters and a ten-year-old boy find themselves in a hotel in a foreign country. The elder one is seriously ill. The younger tries to break out of all restraints in her quest for sensual satisfaction. One of Bergman's most disturbing films, dark and rather fatalistic. Adult viewing. English subtitles. **Distributed by Janus.**

SINGIN' IN THE RAIN, 1952/102 min., color/Gene Kelly and Stanley Donen/**6b, 16.** See Chapter Seven for a commentary on this classic musical. **Distributed by Contemporary/Films, Inc.   PKK 185, 232, 234**

s **SIXTEEN IN WEBSTER GROVES,** 1966/47 min./Art Barron/**8a, 8e, 9.** Teen-age apathy is attacked in this highly controversial and extremely one-sided view of the 16-year-olds in Webster Groves, a wealthy suburb of St. Louis. Conformity to value structures, life goals which amount to large salaries and a two-car family, and attitudes of status quo, all contribute to make the picture of the 16-year-old mentality a dismal and somewhat disturbing one. This film might be seen back-to-back with **Satan's Choice** for two opposing ways in which young people react to the mores and customs of proper society. **Distributed by Mass Media/Roa.   K 145, M2 93**

s **SKYSCRAPER,** 1959/21 min./Shirley Clark and Willard Van Dyke/**5, 6a.** The black and white recounting of the teamwork and planning involved in the erection of a New York high-rise bursts into color as the completed building comes to life. The film was produced by Shirley Clarke, Irving Jacoby, and Willard Van Dyke, in association with Donn Alan Pennebaker and Wheaton Galentine, script by John White. It was a winner in the Venice Film Festival and the San Francisco International Film Festival 1959. **Distributed by Brandon.**

s THE SMALLEST ELEPHANT IN THE WORLD, 1964/6 min., color/NBC-TV/**5, 16. Distributed by Sterling.   M 69**

s THE SMILE, France, 1963/18 min., color/Serge Bourguignon/**2, 5, 8e, 9, 11, 15.** This quiet, simple story of a Buddhist monk and his apprentice looks at the beauty of life around us and effect this beauty has on the person who will stop and notice it. The film, made by the artist of **Sundays and Cybele,** employs vivid color and careful composition as it takes the viewer into the same world of wonder which the young 12-year-old novice is beginning to experience for the first time. **Distributed by Contemporary. K 147, M2 94**

s SMOKING AND YOU, United Kingdom, 1965/11 min., color/**8e. Distributed by Contemporary.   K 149, M 70**

s SO THAT MEN ARE FREE, 1962/27 min./CBS-TV/**8a. Distributed by McGraw-Hill.   M2 95**

STALAG 17, 1952/120 min./Billy Wilder/**2, 3, 4, 8b, 10, 11, 16.** See Chapter Four for a commentary on this film as an execellent example of adaptation from a stage play. **Distributed by Films, Inc.   PKK esp. 349**

STATE OF THE UNION, 1948/124 min./Frank Capra/**8e, 10. Distributed by Contemporary/United World.**

STOWAWAY IN THE SKY, France, 1962/100 min./Albert Lamorisse/**2, 3, 4, 5, 6a, 6b, 9, 15, 16.** An exquisite film by the maker of **The Red Balloon,** this whimsical comedy takes viewers on a completely fresh, exhilarating, and poetic serial balloon tour of France with a little boy and his wise grandfather. The visuals (actually shot from a helicopter) are magnificent, the manipulation of natural sound and music perhaps even better. The sights range from unique shots of Paris, sea and countryside to a forest fire, diving parachutists, and French cowboys driving cattle. But most memorable are flamingos winging over the Mediterranean and a high-speed stag hunt taken from tree-top level. A minor cinematic masterpiece that will delight every age. **Presently not available for U. S. distribution.**

LA STRADA, Italy, 1954/107 min./Federico Fellini/**3, 6b, 8e, 9, 10, 11,**

PROPERTIES OF FILM		
1. Montage	b) Adaptation from Stage, TV	9. Cinema Verite
2. Camera Angle		10. Introceptive Camera
3. Camera Position	c) Adaptation of Novels, Short Stories, Poems	11. Character Development
4. Camera Movement		12. Transitional Phases
5. Color		13. Visual Symbols
6. Sound:	d) Animation	14. Lighting
a) Natural	e) Social/Moral/ Symbolic Commentary	15. Beauty of Photographic Images
b) Music		16. Highly Visual Subject
7. Film Devices	f) Pure Film	
8. Categories		
a) Documentary		

13. For Zampano, life is a road, and life is the sky. This film is a modern morality play concerning the human condition where one must find a way to live out one's existence. A lovable waif, Gelsomina, becomes a traveling companion with a circus performer, Zampano, who often mistreats her. The changing scenery and the visual richness of the film serve to isolate the tender face of Gelsomina. She learns to play a trumpet, a saving factor in her life. Zampano is content to walk around in circles and repeat formulas while he attempts to break the chains which surround his body. The musical score by Nino Rota provides a moving continuity similar to the graphic continuity of the roads. The story progresses very carefully from Gelsomina's innocence to her encounter with religion, to a realization of Zampano's cruelty, to the discovery of the Fool's death, to an insight into love, and to the final emptiness by the lonely sea. It would be an injustice to this film masterpiece to view it only once. See Chapter Nine. Available subtitled or dubbed. **Distributed by Brandon.**   **PKK 318, 351**

STRANGE VICTORY, 1964/77 min./L. Hurwitz/**6a, 7, 8a, 8e.** This film, part one of which was completed in 1948 and part two in 1964, is a documentary with the thesis that the end of World War II and the defeat of Fascism brought after it a strange victory. In this "victory", the poison of racial bigotry and hatred exist into present day. Fast-cut shots and a newsreel effect force the viewer to look at the oppression of the Negro and Jewish people in a forceful and courageous manner. **Distributed by Brandon.**

STRAY DOG, Japan, 1949/122 min./Akira Kurosawa/**4, 11, 13.** Visual commentary is made on the social life of postwar Tokyo in a Japanese version of the detective-in-pursuit. English subtitles. **Distributed by Brandon.**

s **STRESS,** 1967/30 min./Derrick Knight & Partners, Ltd./**6a, 8a, 9, 10, 16.** A sensitive non-sentimental look-in on parents with their handicapped child. **Distributed by Contemporary.**

s **THE STRING BEAN,** France, 1964/17 min., color & black & white/ Edmond Sechan and Marie Marc/**2, 3, 4, 5, 8e, 8f, 9, 13, 14, 15, 16.** An old woman finds a flowerpot and plants a single bean in it. She nurses it as it grows, cares for it lovingly, and finally replants it amid a patch of flowers in the local park. But, before her eyes, the gardeners, having discovered the plant, pull it up. The old woman plucks a few beans, takes the seeds, and begins new plants in the old flowerpot. Like Sechan's **The Golden Fish,** the film is quietly beautiful and tells its story simply, leaving to the viewer the interpretation and the depth of meaning awaiting discovery. **Distributed by Contemporary/Mass Media/Roa.**   **K 151, M 72**

SUNDAYS AND CYBELE, France, 1962/110 min./Serge Bourguignon/ **2, 3, 8e, 9, 10, 11, 13, 15.** What better gift could a girl give her boy-friend than her name? A name is symbolic of a person's total self, especially if the name has nuances of a legendary goddess (Cybele) and a description **(si belle).** This movie is extraordinary in the charming and overwhelming personality of Patricia Gozzi, who can appear at times as if she were 12, and at times as if she were 24. As a young school girl, Cybele meets an ex-pilot suffering from amnesia. The camera sees the world of Cybele and the ex-pilot from different perspectives: from a distance across a lake, through an upturned champagne glass, from the top of a church steeple. The French are not afraid to treat the beauty, the joy, the tragedy of love. English subtitles. **Distributed by Columbia Cinematheque.**

s **SUNDAY LARK**, 1964/11½ min./Sanford Semel/**2, 3, 4, 8e, 16.** A little girl spends twenty minutes in an empty office building one Sunday afternoon. Her childish play is all in the area of discovery and experimentation, but her activities are noticed and the police descend upon the building. The conclusion of the film is a telling and rather emphatic commentary on modern day value structures. **Distributed by Contemporary/Mass Media. K 153**

SUNSET BOULEVARD, 1950/110 min./Billy Wilder/**2, 3, 11, 12.** The silent films were popular, among other reasons, because the actors and actresses had expressive faces. Emil Jannings, Charlie Chaplin, Greta Garbo, and Gloria Swanson were among those who captured their audiences. In this film, Gloria Swanson, as an aging Hollywood actress, attempts a comeback in a world that does not need her talents. When the real world and the imaginary one meet, everyone is involved in the tragedy. The value of this film is to witness a magnificent actress who bridges the silent and modern era of film. It is also a particularly acid, beautifully written view of Hollywood from its inside. **Distributed by Brandon/Films, Inc.   PKK 354-355**

SWEET AND SOUR, France, 1963/93 min./Jacques Baratier/**2, 3, 4, 7, 14, 15, 16.** A highly visual improvisation on experimental film and their makers. English subtitles. **Distributed by Contemporary.**

TALES OF TERROR, 1962/90 min./Roger Corman/**5, 6a, 7, 8c, 14.** Freely adapted from a set of Poe's short stories, **TALES** display Peter Lorre, Vincent Price and Basil Rathbone in an attempted revival of their former glories in horror land. A how-not-to example of effects out of context. Compare to earlier thrillers of these past masters. Screams and goosepimples dubbed in. **Distributed by Brandon.**

A TASTE OF HONEY, United Kingdom, 1962/100 min./Tony Richard-

PROPERTIES OF FILM		
1. Montage	b) Adaptation from Stage, TV	9. Cinema Verite
2. Camera Angle		10. Introceptive Camera
3. Camera Position	c) Adaptation of Novels, Short Stories, Poems	11. Character Development
4. Camera Movement		12. Transitional Phases
5. Color		13. Visual Symbols
6. Sound:	d) Animation	14. Lighting
a) Natural	e) Social/Moral/ Symbolic Commentary	15. Beauty of Photographic Images
b) Music		
7. Film Devices		16. Highly Visual Subject
8. Categories	f) Pure Film	
a) Documentary		

son/**2, 3, 8b, 9, 11, 13.** Honey isn't always sweet. The film **A TASTE OF HONEY** proves it. Shelagh Delaney (age 18) wrote the original play, a story of a girl's longing for a loving relationship and her fears when the Negro sailor who has befriended her sails off, leaving her with the fear that a child soon to be born will be black. The subject matter is honestly but delicately handled, and visually, the film ends on a poignant note of hope. Compare to **A Patch of Blue** and contrast with **Guess Who's Coming to Dinner** and the play **The Great White Hope. Distributed by Contemporary/Continental 16.**

s **THE TENDER GAME,** 1958/7 min., color/John Hubley/**6b, 8d, 5, 7, 8b, 13.** The boy-meets-girl theme is presented in an interesting and delightful cartoon with background music (Ella Fitzgerald's "Tenderly,") strengthening the effect. **Distributed by Brandon/Contemporary.   K 155**

THAT MAN FROM RIO, France, 1964/114 min./Philippe DeBroca/**2, 3, 5, 6b, 9, 15, 16.** This affectionate New Wave spoof of old adventure movies is probably the best of the dozens of super-hero satires produced during the 1960's. Always in good taste, it is not so much anti-heroic as a kind of paean to the indomitable hero of everyone's childhood, presented in the form of comedy. Jean-Paul Belmondo pursues a stolen pagan idol and his kidnapped girlfriend from Paris to the jungles of Brazil. The film has one of the funniest barroom brawls ever staged, and the outdoor shooting in Brazil, especially in the capital city of Brasilia, is fantastic. In content deal for teen-age audiences, **RIO** is also a virtual repertoire of cinematic techniques. **Distributed by United Artists 16.**

s **THAT'S ME,** 1964/15 min./Walker Stuart/**9, 11, 8a.** A thoroughly funny film that tickles you into an illuminating awareness of yourself as a member of corporate society, a society whose consensus ethic has crushed individualism. This is revealed through dialogue of a social worker with a Puerto Rican dropout (artfully portrayed by Alan Arkin). **Distributed by Contemporary/Mass Media.   K 157**

THEY CAME TO CORDURA, 1959/123 min., color/Robert Rossen/**2, 3, 5, 8e, 11, 16.** Gary Cooper, Van Heflin and Rita Hayworth star in this too little known drama. Many Western elements. Highly visual situations and several obvious Christ-symbols throughout. **Distributed by Brandon/Modern Sound/Twyman/Trans-World.**

A THOUSAND CLOWNS, 1965/105 min./Fred Coe/**3, 4, 7, 8b, 11, 13.** Jason Robards repeats his stage role in this screen version of the play, the story of a man whose enormous love for life is only equalled by his hatred of conformity and routine. The camera captures the mood with freewheeling cuts and motion changes, and the characters of Murray and his nephew are indelibly and joyfully established. The visit by the two social workers is nearly a classic in presenting statement through understatement. Discuss comparisons with **Zorba the Greek, Marty** and **The Odd Couple. Distributed by United Artists 16.**

s   **A THOUSAND DAYS,** 1964/25 min./Alan Landsburg/**8a, 9, 10, 11, 12.** This film presents, in newsreel fashion, many of the key situations which are a part of the history of the man we know as JFK. Throughout the 25 minutes of the film, the viewer notices a kind of Kennedy exuberance in the manner of portrayal and, almost, in the selections and editing of these scenes. In addition to being an inspiring study, the film is also a good piece of cinema, and one well worth employing at any grade level in high school. **Distributed by David Wolper Productions.   K 159**

s   **THURSDAY'S CHILDREN,** United Kingdom, 1952/22 min./Guy Brenton and Lindsay Anderson/**6a, 8a, 8e, 9.** This documentary on the work of the teachers in the Margate School for the Deaf in England might well be used as an emphasis after a screening and study of **Helen Keller in Her Story.** It presents the difficulty encountered by children trapped from the world by the wall of deafness. Richard Burton narrates this film, which is not an easy one for immature groups, but which, with preparation and understanding, can be most effective in promoting both a sympathy for the non-hearing population and a heightened appreciation of the gift of hearing which so many of us enjoy but take for granted. **Distributed by Contemporary.   K 161**

s   **A TIME FOR BURNING,** 1966/58 min./William C. Jersey and Barbara Connell/**8a, 8e, 9, 10, 1, 2, 3, 4, 7.** In good cinema and careful documentation, this film presents the ugly truth about self-satisfied Christianity, American style. A pastor tries to bridge the gap existing between his unaware and complacent white parish and the reality of other human beings whose race has somewhat put them out of the accepted society. Set in Omaha, Nebraska, **A TIME FOR BURNING** shows the struggle between a man who sees his duty and a parish which knows only the cry, "You want everything too fast." And the film also presents one man's struggle to remain optimistic in the face of apathy and hypocrisy. In the end, the pastor cannot sacrifice his own integrity nor the truth of universal human dignity, so he resigns his office. The film is most powerful because it is so true. **Distributed by Contemporary/Mass Media.   K 163**

s   **TIME OF THE LOCUST,** 1966/12 min./Peter Gessner/**6a, 7, 8a.** This film is a blunt, somewhat awkward attempt to probe the consciences of the American public with regard to the present Vietnam conflict. It presents

PROPERTIES OF FILM		
1. Montage	b) Adaptation from Stage, TV	9. Cinema Verite
2. Camera Angle		10. Introceptive Camera
3. Camera Position	c) Adaptation of Novels, Short Stories, Poems	11. Character Development
4. Camera Movement		12. Transitional Phases
5. Color		13. Visual Symbols

6. Sound:
   a) Natural
   b) Music
	d) Animation	14. Lighting

7. Film Devices	e) Social/Moral/ Symbolic Commentary	15. Beauty of Photographic Images
8. Categories a) Documentary	f) Pure Film	16. Highly Visual Subject

war activities, with little discrimination between the individuals doing the acting: tormenting prisoners or executing them, building shelters and prisoner traps, extorting information. **TIME OF THE LOCUST** is not a pretty film, nor is it as sophisticated as some viewers would like it. It uses raw footage from the front lines to hammer home its central question: Does anyone really know the motives behind our involvement there? And does anyone really care about the harm being inflicted? **Distributed by American Friends/ Brandon.   K 165**

s   **A TIME OUT OF WAR,** 1954/22 min./Denis Sanders/**8c, 9.** Denis and Terry Sanders present a historically insignificant incident during the American Civil War, a momentary private truce between a Confederate and two Union soldiers on a hot summer day along some nameless stream. Within the lull of battle, the "time out of war," the reality of what war is becomes much clearer. **Distributed by Chicago Public Library/Contemporary/Mass Media.   K 167, M 77**

s   **TIME PIECE,** 1965/8 min., color/Jim Henson/**1, 7, 8e, 10, 13, 8f, 12.** Through rapid editing and the sustained clock motif throughout, this film effectively comments on the crazy, hectic tempo of contemporary society. **TIME PIECE** is both challenging and confusing, and would well be viewed a second time with perhaps a day's lapse between screenings. **Distributed by Contemporary/Mass Media.   K 169**

TO KILL A MOCKINGBIRD, 1962/129 min./Robert Mulligan/**2, 3, 4, 7, 8c, 9, 11, 14.** When does one most easily learn the lesson of love and tolerance if not in childhood? Scout and Jem Finch learn it then, and perhaps the viewer, as he is brought back into a child's world, does too. A wondering, creatively seeing camera brings to life a child's world, and introduces the viewer to the sharp contrast between this world and the harsh reality of modern day prejudice and racial intolerance. **Distributed by Twyman/United World.**

TOM JONES, United Kingdom, 1963/115 min./Tony Richardson/**4, 7, 8c, 11.** Beguilingly alive, the screen version of Fielding's **Tom Jones** does a myriad of astounding things and does them well. It establishes perfectly the 18th century mood of carousal and buffoonery, blends music and fast film slowups and speedups, and establishes one of literature's most rascally rogues with tongue tastefully and impeccably in cheek. It is one of the best technique jobs of the decade. Albert Finney supplies the main playboy role, enjoying every food-stuffing, wench-wrestling moment. Adult humor pulsates the viewer from disapproval to smiles, from "tsk-tsk" to a general re-evaluation of what it means to be happy. **Distributed by United Artists 16.**

s   **THE TOP,** Japan, 1965/8 min., color/Teru Murakami/**8d, 8e, 13, 5.** Everyone wants to get to the top, and in this animated film, the ways in which people struggle to get there are both amusing and disturbingly tragic. The director presents different varieties of people in the struggle to reach the top, and a second and/or third viewing of the film will be useful in getting to the heart of what the director is trying to say. **Distributed by Contemporary.**   **K 171, M2 97**

s **THE TOYMAKER,** 1952/15 min., color/Stevens-Rose Puppet Films/ **5, 8e, 13.** This film attempts to make the point that each of us needs the other guy, and to attack one person means that I really hurt myself because I am somehow hurting humanity. The message is not at all subtle, and the approach is geared to grade school children. One aspect that makes it a bit fascinating is that the actors are two puppets, and at the conclusion, the puppeteer. But the overly obvious message suggests that the viewer is just a bit too stupid to get the point on his own. **Distributed by Anti-Defamation League of B'nai B'rith/Contemporary.**   **K 173, M 78**

s **TOYS ON A FIELD OF BLUE/**20 min./**6a, 8e, 13. Distributed by Brandon.**   **M 79**

THE TRAIN, 1965/133 min./John Frankenheimer/**1, 2, 3, 4, 6a, 9, 11, 16.** An attempt by the Nazis to loot France of her major art treasures after the Allied invasions, and the efforts of the French Resistance to stop them, make both an exciting adventure story and a bitter fable about the futility of war and noble causes. After the final bloody battle, Frankenheimer uses a beautifully edited montage sequence to imply that life has greater value than art. The style is extremely realistic, except perhaps for the exploits of hero Burt Lancaster, and the camera angles and deep-focus effects are especially notable. Most striking perhaps is the splendid use of natural sound: the hissing of steam, the screech of locked wheels, the steady beat of the engine, the scraping fall of a running man on a wooden bridge. Trains, of course, are always highly cinematic subject matter. The fine international cast includes Paul Scofield and Jeanne Moreau. **Distributed by United Artists 16.**

THE TREASURE OF THE SIERRA MADRE, 1948/126 min./John Huston/**2, 3, 6a, 8c, 8e, 9, 11, 12, 13.** Film critics James Agee and Stanley Kaufman have rated this film as one of the best ever made in America. Although originally advertised as such, the film is not strictly a Western. John Huston's adaptation of B. Traven's novel of the same name bears more kin- ship to Chaucer's "Pardoner's Tale." Three men head into the mountains of Mexico in pursuit of gold. In that pursuit, greed tempts them all, finally

---

PROPERTIES OF FILM

1. Montage	b) Adaptation from	9. Cinema Verite
2. Camera Angle	Stage, TV	10. Introceptive Camera
3. Camera Position	c) Adaptation of	11. Character Development
4. Camera Movement	Novels, Short Stories,	12. Transitional Phases
5. Color	Poems	13. Visual Symbols
6. Sound:	d) Animation	14. Lighting
a) Natural	e) Social/Moral/	15. Beauty of Photographic
b) Music	Symbolic	Images
7. Film Devices	Commentary	16. Highly Visual Subject
8. Categories	f) Pure Film	
a) Documentary		

consuming Dobbs, played by Humphrey Bogart. The film can be approached much more positively if one accepts the stylization of characters which the morality play demands. There is a great performance by the director's father, Walter, as the old prospector who comes to terms with his failure with a great gust of human laughter. **Distributed by Brandon/Films, Inc./Trans-World.   PKK esp. 361-362**

THE TRIAL OF JOAN OF ARC, France, 1962/65 min./Robert Bresson/ **3, 9, 11.** Using only the actual record of the saint's trial, Bresson is brilliantly objective, confronting us only with the facts, neither explaining, accusing or defending the Maid of Orleans. We must judge Joan, as John Russell Tyler writes, "not from what we are told about her, but from what she—or the girl playing her—**is.**" There is virtually no "style" at all—everything is shown in eye-level medium shots, alternating between Joan and her judges, and there is no music. The film is excellent subject matter for a discussion on the possibilities of cinematic objectivity and of reducing "form" to a minimum; it is a masterful challenge to all formalistic theories of what makes a good movie. Compare to the much less successful portrayal of Joan by Ingrid Bergman in **Joan of Arc** (1948). English subtitles. **Distributed by Contemporary.**

TRIUMPH OF THE WILL, Germany, 1934-36/80 and 120 min./Leni Riefenstahl/**2, 3, 4, 10, 11.** Available in German or with English subtitles. **Distributed by Contemporary/Museum of Modern Art.**

THE TROUBLE WITH ANGELS, 1966/112 min./Ida Lupino/**7, 13, 14.** The screenplay of Blanche Hanalis was based on the successful novel by Jane Trahey. The large cast includes Rosalind Russell as a sterotyped Mother Superior (often very believable) and Hayley Mills as the little hellion. Several "names" walk through brief parts, including Gypsy Rose Lee who appropriately took off on the part of the school's dance teacher. Reviews were not all favorable on April 7, 1966, in most New York papers, yet it is a harmless example for comparing a novel to its film adaptation. How is it possible for some visual gags to be more effective in print than on film? Have we ever had enough of the nun-as-authority-figure-type film? **Distributed by Columbia Cinematheque/Twyman.**

THE TRUE GLORY, 1945/85 min./Carol Reed and Carson Kanin/**8a.** A new interpretation of war and warring. One of the more striking features of this well-made and energetic retelling of the war in Europe from the Normandy Invasion to the German surrender is the narration made up of bits of comments of the various people who actually participated in the campaign. **Distributed by Contemporary/Museum of Modern Art.**

s A TRUMPET FOR THE COMBO, 1965/8 min./**8e. Distributed by Contemporary/Sterling.   M2 98**

TWELVE ANGRY MEN, 1954/95 min./Sidney Lumet/**2, 3, 4, 6b, 8b, 11, 13.** Noticeably an adapted television play by Reginald Rose (stage version by Sherman Segal). The film does not attempt to move beyond the confines of the single stage set but somehow manages to be visually interesting. The strong character development is intensified by the use of closeups, slow and at times excruciating pans, and carefully timed background music. **Distributed by United Artists 16.**

s **TWO MEN AND A WARDROBE,** Poland, 1958/15 min./Roman Polanski/**8e, 13.** Two men are refused hospitality in a town because they are carrying a large wooden wardrobe. They encounter various examples of evil and non-acceptance, and finally leave the town with their wardrobe, but not until the viewer has seen images and experienced a genuine conflict of ideas and impressions. The film is not recommended for use below the third-year high school level. **Distributed by Contemporary/Mass Media. K 175, M 80**

2001: A SPACE ODYSSEY, 1968/140 min., color, Cinemascope/Stanley Kubrick/**2, 3, 4, 5, 6a, 6b, 7, 8e, 10, 11, 12, 13, 14, 15, 16.** More than a science fiction experience, **2001** considers fundamental concerns of modern man, especially his effort to go forward towards the unknown. There is even a disturbing speculation on the possibilities of man's transcendence. As in **Dr. Strangelove,** Kubrick again touches a somber and controversial subject— nuclear annihilation. Impressionist scenes may surprise viewers who expected no more than another first-man-on-the-moon movie. Pessimism undertones many scenes, but a definite hopefulness triumphs, at least there seems to be "something else," "something after." **Presently not available for distribution.**

UMBERTO D, Italy, 1952/89 min./Vittorio de Sica/**2, 3, 4, 6a, 8a, 9, 10, 11, 12, 13.** One of the best and probably the most polished of the Neo-realist films, **UMBERTO D** is also one of the handful of movies ever made about the problems of old age. It is the story of a lonely old pensioner and his dignified struggle to survive poverty, as well as his affection for a dog who is both a consolation and a burden. The film moves slowly and heart-wrenchingly over the details of daily living. Most memorable are the moments when the hero searches for his lost dog in the city pound, when he tries to bring himself to beg for the first time or, in final desperation, to abandon the dog and destroy its love for him. The Neo-realist style emphasizes problems of real people in real settings. English subtitles. **Distributed by Audio.   PKK esp. 364**

	PROPERTIES OF FILM	
1. Montage	b) Adaptation from Stage, TV	9. Cinema Verite
2. Camera Angle		10. Introceptive Camera
3. Camera Position	c) Adaptation of Novels, Short Stories, Poems	11. Character Development
4. Camera Movement		12. Transitional Phases
5. Color		13. Visual Symbols
6. Sound:	d) Animation	14. Lighting
a) Natural	e) Social/Moral/ Symbolic Commentary	15. Beauty of Photographic Images
b) Music		16. Highly Visual Subject
7. Film Devices		
8. Categories	f) Pure Film	
a) Documentary		

THE UMBRELLAS OF CHERBOURG, France, 1964/92 min., color/ Jacques Demy/**4, 5, 6b, 15, 16.** An all-singing love story. A masterpiece of blending music and film. **Distributed by Audio Film Classics.**

UNCLE TOM'S CABIN, 1926/93 min./Harry Pollard/**8c.** This classic film would be most interesting for serious students to screen before seeing the play-within-a-play in **The King and I,** or in the play **The Great White Hope.** **Distributed by Audio Film Classics.**

s **A UNICORN IN THE GARDEN,** 1953/10 min., color/**5, 8c, 8d, 13.** This cartoon version of James Thurber's classic short story has retained the author's social satire as well as his biting wit and delightful humor. "The unicorn is a mythical being," characters remind one another at various intervals in the play. But the mythical being has a part to play in the downfall of at least one of these characters. **Distributed by Brandon/Columbia Cinematheque/Contemporary/Twyman.**   K 177

VERTIGO, 1958/138 min./Alfred Hitchcock/**2, 3, 4, 6a, 7, 10, 11.** **Distributed by Films, Inc.**

s **VERY NICE, VERY NICE,** 1961/8 min./**4, 6, 7, 8e, 16.** The film is a commentary on the chaotic events of our day as they might look to someone young and rather uncommitted. Dozens of still pictures, seemingly very familiar, are carefully juxtaposed through rapid cutting, thus revealing without any polemics the incongruities of modern life. The fragments of speech which accompany the pictures are trivial, wryly amusing, and both startle and intrigue the observant viewer. **Distributed by Contemporary.**   M 82

A VIEW FROM THE BRIDGE, France and U.S.A., 1961/117 min./Sidney Lumet/**2, 8b, 9, 10, 11.** A sober interpretation of the play by Arthur Miller, shot in Paris and Brooklyn. A longshoreman betrays his family out of love for his niece. Plot-wise, compare to **On the Waterfront.** Also compare the film's shocking ending to the climax scenes in **Twelve Angry Men** and **The Pawnbroker,** both also directed by Lumet. **Distributed by Continental 16.** **PK 155-158**

s **THE VIOLINIST,** 1960/7 min., color/Ernest Pintoff/**8d, 8e, 6b, 13, 11.** Appearances can cause judgments, and the judgments people make can cause individuals to leave off doing what they feel is most right for them. Harry became a violinist, a good violinist, but his efforts took their toll in his appearance. Because of rejection at the appearance level, Harry abandoned violin playing in favor of being fat, happy, and normal. **Distributed by Brandon/Mass Media.**   K 181

THE VIRGIN SPRING, Sweden, 1959/88 min./Ingmar Bergman/**2, 3, 4, 7, 8e, 10, 11, 13, 14, 15, 16.** English subtitles. **Distributed by Janus.**

s **VIVRE!,** France, 1959/8 min./Carlos Vilardebo/**1, 6b, 7, 8a, 8e, 9, 10, 16.** What is this thing called war, and what does it really do to people? At present, this film would be most effective, in what it does not say, in portraying the tragic human results of war. When the viewer realizes that the background music is a continuous use of the "De Profundis," a long musical piece sung in the Roman Catholic funeral rite, he is even more impressed by the film's message. **VIVRE!** is another of the films that would be most effective and most understood if it were screened, thought about, and screened again. It is less a film to be talked about than an experience to be mused over and shared. **Distributed by Contemporary/Mass Media.**   **K 183, M 84**

s   **THE WALL,** Yugoslavia, 1965/4 min., color/Ante Zaninovic/**2, 3, 4, 5, 6, 7, 8d, 8e, 9, 10, 13.** This animated cartoon parable watches a wall and the vain attempts of one little man to get over to the other side while another little man sits quietly by, waiting. The conclusion of this very short, but very powerful, film leaves little to guess at, as to meaning and message. But the message is a brutal one and a telling commentary on "the way things are." **Distributed by Contemporary.**   **K 185**

WAR OF THE BUTTONS, France, 1962/92 min./Yve Robert/**4, 8e, 11, 13.** A not-too-subtle satire on the trophies of war. Boys collect buttons as trophies from their enemies. An interesting ending results from the childlike logic that no clothes = no buttons = no trophies (= no more wars?). **Distributed by Audio.**

s   **WE HAVE NO ART,** 1967/26 min./Baylis Glascock/**2, 3, 4, 5, 7, 9, 16.** A visual experience and record of happy happenings at Immaculate Heart College in Los Angeles (then Sr. M. Corita's scene). Narrated by Sr. Corita (Corita Kent) and Don Dittmer, with excellent photo work by Isadore Mankofsky. Title is from the often quoted "We have no art; we do everything as well as we can." **Distributed by Baylis Glascock.**

WE'LL BURY YOU, 1963/74 min./**8a.** **Distributed by Association/Audio/ Trans-World/Twyman.**

WEST SIDE STORY, 1961/color, Cinemascope/Robert Wise/**8b, 2, 3, 4, 6b, 9, 15.** This film has been called a "cinematic masterpiece" and it is along the lines of photography, editing, choreography, and music that the film should be approached and discussed. Jerome Robbins, Leonard Bernstein, and Robert Wise struggle to put Romeo and Juliet among the Puerto Rican

PROPERTIES OF FILM		
1. Montage	b) Adaptation from Stage, TV	9. Cinema Verite
2. Camera Angle		10. Introceptive Camera
3. Camera Position	c) Adaptation of Novels, Short Stories, Poems	11. Character Development
4. Camera Movement		12. Transitional Phases
5. Color		13. Visual Symbols
6. Sound:	d) Animation	14. Lighting
a) Natural	e) Social/Moral/ Symbolic Commentary	15. Beauty of Photographic Images
b) Music		16. Highly Visual Subject
7. Film Devices		
8. Categories	f) Pure Film	
a) Documentary		

street gangs of New York. Like **The Umbrellas of Cherbourg,** this film comes close to fantasy where a suspension of disbelief is required. Yet, **WEST SIDE STORY** is too rooted in the conflicts of New York to make the complete plunge. It is one of the first musicals to be shot on location. In any comparative film study, the film stands on its merits. The Tony-Maria relationship might be compared with the love relationship in **Ballad of a Soldier,** thus illustrating the universality of film art. **Presently not available for distribution.**   **PK esp. 127-133**

WHISTLE DOWN THE WIND, United Kingdom, 1962/98 min./Bryan Forbes/**2, 3, 4, 6a, 8c, 8e, 9, 11, 13, 12, 14, 15.** In rural England, three farm children find an escaped murderer in their barn and mistake him for Christ. What follows is a touching and ironic parody on the New Testament, with the believing children trying vainly to save the man from his inevitable second crucifixion by the adults. The children, led by Hayley Mills, play it brilliantly, and Alan Bates is memorable in the difficult role of the fugitive. Writer-director Forbes uses the combined power of work and image to deliver a moving sermon on the nature of charity, belief and innocence. The haunting music and misty countryside add greatly to the mood. **Distributed by Janus.**

s   **WHITE MANE,** 1953/39 min./Albert Lamorisse/**2, 3, 4, 13, 14, 15, 5, 7, 9, 16.** Winner of Seven International Awards, this is a film of beauty, tenderness, and photographic mastery. It tells the story of a young boy and his devotion to a proud white stallion as he resists the efforts of men who want to capture and tame the horse. **WHITE MANE** is made with the same delicacy that characterized **The Red Balloon,** also by Lamorisse. **Distributed by Contemporary/Rembrandt.**   **M 94**

WHO'S AFRAID OF VIRGINIA WOOLF?, 1966/130 min./Mike Nichols/ **2, 3, 4, 6a, 7, 8b, 11, 13.** Four excellent actors play out Edward Albee's powerful play. Martha (Elizabeth Taylor) and George (Richard Burton) dominate, while George Segal plays the husband of Sandy Dennis. The main roles have the names of the first American president and his wife by no coincidence; the play is a loud and cruel commentary on many American ways of life. It contained many "firsts": it contained dialogue never before heard in a picture bearing the code seal of the Motion Picture Association of America; the first film directed by Nichols; the first produced by Ernest Lehman; the first film role for Sandy Dennis. It may also have been the first film to cause national excitement about the code held by many Catholics at that time concerning language in a film. Nearly all major periodicals and newspapers reviewed the film in June or July of 1966. Reviewers disagreed on some fine points, but it is at least one of the best Taylor-Burton films. It is loud, crass and cruel as it is powerful, thought provoking and expertly performed. Its closing scene is variously interpreted to make the film a comedy, tragedy or neither one. Sensitive adults will discuss many sides, but the play script will aid in discovering scenes which were regrettably not in the film. **Presently not available for distribution.**

s **WHY DO YOU SMILE, MONA LISA?**, 1967/12 min./**5, 7, 8d.** Well-executed and beautiful animation. Visual puns. **Distributed by Fleetwood Films, Inc.**

WILD STRAWBERRIES, Sweden, 1957/90 min./Ingmar Bergman/**2, 3, 4, 10, 11, 12, 15, 14.** The film reflects the personal vision of a single creative artist. Writer-director Ingmar Bergman shows the emptiness of a life without love and the reasons why a learned professor has retreated within himself and immersed himself in his research. Brilliant techniques—flashbacks and dreams with their free associations—enable Bergman to show how Professor Borg makes an expedition into the labyrinth of his soul during the emotion-arousing journey he takes to receive an honorary degree as a renowned scientist. The nightmare scenes are particularly effective with Bergman using severe black-and-white, over-exposed film in complete silence, while the nostalgic dreams are brightly lit to express the innocence of youth. Victor Sjostrom's portrayal of the professor is subtle and sensitive, and Bergman frequently uses the close-up to capture the revealing expressions on Sjostrom's magnificent face. One of Bergman's least obscure films. English subtitles. **Distributed by Janus.** **PKK esp. 368-369**

s **WILLIE CATCHES ON**, 1962/24 min./Donald Wilder/**8e.** The all-around guy, clean-cut and respectable, is often unaware that he is prejudiced in his thinking about individuals unlike himself. But just how does this manner of thinking develop? The present film seems to think that he "catches on" to opinion patterns, that he molds his attitudes around the attitudes of the powerful group that most influences him: his parents, members in his club, the rich men he envies. **Distributed by Contemporary/ McGraw-Hill/Mass Media.** **K 187, M 86**

WINTER LIGHT, Sweden, 1960-1962/80 min./Ingmar Bergman/**2, 3, 4, 6a, 7, 10, 14.** English subtitles. **Distributed by Janus.**

WOMAN IN THE DUNES, Japan, 1961/123 min./Hiroshi Teshigahara/ **2, 7, 8e, 11, 15, 16.** English subtitles. **Distributed by Contemporary.**

WORLD OF APU, India, 1959/103 min./Satyajit Ray/**8a.** The concluding part of the Apu trilogy, about the physical and spiritual growth of a man,

PROPERTIES OF FILM		
1. Montage	b) Adaptation from Stage, TV	9. Cinema Verite
2. Camera Angle		10. Introceptive Camera
3. Camera Position	c) Adaptation of Novels, Short Stories, Poems	11. Character Development
4. Camera Movement		12. Transitional Phases
5. Color		13. Visual Symbols
6. Sound:	d) Animation	14. Lighting
a) Natural	e) Social/Moral/ Symbolic Commentary	15. Beauty of Photographic Images
b) Music		
7. Film Devices		16. Highly Visual Subject
8. Categories	f) Pure Film	
a) Documentary		

who is himself a part of both the old and the new. India. English subtitles. **Distributed by Brandon.**

WORLD WITHOUT SUN, 1964/93 min./Jacques Cousteau/**4, 6a, 8a, 14, 15, 16.** Besides presenting an interesting and important record of his explorations under the sea, Cousteau has shown the fuller capabilities of the camera. The rhythms which result from the camera following nature are a pleasant contrast to the staged motions of actors following camera. For a study of film techniques, a second viewing might help the action lover who got the message but missed the media during his first screening. **Distributed by Audio.**

s **YEARS OF LIGHTNING, DAY OF DRUMS,** 1966/**2, 3, 4, 6a, 8a, 16. Distributed by Roa.**

THE YOUNG AND THE DAMNED, Mexico, 1951/81 min./Luis Buñuel/ **2, 4, 7, 11.** English subtitles. **Distributed by Brandon.**

THE YOUNG NUN, Italy, 1964/93 min./Bruno Paolinelli/**8c, 10, 11, 13.** Adapted from Giovanni Arpino's novel about a novice who falls in love with a middle-aged man. Sensitive to the tensions of such a relationship, the film visually captures much which **The Nun's Story** missed about convent life. The latter is still by far the better made film. **Distributed by Brandon.**

s **YOU'RE NO GOOD,** 1965/28 min./George Kaczender/**1, 2, 3, 4, 6a, 7, 8e, 9, 10, 11, 12, 13, 14, 16. Distributed by Contemporary.   K 189, M2 100**

ZORBA THE GREEK, Greece, 1964/146 min./Michael Cacoyannis/**8c, 10, 11, 14, 15, 16.** The zesty and incorrigible Zorba is perfectly captured and presented by Anthony Quinn. The primitive Greek village sets the scene for some of the best moments of all Cacoyannis' films. Based on the novel by Nikos Kazantzakis, the film can now be compared to its recent musical show version. The film is a more serious counterpart to **Never on Sunday,** but just as powerful in presenting the East and West in conflict. While the East has more to learn about business and managerial science, it is again in Zorba that we find the West learning to dance the other's tune. Like the philosopher who comes to Greece in **Never on Sunday,** an English writer (Alan Bates) comes to Crete to re-work a mine inherited from his father. The Englishman gradually learns the secret of Zorba's manly beauty; one of the greatest experiences of all the film is the scene of the writer asking Zorba to teach him to dance. Zorba tells him at the end of the film, "A man needs a little madness or else he never dares cut the rope and be free." **Distributed by Brandon.   PKK 160**

WHERE TO RENT AND BUY FILMS

Many of the films mentioned in Appendix I and throughout the book are available on 16mm for rental and/or sale from the sources listed below. Prices and descriptions on the films are usually included in catalogs available free or for a small cost from the distributors. Please note, however, that when a film is to appear on television it is withdrawn from distribution.

A complete list of 16mm libraries is published by the Superintendent of Documents, Government Printing Office, Washington, D.C. However, even this list is not entirely up-to-date. The following addresses and phone numbers were correct at this printing to the best of our knowledge.

Major university film libraries are indicated (*). Many films are available from these sources which are not otherwise distributed.

A summary of current 16mm films available in the United Kingdom was compiled in the 1967 and 1968 *International Film Guide,* edited by Peter Cowie. Films from other countries are often listed in the annual guide.

Academy Film Service
see: Bailey Films

Academy of Motion Picture Arts &
Sciences
9038 Melrose Avenue
Hollywood, California 90069
213-275-1146

American Friends Service
Committee
Audio-Visual Department
160 North 15th Street
Philadelphia, Pennsylvania 19102
215-563-9372

American Radio & TV
Commercials Festival
6 West 57th Street
New York, New York 10019
212-581-7060

Anti-Defamation League of B'nai
B'rith
315 Lexington Avenue
New York, New York 10016
212-689-7400

Association Films (six locations)
600 Madison Avenue
New York, New York 10022
212-421-3900

Athena Films
1545 Broadway
New York, New York
212-CI6-9760

Audio Film Center
34 MacQuesten Parkway South
Mount Vernon, New York 10550
914-664-5051

  2138 East 75th Street
  Chicago, Illinois 60649
  312-684-2531

  406 Clement Street
  San Francisco, California 94118
  415-751-8080

Bailey Films
6509 DeLongpre Avenue
Hollywood, California 90028
213-466-4331

Baylis Glascock
1901 Avenue of the Stars, Suite 700
Los Angeles, California 90067
213-879-2245

Brandon Films
221 West 57th Street
New York, New York 10019
212-246-4867

  Film Center, Inc.
  20 East Huron Street
  Chicago, Illinois 60611
  312-337-2855

  Western Cinema Guild, Inc.
  244 Kearny Street
  San Francisco, California 94108
  415-397-4255

*University of California,
Extension Media Center
2223 Fulton Street
Berkeley, California 94720
415-845-6000

Carousel Films
1501 Broadway, Suite 1503
New York, New York 10036
212-279-6734

*Center for Mass Communications
Columbia University Press
440 West 110th Street
New York, New York 10036
212-865-2000

Chicago Public Library
78 East Washington Street
Chicago, Illinois 60602
312-236-8922

Churchill Films
662 North Robertson Blvd.
Los Angeles, California 90069
213-657-5110

Cinema Inc.
134 Claredon Street
Boston, Massachusetts 02116
617-267-0200

Cinema 16/Grove Press
80 University Place
New York, New York 10003
212-989-6400

Columbia Cinematheque
711 Fifth Avenue
New York, New York 10022
212-751-7529

Contemporary Films/McGraw-Hill
330 West 42nd Street
New York, New York 10036
212-971-6681

    828 Custer Avenue
    Evanston, Illinois 60202
    312-869-5010

    1714 Stockton Street
    San Francisco, California 94133
    415-362-3115

Continental 16
241 East 34th Street
New York, New York 10016
212-683-6300

Creative Film Society
14558 Valerio Street
Van Nuys, California 91405
213-786-8277

Cultural Films
1564 Broadway
New York, New York 10036
212-586-1398

Walt Disney Productions
800 Sonora Avenue
Glendale, California 91201
213-845-3141

Embassy Pictures Corp.
1301 Avenue of the Americas
New York, New York 10019
212-956-5500

*Emory University,
Institute of Communicative Arts
Box 15307
Atlanta, Georgia 30333
404-377-2411

Encyclopaedia Britannica Films
425 North Michigan Avenue
Chicago, Illinois 60611
312-321-6800

The Film Center
915 Twelfth Street, N.W.
Washington, D.C. 20005
202-393-1205

Film Classic Exchange
1926 South Vermont Avenue
Los Angeles, California 90007
213-731-3854

Film Makers' Cooperative
175 Lexington Avenue
New York, New York 10016
212-889-3820

Films, Inc. (ten locations)
4420 Oakton Street
Skokie, Illinois 60076
312-676-1088

Fleetwood Films
34 MacQuesten Parkway South
New York, New York 10550
914-664-5051

Edward Harrison
1501 Broadway
New York, New York 10036
212-LA4-1318

The Grail
Loveland, Ohio

Ideal Pictures
34 MacQuesten Parkway South
New York, New York 10550
914-664-5051

*University of Illinois,
Visual Aids Service
704 South 6th Street
Champaign, Illinois 61820
217-333-1000

*Indiana University
Audio-Visual Center
Bloomington, Indiana 47405
812-332-0211

Institutional Cinema Service
29 East 10th Street
New York, New York 10003
212-673-3990

International Business Machines
Films & TV News Department
590 Madison Avenue
New York, New York 10022
212-573-1900

International Film Bureau
332 South Michigan Avenue
Chicago, Illinois 60604
312-427-4545

International Film Foundation
475 Fifth Avenue
New York, New York 10017
212-685-4998

Jam Handy Organization
2821 East Grand Blvd.
Detroit, Michigan 48211
313-875-2450

Janus Films, Inc.
745 Fifth Avenue
New York, New York 10022
212-753-7100

*Kent State University,
Audio-Visual Center
Kent, Ohio 44240
216-672-2072

Mass Media Ministries
2116 North Charles Street
Baltimore, Maryland 21218
301-727-3270

1714 Stockton Street
San Francisco, California 94133
415-362-7892

McGraw Hill Text-Films
330 West 42nd Street
New York, New York 10036
212-971-3333

*University of Michigan,
Audio-Visual Center, A-3, South
   Campus
Ann Arbor, Michigan
313-764-1817

Modern Sound Pictures
1410 Howard Street
Omaha, Nebraska 68102
402-341-8476

Mogull's
112 West 48th Street
New York, New York 10019
212-757-1414

Museum of Modern Art,
Department of Film
11 West 53rd Street
New York, New York 10019
212-245-8900

National Film Board of Canada
680 Fifth Avenue
New York, New York 10019
212-586-2400

New York Times
Office of Educational Activities
Times Square
New York, New York 10036
212-556-1651

*New York University
Film Library
26 Washington Place
New York, New York 10036
212-777-2000

*Northern Illinois University
Educational Film Library
De Kalb, Illinois 60115
815-753-1000

Pictura Films
565 Fifth Avenue
New York, New York 10017
212-697-9170

Protestant Council,
475 Riverside Drive, Suite 456
New York, New York 10027

Radim Films (Radiant)
220 West 42nd Street
New York, New York 10036
212-279-6653

Rembrandt Film Library
267 West 25th Street
New York, New York 10001
212-675-7220

Roa's Films
1696 North Astor Street
Milwaukee, Wisconsin 53202
414-271-0861

Royal 16
711 Fifth Avenue
New York, New York 10022
212-751-4400

*University of Southern California
Cinema, Film Distribution Division
University Park
Los Angeles, California 90007
213-746-2311

*University of Southern Illinois
Audio-Visual Aids Service
Carbondale, Illinois 62901
618-453-2121

Sterling Educational Films
241 East 34th Street
New York, New York 10016
212-683-6300

Swank Motion Pictures
201 South Jefferson Avenue
St. Louis, Missouri 63166
314-531-5100

Trans-World Films
332 South Michigan Avenue
Chicago, Illinois 60604
312-922-1530

Twyman Films
329 Salem Avenue
Dayton, Ohio 45401
513-222-4014

United Artists 16
729 Seventh Avenue
New York, New York 10019
212-245-6000

United World Films
(Universal Educational & Visual
Arts)
221 Park Avenue, South
New York, New York 10003
212-777-6600

Weston Woods Studios
Weston, Connecticut 06880
203-226-0600

Wolper Productions, Inc.
8720 Sunset Blvd.
Hollywood, California 90069

World Horizons Films
Maryknoll, New York 10545

Xerox Corp., Audio-Visual Services
Midtown Tower, 2nd Floor
Rochester, New York 14604
202-737-8340

Bibliography

The numbers (printed in boldface) following each entry refer to the following categories. Numbers one through thirteen correspond to the content of the 13 chapters in this book.

1. Books on the history of film.
2. On the current situation of film.
3. On film adaptations from literature.
4. On film adaptations from stage plays.
5. On the short films and animation.
6. On the Western.
7. On the Comedy.
8. On the Documentary.
9. On directors, directing. Including (auto) biographies, screenplays, memoirs and recollections by sight-and-sound communicators, "behind-the-scene" reports and books on screen personalities.
10. On editing. Including book recommended for film makers.
11. On film series planning.
12. On programming films. Including books on film criticism, bibliography and basic information sources.
13. On the language and properties of film. Including books on the nature and theories of film and related visual art.
14. On the history of foreign film.

15. On the current foreign film.

16. Indicates the book is well illustrated with "stills."

17. Recommended for teachers.

18. Recommended for students.

19. Not recommended for beginners.

20. Recommended for the students' library in high schools.

Agee, James **Agee on Film.** Gloucester, Massachusetts; P. Smith, 1965. Paperback. Volume One: Reviews and comments. Volume Two: Five Film Scripts—Noa Noa; The African Queen; The Night of the Hunter; The Bride Comes to Yellow Sky and The Blue Hotel. **13**

Agee, James "Comedy's Greatest Era" **Life.** September 3, 1949. **7**

Anderson, Joseph L. and Donald Richie **The Japanese Film.** New York: Grove Press, 1960. **14**

Antonioni, Michelangelo **Screenplays.** New York: Orion Press, 1963. Paperback. **9/15**

Armes, Roy **French Cinema Since 1946.** Cranbury, New Jersey: A. S. Barnes, 1966. Paperback. Volume One: The veterans of the forties and before. Volume Two: The younger directors of the fifties. **14/15**

Arnheim, Rudolf **Film as Art.** Berkeley, California: University of California Press, 1957. Although most of the essays were written in the 1930's, this is a basic reference on the psychology of film. Should be studied along with his **Toward a Psychology of Art** and Lindgreen's **The Art of the Film. 13**

Arnheim, Rudolf **Toward a Psychology of Art.** Berkeley, California: University of California Press, 1967. More valuable and current than his **Art and Visual Perception** (Berkeley, 1966). With the above work highly recommended. **13/19**

Balshofer, Fred and Arthur C. Miller **One Reel A Week.** Berkeley, California: University of California Press, 1967. Reviewed in **Film Quarterly,** Spring, 1968, pp. 50-52. **9**

Barnouw, Erik **A History of Broadcasting in the United States.** New York: Oxford, 1966. Volume One updates his **Mass Communication: Television, Radio, Film, Press** (New York: Holt, Rinehart and Winton, 1956). Both are excellent histories. **1/20**

Barry, Iris and Eileen Bowser D. W. Griffith, **American Film Master.** New York, Doubleday, 1965. A study of the films and career of this pioneer director of film. **9**

Battack, Gregory (editor) **The New American Cinema.** New York: Dutton, 1967. Paperback. An anthology of twenty-nine critical essays on underground film mostly by their film makers. **2/16**

Bazin, Andre **What is the Cinema?** Berkeley, California: University of California Press, 1967. Paperback. Clear and direct essays by a foremost French critic. **13**

Beck, Bob **Light Show Manual.** Los Angeles: Perisles Press, 1966. **2/10**

Bergman, Ingmar **Four Screenplays of Ingmar Bergman.** New York: Simon and Schuster, 1965. **9/15**

Blesh, Rudi **Keaton.** New York: Macmillan, 1966. **7/9**

Blum, Daniel **A Pictorial History of the Talkies.** London: Secker and Warburg, 1968. **1/20**

Bluem, A. W. **Documentary in American Television.** New York: Hastings House, 1964. Contains a significant chapter on film documentaries. Excellent historical approach. **8/12**

Bluestone, George **Novels into Films.** Berkeley, California: University of California Press, 1961. Paperback. Not throughly convincing but a valuable contribution to the relationships between the novel and film. **3**

Bogdanovich, Peter **Cinema of Alfred Hitchcock.** New York: Museum of Modern Art, 1963. **9/16**

Bogdanovich, Peter **Cinema of Howard Hawks.** New York: Museum of Modern Art, 1962. **9/16**

Bogdanovich, Peter **Cinema of Orson Welles.** New York: Museum of Modern Art, 1961. **9/16**

Bowman, W. Dodgson **Charlie Chaplin, His Life And Art.** New York: John Day Company, 1931. **7/9**

Budgen, Susanne **Fellini.** London: British Film Institute, 1966. **9/15**

Calder-Marshall, Arthur **The Innocent Eye.** New York: Harcourt, Brace, 1966. The life of Robert J. Flaherty, the great documentary film maker. **8/9**

Callenbach, Ernest **Our Modern Art, The Movies.** Chicago: Center for Study of Liberal Education for Adults, 1955. **1**

Capa, Robert **Images of War.** New York: Grossman Publishers, 1964. The wars in documentary film discussed intelligently. **8**

Ceram, C. W. **Archaeology of the Cinema.** New York: Harcourt, Brace, 1965. An illustrated pre-history of the cinema up to 1897. **1/16**

Chaplin, Charles **My Autobiography.** New York: Simon and Schuster, 1964. **7/9/18/20**

Chaplin, Charles Jr. **My Father, Charlie Chaplin.** New York: Random House, 1960. **7/9/18**

Chayefsky, Paddy **Television Plays.** New York: Simon and Schuster, 1955. **4**

Chocilowski, Jerzy (editor) **Contemporary Polish Cinematography.** New York: W. S. Heinman, 1963. **1/16**

Clarens, Carlos **An Illustrated History of the Horror Film.** New York: Capricorn Books, 1968. Paperback. **1/18/16/20**

Costello, Donald P. **The Serpent's Eye.** South Bend, Indiana: Notre Dame Press, 1967. **17**

Cowie, Peter **Antonioni, Bergman, Resnais.** New York: A. S. Barnes, 1964. Paperback. **9/13/15**

Cowie, Peter "The Growth of the Western" **International Film Guide, 1966. 6/1**

Cowie, Peter (editor) **International Film Guide.** New York: A. S. Barnes and Co. (annual) These paperbacks are indispensable for current information on film. Back issues remain very helpful. **12/14/15/16/17/20**

Cowie, Peter **Swedish Cinema.** New York: A. S. Barnes and Co., 1966. Paperback. **14/15**

Cox, Alva I. and Janet Isabell (editors) **Audio Visual Resource Guide.** New York: National Council of the Churches of Christ in the U.S.A., Department of Audio-Visual and Broadcast Education of the Division of Christian Education, 1965. 7th edition. **12/20**

Cross, A. J. F. and Irene F. Cypher **Audio-Visual Education.** New York: Crowell, 1961. **17**

Culkin, John "Film Study in the High School" **Catholic High School Quarterly Bulletin,** October, 1965. Basic information. Remainder of the issue much less valuable. **17**

Culkin, John "The Motion Picture as an Art Form" **Catholic High School Bulletin.** XXIII, Number 3, October 1956. **17**

Deren, Maya "Cinematography: The Creative Use of Reality," **Daedalus** (Journal of the American Academy of Arts and Sciences) LXXXIX, Winter, 1960, pp. 150-67. This special issue of **Daedalus** is on the visual arts today. The Deren article is outstanding. **13/17/19**

Dimmitt, Richard B. **A Title Guide to the Talkies.** New York: Scarecrow, 1965. Two volume comprehensive listing of 16,000 feature-length films from 1927 to 1963. **12/20**

Donner, Jorn **The Personal Vision of Ingmar Bergman.** Bloomington, Indiana: Indiana University Press, 1964. The best on Bergman. Extensive bibliography. **9**

Duprey, Richard A. **Just Off the Aisle.** Westminster, Maryland: Newman Press, 1962. Subtitled "The Ramblings of a Catholic Critic." **17/12**

Education Film Library Association **Film Evaluation Guide, 1946-1964.** New York: The Association, 1965. **12**

Eisenstein, Sergei **The Film Form and The Film Sense.** New York: Meridan Press, 1960. Both are available as a single paperback. A required reading for serious students of film. **17/9/13/1/19**

Everson, William K. **The Bad Guys.** New York: The Citadel Press, 1964. A pictorial history of the movie villain. **6/1/18/20**

Eyles, Allen **The Marx Brothers.** New York: A. S. Barnes, 1966. International Film Guides Series. Paperback. **7/9/18**

Eyles, Allen **The Western.** New York: A. S. Barnes, 1967. International Film Guide Series. Paperback. **6/12**

Fellini, Federico **Juliet of the Spirits.** New York: Ballantine Books, 1965. Paperback. The screenplay and final transcription of Fellini's first color film. An interview with Fellini is included. **9/15**

Fellini, Federico **La Dolce Vita.** New York: Ballantine Books, 1961. Paperback. Illustrated with full script of the film. **9/15**

Fenin, George N. and William K. Everson **The Western.** New York: Orion Press, 1962. From silents to cinerama with emphasis on the personalities and the historical evolution of the western film. **6/1/18/16/20**

Fielding, Raymond (editor) **A Technological History of Motion Pictures and Television.** Berkeley, California: University of California Press, 1967. Compiled from the Journal of the society of Motion Pictures and Television Engineers. The best and most reliable information in the field. **1/10/20**

Finler, Joel **Stroheim.** London: Studio Vista, 1967. The first study in English of the man and his films. **16/9/15**

Fischer, Edward **The Screen Arts.** New York: Sheed and Ward, 1960. An introductory guide to film and television appreciation. **17/12/13/18/20**

Friendly, Fred W. **Due to Circumstances Beyond Our Control.** New York: Random House, 1967. **9/17**

Gallez, Douglas W. "Patterns in Wartime Documentaries" **The Quarterly of Film, Radio and Television,** X (Winter, 1955) pp. 125-35. **8**

Gaskill, Arthus L. and David A. Englander **How To Shoot A Movie Story** Third Edition (revised) New York: Morgan and Morgan, 1967. Subtitle: the technique of pictorial continuity. A simple introduction with helpful illustrations. Recommended for the high school film maker. **10/13/18**

Geduld, Harry M. (editor) **Film Makers and Film Making.** Bloomington, Indiana: Indiana University Press, 1967. Statements on their art by thirty directors. **9/13**

Gibson, William **Dinny and the Witches, The Miracle Worker, Two Plays.** New York: Atheneum, 1960. **4/9**

Graham, Peter. **A Dictionary of the Cinema.** New York: A. S. Barnes, 1968. Revised edition. Paperback. Very helpful and informative guide to films and film makers. The most useful paperback in popular film research. **12/17/9/11/14/15/18/20**

Grau, Robert **The Theatre of Science: A Volume of Progress and Achievement in the Motion Picture Art.** New York: out of print, 1914. Included here because it is the first comprehensive history of the film. (Available from Gotham Book Mart, 41 W. 47th St., New York City 10036, at rare book price.) **1**

Griffith, D. W. **The Rise and Fall of Free Speech in America.** California: Larry Edmunds Bookshop, 1968. Number one in a series of cinema classics in reprint. **13/17**

Griffith, D. S., Mrs. (Linda Arvidson) **When the Movies Were Young.** New York: Dutton, 1925. **1/9**

Griffith, Richard **Cinema of Gene Kelly.** New York: Museum of Modern Art, 1962. **7/9**

Griffith, Richard and Arthur Mayer **The Movies.** New York: Simon and Schuster, 1957. Sixty-year story of Hollywood and its effect on America in a popular style by one who knows. **9**

Griffith, Richard **The World of Robert Flaherty.** New York: Duell, Sloan and Pearce, 1953. See also **The Innocent Eye** by Calder-Marshall. **8/9**

Halas, John **Film and TV Graphics.** New York: Hastings House, 1967. Beautifully designed commentary on the artwork in cinema and television. Excellent illustrations and survey of animation. **16/5/10/13/17/18/20**

Hall, Mary Harrington "The Fantasy Makers" **Psychology Today,** April, 1968, p. 28-37, 70. An insightful interview with Ray Bradbury and Chuck Jones. Thoughts on the role of fantasy in film, etc. Highly recommended reading, along with the entire issue, including the editorial. **17**

Halliwell, Leslie **The Filmgoer's Companion.** New York: Hill and Wang, 1967. Revised edition. An interesting and surprisingly readable cyclopedia of film personalities, some films and a few terms. Slightly opinionated. **12/17/20**

Hampton, Benjamin B. **A History of the Movies.** New York: out of print, 1931. Included here because of its important contribution to early film history. (Available from Cinemabilia, 10 Cornelia St., New York City, 10014, at rare book price.) **1**

Harcourt, Peter "The Secret Life of Federico Fellini" **Film Quarterly** XIX Spring, 1966, pp. 4-19.**9/15**

Hardy, Forsyth (editor) **Grierson on Documentary.** Berkeley, California: University of California Press. Revised edition, 1966. Articles on all aspects of the documentary. **8**

Haselden, Kyle **Morality and the Mass Media.** Nashville: Broadman Press, 1968. Compare with **Movies and Morals** by Anthony Schillaci. **17**

Herman, Lewis **Educational Films.** New York: Crown, 1965. Writing, directing and producing for the classroom, television and industry. See also his **A Practical Manual of Screen Playwriting,** Cleveland: World Publishing Co., 1963. **17/10/20**

Hill, Derek "The Short Film Situation" **Sight and Sound,** XXXI (Summer, 1962), pp. 108-12. **5**

Horowitz, Murray **TV 69.** New York: Media Books, 1968. Paperback. An attractive projection of the next season of television viewing. Not a substitute, however, for **TV Guide** or other sources which help plan the season's viewing. **11/18/20**

Houston, Penelope **The Contemporary Cinema.** London: Penguin Books Limited, 1963. Paperback. A fine study of cinema since World War II. **1**

Huaco, George A. **The Sociology of Film Art.** New York: Basic Books, 1965. On the inter-relationships of cinema to society, especially in Germany, Russia and Italy. **1/13/19**

Hughes, Robert (editor) **Film.** New York: Grove Press. Book One: The audience and the film-maker (1959). Book Two: Films of peace and war (1962). **13/9/17**

Hulfish, James W., Jr. **The Audio-Visual Equipment Directory.** Fairfax, Virginia: National Audio-Visual Association. Twelfth edition, 1966. **10/17/20**

Jacobs, Lewis (editor) **Introduction to the Art of the Movies.** New York: Noonday Press, 1960. An anthology of ideas on the nature of movie art. **17/18/13**

Jacobs, Lewis **The Rise of the American Film.** New York: Harcourt Brace, 1968. A standard reference now updated with a section on experimental film in America (1920-1947) and a new introduction by M. S. Dworkin. **1/2/17/20**

Jacobson, Howard B. (editor) **A Mass Communications Directory.** New York: Philosophical Library, 1961. **12/17/20**

Jones, William G. **Sunday Night at the Movies.** Richmond, Virginia: John Knox Press, 1967. A valuable paperback for church workers who use film. Hopefully a prototype of even better aids to come. **17/18/13**

Kael, Pauline **I Lost It at the Movies.** New York: Bantam Books, 1965. Paperback. Delightfully entertaining collection of her famous film reviews and articles. Highly recommended. **12/17/18/20**

Kael, Pauline **Kiss, Kiss, Bang, Bang.** New York: Atlantic, Little, Brown, 1968. Perceptive essays on past and current trends. Current films reviewed at length and short reviews of 280 older films. **12/17/18/20**

Kaplan, Abraham "Realism in the Film: A Philosopher's Viewpoint" **Quarterly of Film, Radio and Television** VII (1952-1953) pp. 360-84. Even ten years ago the documentary approach to reporting led to ideological conflicts. This article is still a firm basis for discussion. **13/17**

Kauffman, Stanley **A World on Film.** New York: Harper and Row, 1966. Valuable comments on films of the late 50's and early 60's. **1/12/17**

Kelly, Terence and others **A Competitive Cinema.** London: Institute of Economic Affairs, 1966. **13/14/15/19**

Kepes, Gyorgy (editor) **Education of Vision.** New York: George Braziller, Publisher, 1965. An inter-disciplinary approach to the question of contemporary art and education. To be seriously considered with the following. **13/17/19/20**

Kepes, Gyorgy (editor) **The Nature and Art of Motion.** New York: George Braziller, Publisher, 1965. Like **Education of Vision** this excellent collection of theoretical studies is worth the mental effort. **13/17/19/20**

Kirby, Michael **Happenings.** New York: E. P. Dutton and Co., 1965. **2/16/18**

Kitchen, Laurence "Decline of the Western" **The Listener** July 14, 1966. London, B.B.C. Publications. Have we thrown out the baby with the wash as we glorify the cowboy of yesterday? **6**

Knight, Arthur **The Liveliest Art.** New York: New American Library, 1957. Paperback. Recommended for students as a good introduction to the history of film. Data in the appendix slightly dated. **18/17/1/12**

Knight, Derrick and Vincent Porter **Long Look at Short Films.** Oxford: Pergamon Press, 1966. Criticism of current situations of short films in Britain. Attempts to be empirical. A fine basis for a similar study in America. See Derek Hill's article "The Short Film Situation." **15/5**

Kracauer, Siegfried **Theory of Film.** New York: Oxford, 1960. Paperback.

A difficult and theoretical presentation. Critically reviewed by Pauline Kael in **I Lost It at the Movies. 13/12/19**

Kuhns, William **Environmental Man.** New York: Harper and Row, 1969. A serious probe into the forces of technology which have formed contemporary man. Not only the section on movies, but the whole work is a contribution to film educators and lovers. This work brings together many relevant issues, not the least of which is film. **17/13/19/20**

Kuhns, William and Robert Stanley **Exploring the Film.** Dayton, Ohio: Geo. A. Pflaum, Publisher, Inc., 1968. Teaching manual and a "nontext" for students. Probably the best set of aids on teaching and experiencing film in high school. Five 16mm. commercials are available for coordination with the program. **17/13/16/19**

Kuhns, William **Short Films in Religious Education.** Dayton, Ohio: Geo. A. Pflaum Publisher, Inc., 1967. A loose-leaf, on-going service of teaching guides on short films. Additional pages are published regularly. The best service of its kind. **17/5**

Kuhns, William **Themes: Short Films for Discussion.** Dayton, Ohio: Geo. A. Pflaum, Publisher, Inc., 1968. Practical guide to available short films with excellent discussion starters for 82 films. **17**

Kyrou, Adonis **Luis Buñuel.** New York: Simon and Schuster, 1963. An introduction to the work of a controversial director. **9/15**

Lacy, Dan **Freedom and Communications.** Urban, Illinois: University of Illinois Press, 1965. Second Edition. **17**

Lahue, Kalton C. **World of Laughter.** University of Oklahoma Press, 1966. Excellent study of the short comedies which dominated the early history of American film. **7**

Larson, Rodger **A Guide for Film Teachers to Filmmaking by Teenagers.** New York: Department of Cultural Affairs, 1968. Available from Educational Film Library Association, 250 West 57th Street, New York City, 10019. After four years of experimental work with teenagers in the production of their own 16mm movies, the author presents practical advice. A longer work would have been more helpful. **12/10/17/18/20**

Lauritzen, Elinar **Swedish Films.** New York: Museum of Modern Art, 1962. **14/15**

Lauter, Paul **Theories of Comedy.** New York: Doubleday Anchor Books, 1964. **7/18**

Lawson, John Howard Film: **The Creative Process.** New York: Hill and Wang, 1964. Timely, valuable and readable theory. **13**

Leahy, James **The Cinema of Joseph Losey.** New York: A. S. Barnes and Co., 1967. Stresses his films **Eve** (62) and **King and Country** (64). **9/15**

Leavitt, Hart Day and David A. Sohn **Stop, Look, and Write.** New York: Bantam Books, 1964. Paperback. Presents a creative approach to effective writing through viewing and discussing photographs. It could be a logical springboard for a similar approach to and from film. **17/18**

Lenning, Arthur (editor) **Classics of the Film.** Madison, Wisconsin: Film Society Press, 1965. **1**

Leprohon, Pierre **Michelangelo Antonioni.** New York: Simon and Schuster, 1963. Includes interviews and writings of Antonioni. **9/15**

Lewin, William and Alexander Frazier. **Standards of Photoplay Appreciation.** New Jersey: Educational and Recreational Guides, 1957. Dated but helpful. **12/17**

Leyda, Jay **Films Beget Films.** New York: Hill and Wang, 1964. Subtitle: Compilation Films from Propaganda to Drama. As with a play within a play, film within film has a history and an interesting pattern. Very worthwhile study and probably the only one on the subject. **10/17/19**

Leyda, Jay **Kino.** New York: Macmillan, 1960. A well-documented history of the Russian and Soviet film from 1896 to 1958. **14/20**

Limbacher, James L. (editor) **Feature Films on 8 and 16.** New York: Educational Film Library Association, Inc., 1968. A comprehensive directory of feature films available on 16 mm, with a list of distributors' addresses. Many services and publications for educators also available from the Education Film Library Association, 250 West 57th Street, New York, New York, 10019. **11/12/20**

Lindgren, Ernest **The Art of the Film.** New York: Macmillan, 1963. Second Edition. An introduction to film appreciation. Excellent reference on the nature of film and its requirements for creative expression. **13**

Lindgren, Ernest **A Picture History of the Cinema.** New York: Macmillan, 1961. **16/1/20**

Losey, Joseph **Losey on Losey.** (edited by Tom Milne) London: Secker and Warburg, 1967. The film-maker who left America for England during the McCarthy hearings comments on his own work. **9**

McAnany, Emile G. and Robert Williams **The Film Viewer's Handbook.** Glen Rock, New Jersey, Paulist Press, 1965. Valuable source book of practical information. **11/17/12/18**

McBride, James **The Contemporary American Avant-garde Program Notes.** New York: The Gallery of Modern Art, 1964. **2**

McBride, Joseph (editor) **Persistence of Vision—A Collection of Film Criticism.** Madison, Wis.: Wisconsin Film Society Press, 1964. **12/13**

McCabe, John **Mr. Laurel and Mr. Hardy.** New York: Doubleday, 1961. Also in Paperback. **7/9/18**

McCaffrey, Patrick J. **A Guide to Short Films for Religious Education Program,** and **A Guide to Short Films for Religious Education II.** South Bend, Indiana: Fides Press, 1967 and 1968. Brief synopsis of short films with basic information on each. Uneven quality. **5/17**

McCann, Richard Dyer **Film and Society.** New York: Charles Scribner's Sons, 1964. A brief anthology on important questions. **17/13/19**

McCann, Richard Dyer **Film: A Montage of Theories.** New York: Dutton, 1966. Highly recommended anthology on film theory. Excerpts from leading film theorists. **13/17/19**

McDonald, Gerald with Michael Conway and Mark Ricci (editors) **The Films of Charlie Chaplin.** New York: Citadel Press, 1965. **7/9**

McLuhan, Marshall **The Gutenberg Galaxy.** Toronto: University of

Toronto Press, 1962. Paperback. A reprint of his now famous thesis that the printing, printing, printing of words, words, words has created a new pattern of perception. To be read if one is to see the evolution of his thought. **13/17/18/20**

McLuhan, Marshall **The Mechanical Bride, Folklore of Industrial Man.** Boston: Beacon Press, 1951. Paperback. The earliest writing of his explorations of popular culture. Updating with current commercials would be very revealing. **13/17/18/20**

McLuhan, Marshall **The Medium is the Massage.** New York: Bantam Books, 1967 Paperback. (Hard-cover edition is available and silghtly different from the less expensive paperback.) A palatable version of his key notions in **Understanding Media. 13/17/18/20/16**
A phonograph record version available on Columbia Records, CL-2701 (monaural) and CS-9591 (stereo). The stereo version is nearly essential for a proper massage. **13/17/18**
A 60-minute film from Mass Media Ministries is available titled "This is Marshall McLuhan: The Medium is the Massage." Originally shown on NBC-TV. **13/17/18**

McLuhan, Marshall and Harley Parker **Through the Vanishing Point: Space in Poetry and Painting.** New York: Harper and Row, 1968. Volume 37 of the **World Perspective** series. Surprisingly clear probings and nearly explicit descriptions of the sensory phenomenon. Highly recommended, but not as an introduction to McLuhan. **13/19/20**

McLuhan, Marshall **Understanding Media: The Extensions of Man.** New York: McGraw-Hill, 1964. Paperback. The book which brought the Mc-Luhan message (message) to the masses (mass-age). The last section (best to be read first) is especially helpful in grabbing his thesis. **13/17/19/20**

McLuhan, Marshall and Edmund Carpenter (editors), **Verbi-Voco-Visual Explorations.** New York: Something Elso Press, Inc., 1967. Originally issued as Number 8 of **Explorations,** a periodical edited by McLuhan and Carpenter. Later printed by Beacon Press of Boston, 1960, under the title **Explorations in Communications.** Mysterious and intriguing (see Webster) probings which describe, not prescribe. Many consequences for film. **13/17/18/20**

McVay, Douglas **The Musical Film.** New York: A. S. Barnes, 1967. A sketchy and superficial survey of major American musical films from 1927 to 1966, included here for the unique view of this area by a European and a good collection of stills. **16**

MacGowan, Kenneth **Behind the Screen.** New York: Delacorte Press, 1965. Paperback. The history and techniques of the motion picture. Updates other histories of film with an original approach to the interrelated elements of film. **7/9/10**

Mallery, David **The School and the Art of Motion Pictures.** Boston, National Association of Independent Schools, 1966. Paperback. Valuable guide to feature films and their use in high schools. **17/11**

Manchel, Frank "The Archetypal American" **Media and Methods** (Educators Guide) Vol. 4, No. 8 (April 1968) 36-40, 48. A study of the Western genre as essential to the understanding of America. **6**

Manoogian, Haig P. **The Film-Maker's Art.** New York: Basic Books, 1966.

Practical technical data. Reviewed in **Cinema** Vol. 1, No. 2, Summer, 1968, p. 60. **10**

Manvell, Roger (editor), **Experiment in the Film.** London: Grey Walls Press, 1949. **2**

Manvell, Roger **New Cinema in the U.S.A.** New York: Dutton, 1968. Even less valuable than his 1966 **New Cinema in Europe.** A European view of American films since 1946. Superficial commentary. Included here for its excellent stills. **16/14/15**

Mayer, Michael F. **Foreign Films on American Screens.** New York: Arco, 1965. Well-illustrated paperback in magazine form concerned with censorship. **14/15/16**

Montagu, Ivor G. **Film World.** Baltimore, Penquin, 1965. Paperback. Film as science, art, commodity, media and especially as business is discussed in this interesting guide. **13/17/19**

Montgomery, John **Comedy Films.** London: George, Allen and Unwin, 1954. **7**

Newhall, Beaumont **The History of Photography from 1839 to the Present Day.** New York: Museum of Modern Art, 1949. **1/20**

Nilsen, Vladimir **The Cinema as a Graphic Art.** New York: Hill and Wang, 1959. With a foreward by his teacher S. M. Eisenstein. Valuable but heavy theory. First published in 1936. **13/17/19**

Nizhnii, Vladimir B. **Lessons With Eisenstein.** New York: Hill and Wang, 1963. **13/17**

Nowell-Smith, Geoffrey **Luchino Visconti** London: Secker and Warburg, 1967. Paperback. First study of his films in English. **9/15**

O'Gara, James "Battle of Newburgh: NBC's White Paper" **Commonweal,** LXXV (February 16, 1962) p. 532. A commentary on one of television's most dramatic documentaries. A model for criticism. **8**

O'Leary, Liam **The Silent Cinema.** New York: Dutton Books, 1965. Paperback. Informative and well-illustrated history of early films. **16/1/17/18/20**

Parrington, Ruth **An Educator's Guide to the Use of Film.** Chicago: Argus Communications, 1967. Paperback. **5/17**

Perry, George **The Films of Alfred Hitchcock.** New York: Dutton Books, 1965. Paperback. A tour through the 49 films of four decades and the man who directed them. **9/18**

Peters, J. M. L. **Teaching About the Film.** New York: Columbia University Press, 1961. Some data already outdated, yet one of the most worthwhile resources on the teaching of film. **17/12**

Pike, Robert Marvin **A Critical Study of the West Coast Experimental Film Movement.** Los Angeles, 1960. A Master's thesis included here because of its (indirect) influence on other film-makers. Pike since 1958 has headed the Creative Film Society. **2**

Pudovkin, V. I. **Film Techniques and Film Acting.** New York: Evergreen

Press, 1960. Paperback. The great Russian film theorist shares his insights into the distinctions between film and the art of stage drama. **4/19**

Ramsaye, Terry **A Million and One Nights.** New York: Simon and Schuster, 1964. Paperback. A standard classic history of motion pictures. **1/17/20**

Reisz, Karel **The Technique of Film Editing.** New York: Focal Press, 1958. Best available information on film editing. Glossary of technical terms. **10**

Renan, Sheldon **An Introduction to the American Underground Film.** New York: E. P. Dutton, 1967. Paperback. The best available survey of American experimental films. Well-illustrated and very helpful appendix. **2/12/17/16/18**

Richie, Donald **The Films of Akira Kurosawa.** Berkeley, California: University of California Press, 1965. **14/15/9**

Richie, Donald **The Japanese Movie.** Rutland, Vermont: Japan Publications, 1965. An illustrated history and analysis against the philosophical, social and artistic background it reflects. See also his work with Joseph L. Anderson listed above. **14/9/16**

Rondi, Gian L. **Italian Cinema Today.** New York: Hill and Wang, 1966. An illustrated survey of Italian film from 1952-1965. **14/15/16**

Ross, Lilian **Picture.** New York: Holt, Rinehart, Winston, 1965. An interesting and informative description of the filming of **The Red Badge of Courage. 9/3/18**

Rosten, Leo "The Intellectual and the Mass Media: Some Rigorously Random Remarks" **Daedalus,** XXIX (Spring, 1960), pp. 33-46. **17/19**

Rotha, Paul and Sinclair Road and Richard Griffith **Documentary Film.** New York: Hastings House, 1964. Third edition, revised and enlarged. Subtitled: "The use of the film medium to interpret creatively and in social terms the life of the people as it exists in reality." Much of the situation described still exists and many of the proposals still very timely. Over 800 pages. **8/13/16/17**

Rotha, Paul and Roger Manvell **The Film Till Now.** New York: Funk and Wagnalls, 1949. Revised edition. A basic world survey of film history up to 1948, with additional materials by Richard Griffith on developments during 1948-1958. **1/12/17/20**

Sarris, Andrew **The Films of Josef Von Sternberg.** Garden City: Doubleday, 1966. **9**

Schever, Steven H. (editor) **Movies on TV** (formerly **TV Key Movie Guide**). New York: Bantam Books, 1968. A handy list of films released for viewing on television. Includes usually correct dates, performers, brief commentary and evaluations. More foreign films are listed in this edition than the former three. **12/18/20**

Schickel, Richard and John Simon (editors) **Film 67/68.** New York: Simon and Schuster, 1968. The best collection of critical reviews of current films. By top critics. **12/17/18/20**

Schickel, Richard **Movies.** New York: Basic Books, 1964. The history of an art and an institution written in direct and clear language. **1/18**

Schillaci, Anthony **Movies and Morals.** Notre Dame: Fides Press, 1968.

Sections helpful and provocative. Not a definitive study. Read along with **Morality and the Mass Media** by Kyle Haselden. **17**

Seldes, Gilbert **The Public Arts.** New York: Simon and Schuster, 1964. Paperback. A discussion-starter which probes the economics, personalities and exciting world of movies, radio and television. **13/17/19**

Sennett, Mack **King of Comedy, As Told to Cameron Shipp.** Garden City: Doubleday, 1954. **7/9/18**

Sheridan, Marion C. and others (editors for this study by the National Council of Teachers of English) **The Motion Picture and the Teaching of English.** New York: Appleton, 1965. Paperback. Recommended for all teachers interested in film teaching or communication in general. **17/3/4**

Sontag, Susan **Against Interpretation.** New York: Delta Books, 1967. Paperback. Especially good commentary on science-fiction films. Other essays worth a fast reading. **9/17/18**

Speed, F. Maurice (editor) **The Western Film Annual** (1951-1959) and **The Western Film and TV Annual** (1960-   ). London: MacDonald Press. Illustrated volumes with articles on Westerns and records of the year's new films in this area. **6/12/20**

Spottiswoode, Raymond **Film and its Techniques.** London: Faber and Faber, 1967. Written in 1950, could be a companion to his much earlier **A Grammer of the Film,** published by the University of California Press in 1957. Both are badly in need of updating, but excellent references. **13/12/17**

Springer, John **All Talking! All Singing! All Dancing!** New York: Citadel Press, 1966. A fascinating pictorial and history of the musical. **16/7/1/20**

Stauffacher, Frank (editor) **Art in Cinema.** San Francisco: San Francisco Museum of Art, 1947. **2**

Stearn, Gerald Emmanual **McLuhan Hot and Cool.** New York: Dial Press, 1967. Probing the prober and describing the describer. **13/17**

Steinberg, Charles S. **Mass Media and Communication.** New York: Hastings House, 1966. Timely, informed and informative. **13/17**

Stephenson, Ralph **Animation in the Cinema.** New York: A. S. Barnes and Co., 1967. Paperback. A well-illustrated survey of animation's history. **5/17/18/16**

Stephenson, Ralph and Jean R. Debrix **The Cinema as Art.** Baltimore: Penguin Books, 1965. Paperback. A good introduction to fiim form. Describes several technical devices and suggested ways they may be used. **10/12/19**

von Sternberg, Josef **Fun In A Chinese Laundry.** London: Secker and Warburg, 1965. Paperback. Austrian born director reflects on his film-making experiences (**The Blue Angel, Crime and Punishment,** etc.). **7/9/17/18**

Stewart, David C. **Film Study in Higher Education.** Washington: American Council on Education, 1966. Paperback. For, by and on educators and film education. In one essay Pauline Kael applies her critical art to an embarrasing evaluation of film education. **17**

Sugy, Catherine "Black Men or Good Niggers?" **Take One** Vol. 1, No. 8

(1968), pp. 18-21. An outspoken look at race in the new movies. Would definately provoke discussion among young people. **17/18**

Sullivan, Bede **Movies, The Universal Language.** South Bend, Indiana: Fides Press, 1967. Paperback. A unique contribution drawn from practical experience with student-made films. **10/17/18/5/20**

Swing, Raymond **Good Evening!** New York: Harcourt, Brace and World, Inc., 1964. Timely comments on television viewing also applicable to film screening. **17/18**

Talbot, Daniel (editor) **Film.** New York: Simon and Schuster, 1959. Paperback. An anthology including invaluable essays by experts. **13/17/18**

Taylor, Deems (editor) **Fantasia.** New York: out of print, 1940. An elaborate folio of illustrations from the famous Disney animated feature. A foreward by Stokowski. Included here to encourage a reprinting. (Available from Cinemabilia, 10 Cornelia St., New York, New York, 10014, at rare book price.) **5/20**

Taylor, John Russell **Cinema Eye, Cinema Ear.** New York: Hill and Wang, 1964. Paperback. Studies of nine key film-makers of the sixties: Fellini, Antonioni, Bresson, Brunuel, Hitchcock, Bergman, Truffaut, Godard and Resnais. **9/17/18**

Taylor, Robert Lewis **W. C. Fields, His Follies and Fortunes.** New York: New American Library, 1967. Paperback. **7/9/17/18**

Thompson, Denys (editor) **Discrimination and Popular Culture.** Baltimore: Penguin Books, 1964. Paperback. Studies on the individual and corporate response to mass media. Admirable lack of ax-grinding. **13/17/19**

Tucker, Nicholas **Understanding the Mass Media.** New York: Cambridge, 1966. A practical approach for teachers. **17**

Tyler, Parker **Classics of the Foreign Film.** New York: Citadel Press, 1962. A pictorial and discussion of non-American film classics. **14**

UNESCO: **Screen Education.** New York: UNESCO Publications Center, 1964. Paper. Number 42 of the reports and papers on Mass communications. On teaching a critical approach to cinema and television. Many addresses and materials mentioned no longer apply. **12/17**

UNESCO: **The Influence of the Cinema on Children and Adolescents.** Paris: Mass Communication Techniques Division, UNESCO, 1961. An annotated international bibliography. Number 31 of the series of reports and papers on mass communication. **12/17**

UNESCO: **World Communications.** New York: UNESCO Publications Center, 1964. Paper. On press, radio, television and film around the world. Many addresses and materials listed no longer apply. **12/17**

Vallance, Tom **Westerns: A Preview Special.** London: Golden Pleasure Books, 1964. Popular short articles. **6**

Vardac, Nicholas "Documentary Film as an Art Form" **Sight and Sound,** XIX (April, 1951), pp. 477-80. **8/10**

Warshow, Robert **The Immediate Experience.** Garden City, New York:

Doubleday, 1964. Movies, comics, theatre and other aspects of popular culture considered anthropologically, psychologically and, in general, very informatively. His article "The Western" originally appeared in **The Partisan Review** (March-April, 1954) and highly recommended. ("The Western" has been reprinted also in Daniel Talbot's **Film: An Anthology.)** **6/7/17/18**

Weinberg, Herman G. **Josef von Sternberg.** New York: E. P. Dutton, 1967. A study of the director and his discovery of Marlene Dietrich. **9**

White, David Manning and Richard Averson (editors) **Sight, Sound, and Society.** Boston: Beacon Press, 1968. On motion pictures and television in America. One of the most valuable anthologies in English. A confusing style of appendix and index. Otherwise faultless. **9/13/17**

Whitehall, Richard "The Heroes Are Tired" **Film Quarterly.** Winter, 1966-1967. Berkeley, California: University of California Press. On the recent happenings in Westerns. **6/17/18**

Wigal, Donald "Feature Book Review" **Ave Maria.** December 2, 1967, p. 23-24. A review of **A Guide to Short Films** by Patrick J. McCaffrey and **Short Films in Religious Education** by William Kuhns. (Both books have since supplemented their original form, but the basic praise and/or criticism remains the same. DW) **5/17**

Wiseman, Thomas **Cinema.** New York: A. S. Barnes, 1965. Paperback. **17**

Wood, Michael **The Fabulous Films of the Twenties.** New York: Archer House, 1960. **1**

Wood, Robin **Hitchcock's Films.** New York: A. S. Barnes and Co., 1965. Paperback. Film criticism at its best. Adequately illustrated. **9/13/17/18**

Wright, Charles **Mass Communications: A Sociological Perspective.** New York: Random House, 1959. Paperback. The inter-relationship of media to society well treated. **13/17/19**

Wycoff, Gene **The Image Candidates.** New York: Macmillan, 1968. **13/17**

Yoakem, Lola Goelet (editor) **TV and Screen Writing.** Berkeley, California: University of California Press, 1959. **10**

RECOMMENDED PERIODICALS

AFTER DARK, monthly, published by DANCE magazine, Inc., 268 West 47th Street, New York, 10036. One year $4; two years $6 in U.S.A. While concerned mainly with the New York City world of entertainment, especially the dance, AFTER DARK is often a good source for current comment on film.

BACKSTAGE, weekly, 155 West 46th Street, New York, New York, 10036. $15 a year; $8 for six months. Current film news included with popular coverage of stage and television. Primarily concerned with casting, especially in New York City.

CANYON CINEMANEWS, 263 Colgate, Berkely, California 94708. $3 for 12 issues. An occasional hectograph of valuable information for and on film-makers. Especially interested in festivals. Canyon Cinema Co-operative films listed. The latter address: 756 Street, San Francisco, California 94133. Concerned mainly with "experimental" film.

CINEMA, quarterly, 9667 Wilshire Boulevard, Beverly Hills, California. $4 for four issues; $6 for six, etc. Slick coverage, high quality lay-out and illustrations.

CONTINENTAL FILM REVIEW, monthly, Eurap Publishing Co., Ltd., 71 Oldhill Street, London, N. 16. Adults may find an occasional paragraph of helpful information amid many stills which are consistently the most suggestive shots in current foreign film.

CTVD: Cinema-TV-Digest, quarterly, Hampton Books, Drawer H, Hampton Bays, New York. $3 a year. (Group rates on request.) Very worthwhile review of serious foreign-language cinema and television press. Foreign periodicals surveyed.

FILMSURVEY, annual. First two issues (1966, 1967) were $1.50 each (10s 6d). The Yearbook of the Federation of Film Societies intended as a reference book for film groups and enthusiasts. Many features and shorts listed with availability in England and, sometimes, U.S.A. Published by the Federation of Film Societies, 102 Dean Street, London W1. Beautiful stills, lists of books, records, equipment related to film.

PSYCHOLOGY TODAY, Monthly, 1330 Camino Del Mar, Del Mar, California 92014. $9 a year in U.S.A. A film-review column began with the May, 1968 issue.

SHOWCASE MAGAZINE, 220 East 57th Street, New York, New York, 10022. A small booklet distributed at major theatres in New York City. Often timely information offered not otherwise available.

VARIETY, weekly. $20 year in U.S.A. 154 West 46th Street, New York, New York, 10036. Standard news on films, television, radio, stage, etc. Basic reference for contemporary information.

THE VILLAGE VOICE, weekly. Sheridan Square, New York, New York, 10014. $5 a year in U.S.A. The largest community weekly newspaper in U.S.A. Indispensable source on current "underground" and "experimental" film. Jonah Mekas is a regular columnist.

See: The list given by William Kuhns in the TEACHING PROGRAM which accompanies EXPLORING THE FILM, pp. 73-76.

FILM BOOK CATALOGS

Many bookstores publish catalogs of their offerings on film. Some of the best of these are available from:

Cinemabilia
10 Cornelia Street
New York, New York 10014

Gotham Book Mart
41 West 47th Street
New York, New York 10036

Harold's Foto Spot
100 West 42nd Street
New York, New York
(no mail or phone orders)

New Yorker Books
250 West Eighty-ninth Street
New York, New York 10024

SINGIN' IN THE RAIN, *1952, Gene Kelly*

Index of Film Titles

Films which are usually referred to only by their foreign title are listed here without translation. Films which have English and foreign titles are listed both ways.

The availability details of many of these films are given in Appendix I. Some films not listed in Appendix I may also be available; current distributors' catalogues should be consulted.

In the case of variants of certain titles this list follows the authority of Peter Graham's **A DICTIONARY OF THE CINEMA** New York: A.S. Barnes, Revised 1968.

Dr